THE KWAIDAN OF THE LADY OF TAMIYA

T0352811

Kwaidan are what Lafcadio Hearn called 'stories and studies of strange things' – eerie tales which convey the enduring mystery of traditional Japanese culture and the world of the samurai. In this volume, de Benneville's rendition of the Yotsuya Kwaidan of Shunkintei Ryuo paints a picture of life in the capital city of Edo among the samurai of the highest class, jostling for power at the court of the Shogun. At the heart of the story is the Lady of Tamiya, a daughter of the samurai who is sold by her brutal husband into the floating world of the brothels, from which she escapes only in death. Thereafter, the Lady is avenged as misfortune relentlessly overtakes all who betrayed her, and she is still remembered today in a Tokyo shrine popular with women who seek her protection. More than any history, *kwaidan* reveal the inner morality of the samurai code.

The late JAMES S. DE BENNEVILLE, American author, translator and scholar, and long-time resident of Japan is well known for his superb renditions of Japan's great historic literary classics. Among his works is *Tales of the Samurai*, also published by Kegan Paul.

田宮稲荷大神

THE O'IWA OF THE TAMIYA INARI JINJA
OF ECHIZENBORI, TOKYO

THE KWAIDAN OF THE LADY OF TAMIYA

SAMURAI TALES OF THE TOKUGAWA

JAMES S. DE BENNEVILLE

Routledge
Taylor & Francis Group

LONDON AND NEW YORK

First published in 2001 by
Kegan Paul International

This edition first published in 2010 by
Routledge
2 Park Square, Milton Park, Abingdon, Oxfordshire OX14 4RN

Simultaneously published in the USA and Canada
by Routledge
711 Third Avenue, New York, NY 10017

First issued in paperback 2016

Routledge is an imprint of the Taylor & Francis Group, an informa business

British Library Cataloguing in Publication Data
A catalogue record for this book is available from the British Library

ISBN 13: 978-1-138-99296-2 (pbk)
ISBN 13: 978-0-7103-0700-2 (hbk)

Publisher's Note
The publisher has gone to great lengths to ensure the quality of this reprint
but points out that some imperfections in the original copies may be
apparent. The publisher has made every effort to contact original copyright
holders and would welcome correspondence from those they have been
unable to trace.

PREFACE

T ALES of the Tokugawa can well be introduced by two " won-der-stories " of Nippon. One of these, the Yotsuya Kwaidan,[1] is presented in the present volume, not so much because of the incidents involved and the peculiar relation to a phase of Nip-ponese mentality, as from the fact that it contains all the machinery of the Nipponese ghost story. From this point of view the reading of one of these tales disposes of a whole class of the native literature. Difference of detail is found. But unless the tale carries some particular interest, as of curious illustration of customs or history—the excuse for a second presentation—a long course of such reading becomes more than monotonous. It is unprofitable. Curiously enough, it can be said that most Nip-ponese ghost stories are true. When a sword is found en-shrined, itself the malevolent influence—as is the Muramasa blade of the Hamamatsu Suwa Jinja, the subject of the Komatsu Onryu of Matsubayashi Hakuchi—and with such tradition attached to it, it is difficult to deny a basis of fact attaching to the tradition. The ghost story becomes merely an elaboration of an event that powerfully impressed the men of the day and place. Moreover this naturalistic element can be detected in the stories themselves. Nipponese writers of to-day explain most of them by the word *shinkei*—" nerves "; the working of a guilty con-science moulding succeeding events, and interpreting the results to the subsequent disaster involved. The explanation is some-what at variance with the native Shinto doctrine of the moral perfection of the Nipponese, and its maxim—follow the dictates of one's heart; but that is not our present concern.

---

[1] *Kwaidan* means "Wonder Tale." The word is of general mean-ing, requiring limitation for the specific case.

Their theory, however, finds powerful support in the nature of the Nipponese ghost. The Buddhist ghost does not remain on earth. It has its travels and penalties to go through in the nether world, or its residence in Paradise, before it begins a new life—somewhere. The Shintō ghost, in the vagueness of Shintō theology, does remain on earth. If of enough importance it is enshrined, and rarely goes abroad, except when carried in procession at the time of the temple festival. Otherwise it finds its home in the miniature shrine of the *kami-dana* or god-shelf. There is a curious confusion of Nipponese thought on this subject; at least among the mass of laity. At the Bon-Matsuri the dead revisit the scene of their earthly sojourn for the space of three days; and yet the worship of the *ihai*, or mortuary tablets, the food offerings with ringing of the bell to call the attention of the resident Spirit is a daily rite at the household Buddhist shrine (Butsu-dan). When, therefore, the ghost does not conform to these well-regulated habits, it is because it is an unhappy ghost. It is then the *O'Baké* or *Bakémono*, the haunting ghost. Either it has become an unworshipped spirit, or, owing to some atrocious injury in life, it stays to wander the earth, and to secure vengeance on the living perpetrator. In most cases this is effected by the grudge felt or spoken at the last moment of life. The mind, concentrated in its hate and malice at this final crisis, secures to the Spirit a continued and unhappy sojourn among the living, until the vengeance be secured, the grudge satisfied, and the Spirit pacified. There are other unhappy conditions of this revisiting of life's scenes; as when the dead mother returns to nurse her infant, or the dead mistress to console a lover. In the latter case, at least, the expressed affection has a malignant effect, perhaps purpose—as in the Bōtan Dōrō of Sanyūtei Enchō, a writer most careful in observing all the niceties called for by the subject.

In the Nipponese ghost story the vengeful power of the ghost acts through entirely natural means. The characters involved suffer through their own delusions aroused by conscience. In the old days, and among the common people in Nippon to-day, the supernatural was and is believed in, with but few exceptions. Such stories still are held to be fact, albeit the explanation is modern. Hence it can be said that the "Yotsuya Kwaidan" is a true story. O'Iwa, the Lady of Tamiya, really did exist in the Genroku and Hōrei periods (1688–1710); just ante-dating the reforming rule of the eighth Tokugawa Shōgun, Yoshimune Kō. Victim of an atrocious plot of her husband and others, she committed suicide with the vow to visit her rage upon all engaged in the conspiracy. The shrine of the O'Iwa Inari (Fox-witched O'Iwa) in Yotsuya was early erected (1717) to propitiate her wrathful ghost; and the shrines of Nippon, to the shabbiest and meanest, have their definite record. On the register the name of the husband appears as Ibei; "probably correct," as Mr. Momogawa tells us. With him the name of Iémon is retained in the present story. Iémon is the classic example of the wicked and brutal husband, on the stage and in the *Gidayu* recitation of Nippon. There was but little reason to revert to the record. The shrine always prospered. It appears on the maps of the district as late as Ansei fourth year (1857); and the writer has had described to him by a friend a visit to this shrine some twenty years ago. The lady in question referred to it rather vaguely as beyond Samegafuchi: *i.e.*, at Yotsuya Samonchō. It was particularly favoured by the hair dressers, and to the eyes of a young girl was a gorgeous structure in its continually renewed decoration. Inquiry of late in the district elicited the information that the shrine had been removed. Many changes have been made on the southern side of Yotsuya by the passage of the railway from Iidamachi to Shinjuku. The Myōgyōji, with other temples there located, has been swept away. In fact the Meiji period handled all those institutions established by deceased piety with great roughness. Teramachi—Temple Street—is now but a name. The temples of eastern Yotsuya have nearly all disappeared. Have public institutions occupied this "public land"? Of course: the sites were sold for the secular purpose of profit, and poverty spread wide and fast over them. Yotsuya got the shell of this oyster.

About the middle of Meiji therefore (say 1893) the shrine disappeared from Yotsuya Samonchō; to be re-erected in Echizenbori near the Sumidagawa. Local inquiry could or would give but little information. A fortunate encounter at the Denzu-In with an University student, likewise bent on hunting out the old sites of Edo's history, set matters right. Subsequent visits to the newer shrine were not uninteresting, though the presence of the mirror of O'Iwa and of the bamboo tube inclosing her Spirit (Mr. Momogawa) was strenuously denied by the incumbent. In the presence of the very genuine worship at the lady's shrine much stress need not be laid on the absence.

The present story practically is based on the "Yotsuya Kwaidan" of Shunkintei Ryuō, a famous story-teller of the Yoshiwara, and an old man when the "Restoration" of the Meiji period occurred. The sketch given in the "O'Iwa Inari Yūrei" of Momogawa Jakuen filled in gaps, and gave much suggestion in moulding the story into a consistent whole. Parts merely sketched by the older story-teller found completeness. This collection of ghost stories—the "Kwaidan Hyaku Monogatari" published by the Kokkwadō—is in the main written by Mr. Momogawa, and can be recommended as one of the best of these collections, covering in shorter form the more important stories of this class of the native literature. The "Yotsuya Kwaidan" of Shinsai Tōyō, one of the older and livelier of the Kōdan lecturers, gives the scene at the house of Chōbei, and his quarrel with Toémon. It is found in the "Kwaidan-Shū" published by the Hakubun-kwan. The gidayu (heroic recitation) and the drama handle all these stories for their own peculiar purposes The incidents of a tale are so distorted, for stage use and dramatic effect, as to make these literary forms of small avail. The letter of O'Hana, however, is practically that of the play of Tsuruya

Namboku (Katsu Byōzō). It has been thought well to append to the story the *gidayu* of this writer, covering the scene in Iémon's house. Also the strange experience of the famous actor' Kikugorō, third of that name, is put into English for the curious reader. Kikugorō was the pioneer in the representation of the Namboku drama. This life history of the O'Iwa Inari—the moving cause of the establishment of her shrine—is no mere ghost story. It is a very curious exposition of life in Edo among a class of officials entirely different from the fighting *samurai* who haunted the fencing schools of Edo; from the men higher up in social status, who risked heads, or rather bellies, in the politics of the day and the struggle to obtain position, which meant power, in the palace clique. These latter were men who sought to have a share in the government of the Shōgun's person, and hence of the nation. They strove to seat themselves in the high posts of the palace. Here was a rapidly revolving wheel to which a man must cling, or be dashed to pieces. To prevent being shoved off into destruction they used every means of slander and intrigue, and fought against such, that the life of a rich and luxurious court afforded. The result, too often, was the present of a dagger from the suzerain they sought to please. Trapped into some breach of the harsh discipline, or even of mere form of etiquette, the gift was "respectfully received" with the mocking face of gratitude, even from the hand of the successful rival in office. At his home the defeated politician cut his belly open. His obedience to the suzerain's will was duly reported. His family was ruined or reprieved according to a capricious estimation of its power of resentment—and it became a question of " who next? " to try for a place on the wheel. On the contrary those lower officials,[2] engaged in the dull routine of bureaucratic office, had a much less dangerous

---

[2] The *go-kenin*, for the most part; although some *hatamoto*, whose incomes ran as low as 300 koku could be classed with them. In English—cf. T. H. Gubbins—Trans. Asiatic Soc, of Japan, xv.

service and etiquette to deal with. In insignificant ease they lived and intrigued in their petty way, under no obligation to take sides in the politics of the truly great. If they fell, it was largely their own fault. Such was the position of those in immediate contact with the working wheels of the Shōgun's Government. The great *bugyō* (magistrates) were continually shifting. Their court staff was the solid foundation of unyielding precedent in form. The one was a court officer; the others court officers.

Hence the Kwaidan possesses value for the social lesson it conveys. The admittance of a stranger to the ward, his evil bond with the Lady of Tamiya, the previous passion for O'Hana and thereby the entanglement of Kwaiba in the plot; all form a network in which the horror of the story is balanced by the useful lessons to be drawn by the mind of Nippon from its wickedness. Perhaps this belief in the effect of the curse of the suicide acts both in deterring or bringing back the erring husband, and in saving the wife from the extremities of her despair in abandonment. The story of O'Iwa, the belief in her power, to-day has a strong influence on a certain class of the Nipponese mind; especially among the women. If the present writer might have felt momentarily an amused feeling at sight of her worshippers, it was quickly lost at sight of the positive unhappiness expressed in these faces of the abandoned. A visit to the Tamiya Inari is not necessarily either one of idle curiosity or without results. Some exceedingly painful impressions can be brought away in the mind.

It is not entirely in jest therefore that apology is made for the reproduction of the story. It is well in such matters to follow one's predecessors. Moreover, public sentiment is not to be derided nor disregarded. It has a certain title to respect, even when superstition is involved. Hence the statement can be made, that in telling this story of the "Yotsuya Kwaidan" no derogatory motive is involved—to people, class, or person; least of all in reference to the dread Lady of Tamiya.

OMARUDANI—4th July, 1916.

CONTENTS

[The pronunciation of the Japanese vowels and consonants follows closely the Italian; in diphthongs and triphthongs each vowel is given full value.

a = a as in father, e = a as in mate, i = e as in meet, o = o as in soap, u = oo as in fool.

g is always hard. In the Tōkyō district it has the sound ng.

ch has full value, as in church. It is *not* k; c is only found as ch; *i.e.* cha, chi, cho, chu.

The vowels also have long (continued) sounds, marked by the accent -.

At times a vowel is elided; or rather but faintly touched by the voice. Thus Sukéshigé is pronounced Skéshigé; Sukénaga = Skénaga; Kuranosuké = Kuranoské. *Bu* and *mu* at the end of word lose the vowel sound—Shikibu = Shikib.

Kami used in connection with a man means "lord," Wakasa no Kami = Lord of Wakasa province.

Reprinted from the "Oguri Hangwan."]

(Kami also means "God" or divinized person; including the spirits of the dead. Even a living man can be regarded as a *kami*, in cases of some very unusual service rendered to the public welfare. Professor Imai recently—at Karuizawa—called attention to the fact that originally *kami* was written 上,

i.e. "superior." The divine attribute 示申 was introduced with Buddhism.)

PROEM

READER, pray take not the story of the O'Iwa Inari, the Yotsuya Kwaidan, as a mere fairy tale or novel of the day. The shrine of the Tamiya Inari stands now to attest the truth of the tradition. Let the doubter but witness the faith of the believer in the powers of the fearful lady; and, if doubt still continues to exist, the salutary fear of others at least will inspire respect.

THE YOTSUYA KWAIDAN
OR O'IWA INARI

CHAPTER I

O'MINO AND DENSUKÉ

YOTSUYA is a suburb—at the extreme west of Edo-Tōkyō. Its streets are narrow and winding, though hilly withal; especially on the southern edge toward the Aoyama district, still devoted to cemeteries and palaces, sepulchres whited without and within. Echizenbori would be at the other extremity of the great city. It fronts eastward on the bank of the Sumidagawa. The populous and now poverty stricken districts of Honjō and Fukagawa beyond the wide stream, with other qualities, deprive it of any claim of going to extremes. In fact Echizenbori is a very staid and solid section of Edo-Tōkyō. Its streets are narrow; and many are the small shops to purvey for the daily needs of its inhabitants. But these rows of shops are sandwiched in between great clumps of stores, partly warehouses and partly residences of the owners thereof. These stores line the canals of Echizenbori, water courses crowded with junks carrying their ten tons, or their hundreds of tons, of freight—precious cargoes of rice to go into these stores in bulk, of *shoyu* (soy) by the hundred kegs, of sakarazumi (charcoal from Shimosa) by the thousand *tawara* (bale), of fish dried and fresh, of *takuan* or *daikon* (the huge white radish) pickled in salt and rice bran, of all the odds and ends of material in the gross which go to make up the necessities of living in a great city. If Echizenbori then can make its show of poverty, and very little *display* of wealth, it is not one of the poor quarters of this capital city of Nippon.

2   17

Crossing the Takabashi from Hachōbori and plunging down
the narrow street opposite; a short turn to the right, a plunge
down another narrow street and a turn to the right; one comes to
the high cement wall, in its modernness of type a most unusual
attachment to shrine or temple. The gate is narrow and formal;
almost like the entrance to a garden or smaller burying ground.
Within all is changed from the busy outside world. The area in-
closed is small—perhaps a square of a hundred and fifty feet—
but marked in lines by a maze of lanterns of the cheap iron
variety, set on cheap wooden posts. On the right is seen a minor
shrine or two dedicated to the Inari goddess. On the left is a
small building devoted to votive offerings, the crude and the more
elaborate. The most striking is the offering of a little geisha
lady, and portrays an heroic scene of early days. There are
other portraitures, in which perhaps a wandering lover is seen
as a hero, to the lady's eyes, of these later times. On the outside
of the structure are posted up by the hundred pictures of once woe-
begone ladies, now rejoicing in the potent influence of the Tamiya
shrine to restore to them the strayed affections of husband or
lover. Next in line is an open, shed-like structure. It is a poor
chance if here the casual visitor does not encounter one or two
of the petitioners, patiently trotting round in a circle from front
to back, and reciting their prayers in this accomplishment of " the
hundred turns." Just opposite, and close by, is the shrine itself.
This is in part a massive store-house set back in the domestic
structure, with the shrine of the Inari facing the visitor. The
floor space at the sides and before it often is piled high with tubs
of *shoyu* and *saké,* with bundles of charcoal, such negotiable
articles as the wealthier shopkeeper can offer to the mighty lady;
and long tresses of hair of women too poor to offer anything
else, or wise enough to know that a woman could make no greater
sacrifice. And is not the object of their worship a woman? Numerous are these severed strands. Entering the shrine and passing
the pleasant spoken warden at its entrance, peddling his charms and

giving advice where often it is sadly needed—perhaps the more valuable of his two public duties—to the left within is the Okuno-In, the inner shrine containing the *ihai* or memorial tablet of O'Iwa. That the shrine is popular and wealthy; that the lady is feared, venerated, and her dreadful powers much sought after; this is plain to the eye in the crowded elaborateness of this inner holy place of the larger sacred structure.

Now Echizenbori is not a particularly old quarter of the city. Long after Edo was established, the city, step by step, fought its way down to the river; filling in lagoons and swamps, and driving their waters into the canals which were to furnish very largely the means of communication for its traffic. Yotsuya on the contrary is old. Its poverty is of later date. In the Edo days it was a favourite site for the homes of *dōshin, yakunin,* and a whole herd of the minor officials who had the actual working of the great Tokugawa machine of government in their hands. In the maps of Ansei 4th year (1857) the shrine of the O'Iwa Inari figures in Samonchō, in its Teramachi; a small part of the great mass of red, indicating temples and shrines and their lands, which then covered a large part of Yotsuya. How then did it come to pass that the shrine was removed to this far off site in Echizenbori, with such incongruous surroundings? The explanation must be found in our story.

When the Tenwa year period (1681–83) opened, long resident at Yotsuya Samonchō had been Tamiya Matazaémon. By status he was a minor official or *dōshin* under the Tokugawa administration. These *dōshin* held highest rank of the permanent staff under the bureaucratic establishment; and on these men lay the main dependence for smoothness of working of the machinery of the Government. Matazaemon was the perfect type of the under-official of the day; smooth, civilly impertinent to his equals, harsh to his inferiors, and all unction and abjectness to his superiors. Indeed, he laid more stress on those immediately above him than on the more removed. To serve the greater lord he served his immediate officer, being careful to allow to the latter all the credit. No small part of his function was to see that ceremonial form and precedent were carried out to the letter. It was the accurate and ready knowledge of these which was of greatest import to his chief, indeed might save the latter from disaster. Matazaémon's readiness and conduct rendered him deservedly valued. Hence he enjoyed the double salary of thirty *tawara* of rice, largely supplemented by gifts coming to him as teacher in *hanaiké* (the art of flower arrangement) and of the *cha-no-yu* (tea ceremony). He had a more than good house, for one of his class, facing on the wide Samonchō road, and with a garden on the famous Teramachi or long street lined with temples and which runs eastward from that thoroughfare. The garden of Tamiya almost faced the entrance to the Gwanshōji, which is one of the few relics of the time still extant. It was large enough to contain some fifteen or twenty fruit trees, mainly the *kaki* or persimmon, for Matazaémon was of practical mind. Several cherry trees, however, periodically displayed their bloom against the rich dark green foliage of the fruit trees; and in one corner, to set forth the mystic qualities of a small Inari shrine relic of a former owner, were five or six extremely ancient, gnarled, and propped up plum trees, sufficient in number to cast their delicate perfume through garden and house in the second month (March).

Such was the home of Matazaémon; later that of O'Iwa San. It was pretentious enough to make display with a large household. But the master of Tamiya was as close-fisted and hard and bitter as an unripe *biwa* (medlar). His wealth was the large and unprofitable stone which lay within; the acid pulp, a shallow layer, all he had to give to society in his narrow minded adherence to official routine; the smooth, easily peeled skin the outward sign of his pretentions to social status and easily aroused acidity of temper. With most of his neighbours, and all his relatives, he had a standing quarrel. Secure in his lord's favour as

an earnest officer, so little did he care for the dislike of the
ward residents that he was ever at drawn swords with the head
of his ward-association, Ito Kwaiba. As for the relatives, they
were only too ready to come to closer intimacy; and Matazaémon
knew it.

His household consisted of his wife O'Naka, his daughter
O'Mino, and the man servant Densuké. The garden Matazaémon
would allow no one to attend to but himself. The two women
did all the work of the household which ordinarily would fall
to woman-kind, with something more. Densuké performed the
heavier tasks, accompanied his master on his outings, and represented his contribution to the service of the ward barrier, the
Ōkidō, on the great Kōshū-Kaidō and just beyond the Ōban-
gumi. The barrier cut off Yotsuya from the Naitō-Shinjuku district, and, as an entrance into Edo, was of considerable importance.
When the time of service came Densuké appeared in full uniform
and with his pike. A handsome young fellow of nineteen years,
the women, especially O'Mino, saw to it that his appearance should
be a credit to the House. His progress up the wide Samonchō,
up to his disappearance into the great highway, was watched by
O'Mino—and by the neighbours, who had much sharper eyes and
tongues than Matazaémon and his wife. They marvelled.

With ground for marvel. In the eyes of her parents O'Mino
was the most beautiful creature ever created. Occasionally
Matazaémon would venture on criticism. " Naka, something is
to be said to Mino. Too much powder is used on the face. Unless the colour of the skin be very dark, the use of too much
powder is not good. Mino is to be warned against excess." Thus
spoke the official in his most official tone and manner. Wife
and daughter heard and disobeyed; the wife because she was
ruled by her daughter, and the daughter because she would emu-
late the fair skin of Densuké and be fairer in his eyes. O'Mino
had suffered both from fate and fortune. She had been born
ugly; with broad, flat face like unto the moon at full, or a dish.

Her back was a little humped, her arms disproportionately long, losing in plumpness what they gained in extension. She seemed to have no breasts at all, the chest forming a concavity in correspondence to the convexity of the back, with a smoothness much like the inner surface of a bowl. This perhaps was no disadvantage—under the conditions. So much for fate. But fortune had been no kinder. "Blooming" into girlhood, she had been attacked by smallpox. Matazaémon was busy, and knew nothing of sick nursing. O'Naka was equally ignorant, though she was well intentioned. Of course the then serving wench knew no more than her mistress. O'Mino was allowed to claw her countenance and body, as the itching of the sores drove her nearly frantic. In fact, O'Naka in her charity aided her. The result was that she was most hideously pock-marked. Furthermore, the disease cost her an eye, leaving a cavity, a gaping and unsightly wound, comparable to the dumplings called *kuzumanju*, white puffy masses of rice dough with a depression in the centre marked by a dab of the dark-brown bean paste. The neighbours used to say that O'Mino was *nin san baké shichi*—that is, three parts human and seven parts apparition. The more critical reduced her humanity to the factor one. The children had no name for her but "Oni" (fiend). They had reason for this. They would not play with her, and treated her most cruelly. O'Mino, who was of no mild temperament, soon learned to retaliate by use of an unusually robust frame, to which was united by nature and circumstances her father's acidity of character. When the odds were not too great all the tears were not on O'Mino's side; but she suffered greatly, and learned with years that the Tamiya garden was her safest playground.

O'Mino grew into a woman. Affection had to find some outlet. Not on the practical and very prosaic mother; not on the absorbed and crabbed father; but on Densuké, on the *samurai's* attendant or *chūgen*, it fell. All manner of little services were rendered to him; even such as would appropriately fall within his own performance. At first O'Mino sought out little missions for him to perform, out of the line of his usual duties, and well rewarded in coin. This was at his first appearance in the house. Then she grew bolder. Densuké found his clothing undergoing mysterious repairs and replacement. His washing, even down to the loin cloths, was undertaken by the Ojōsan. Densuké did not dare to question or thwart her. Any trifling fault O'Mino took on herself, as due to her meddling. She became bolder and bolder, and sought his assistance in her own duties, until finally they were as man and maid employed in the same house. Matazaémon noted little increases in the house expenses. O'Mino took these as due to her own extravagance. The father grunted a little at these unusual expenditures. "What goes out at one end must be cut off at the other end. Densuké, oil is very expensive. At night a light is not needed. Be sure, therefore, on going to bed to extinguish the light." Densuké at once obeyed his master's order; and that very night, for the first time, O'Mino boldly sought his couch. Confused, frightened, overpowered by a passionate woman, Densuké sinned against his lord, with his master's daughter as accomplice.

Henceforth Densuké had what O'Mino was willing to give him. On Matazaémon's going forth to his duties, O'Mino, and O'Naka under her orders, did all his household work. The only return required was submission to the exigencies of the Ojōsan. This was no slight obligation. Densuké at times thought of escape, to his home at Tōgané village in Kazusa, to his uncle Kyūbei in the Kanda quarter of Edo. O'Mino seemed to divine his thoughts. She would overload him with favors; or openly express her purpose of following wherever he went in life. Kanda? Kyūbei was a well-known hanger-on at the Tamiya. Matazaémon entered him up in his expense book at so much a year. Tōgané? He could not get there except through Kyūbei. Matazaémon had farms there, and the *nanushi* or village bailiff was his servant. Besides, he would be a runaway. Matazaémon surely would come down on Kyūbei as the security. So the months passed, and matters were allowed to drift. Perhaps it was some gossip of the quarter which reached the deaf ears of Matazaémon. As he was about to go forth one day he followed the figure of O'Mino sharply with his little eyes all screwed up. "Naka, there seems change in the figure of Mino. Surely the gossip of the neighbours as to Densuké is not true? Mino is said to harbour a child by him. In such case it would be necessary to kill them both. Warn Mino in time; a *chūgen* is not one to become the adopted son (*muko*) of the Tamiya. He is an excellent lad, and costs but little. His habits are not riotous. To dismiss him thus causelessly would not only be unjust, but to no profit. Mino giving heed to the warning, all will be well." With this the lord of the household stalked forth to the house entrance. Receiving his clogs from O'Mino, he stalked forth to his official attendance. The two women, prostrate in salutation at his exit, raised their heads to watch him stalk.

It was a frightened face that O'Naka turned to her daughter. In whispering voice—"The honoured father's words have been heard? If not, it is to be said that gossip of the neighbourhood has come to his ears as to relations with Densuké. He notices that an *obi* is not often worn; and when worn is soon discarded. However, a man's eye is not so apt in such matters. Even in this Naka cannot speak positively. Doubtless the report is not true." O'Mino, if ugly, was anything but obtuse. Her mother must know; and yet not know. "My honoured father does not consider the difference of age and status in Densuké. Densuké is but a boy. This Mino has passed her twenty-third year. Moreover,. surely she deserves a better husband than a *chūgen*. Least of all would she give her father cause for regret or painful thoughts. Can a woman be pregnant otherwise than by a man?" O'Mino, respectfully prostrate, with this raised her head. The two women looked each other in the face. Finally O'Naka said—"With joy is the answer heard. But Matazaémon San is of hasty temper.

In his suspicions even he is to be avoided. However, the business of the house is to be performed. This will take the time until late in the day. Tradesmen may come for payments of the month. In the closet ten *ryō* in silver will be found. Here are the keys to the chests. It would be well to take an inventory of the effects. The winter is at hand. It is time to make warmer provision for it. Be sure to observe circumspection." With these words, and a sad look at her erring daughter, O'Naka donned street garb, threw a *haori* (cloak) over her shoulders, climbed down into her clogs, and their patter soon disappeared down the street.

Her departure was almost coincident with the reappearance of Densuké. His attendance on the master to the offices of the palace stables accomplished, for the time being he had returned. Thus did Matazaémon effect an outward state and an household economy. None too willing was the presence of Densuké. He was faithful in his way to O'Mino, and much afraid of her. Even in the most private intercourse to him she was the Ojōsan, the daughter of the House; but he had no other recourse than the Tamiya. Once assured of him, O'Mino had cut off all the previous flow of coin, and with it the means of his rare indiscretions at the Shinjuku pleasure quarter. Besides, their interviews took place in the darkness of night. In the daytime O'Naka usually was present, who, lacking other company, sought that of her daughter, and moreover was unwilling to be too complacent in the intrigue she saw going on. As soon as the sound of Densuké's steps was heard, O'Mino called him. There was a sharpness in her tone, a note of alarmed decision, that frightened and chilled him. Humbly he sought her presence. A glance showed the absence of O'Naka, yet as usual he prostrated himself in salutation. In that position he did not see her face. She said impatiently—" For salutation there is no time nor occasion. It is no longer the Ojōsan who speaks; it is the wife. My father knows all concerning this Mino and Densuké. On his return he is sure to take the occasion of the presence of both to kill us. It is his right and our duty to submit to his punishment. But to do so consigns the infant in the womb from darkness to darkness. This is too dreadful to contemplate. Unfilial though it be, we must run away. Make up your mind to do so." Densuké looked up. She was bent in meditation over this flight. The corners of the mouth widened out, the eyelid drooping more conspicuously than ever and forming a heavy fold over the empty socket, the bald brow, the scanty hair at the sides in disordered whisps and strands, all these made her a hideous mask. He could not endure the sight. Timidly he said—"Terrible news indeed! How has it happened? Surely, honoured lady, you have been very rash; nay, somewhat clumsy withal. Cannot women take their pleasure with whom they please without such dire results? Ah! Such luxury, such pleasant surroundings! All must be abandoned. This Densuké will seek his native village in Kazusa. And the Ojōsan whither will she go; what will she do?"

Was the question asked in innocence, or in deepest guile? O'Mino could not have answered, well as she thought she knew Densuké. He felt a hand on his shoulder. He sprang up in fright, hardly knowing whether it was a demon, or O'Mino turned demon, who confronted him. Her mouth half open, her large, white, shining, even teeth all displayed, her single eye darting malignant gleams, and the empty socket and its fold quivering and shaking, she was a frightful object. "To speak of pleasure without the consequences, such talk is that of a fool. Densuké was taken for the relationship of the two worlds. Now you would abandon me. Very well—do so. But this Mino does not perish by her father's sword. The well is at hand. Within three days I shall reappear and hunt you out. Torn to pieces the wretched man shall die a miserable death. Better would it be now to die with Mino. A last salutation . . ." Two vigorous arms seized his neck. Densuké gave a cry of anguish as the sharp teeth marked the ear. Letting him go, she sprang to the *rōka* (verandah). Frightened as he was, Densuké was too quick for her. He grasped her robe. " Nay! The Ojōsan must not act so desperately. Densuké spoke as one clumsy, and at a loss what to do . . . yes . . . we must run away . . . there is the uncle, Kawai, in Kanda. To him Densuké will go, and there learn the will of Tamiya Dono." O'Mino's tragic attitude lapsed. At once she was the practical woman of the house. She gave thanks for her mother's foresight. " The escape is not as of those unprovided. Here are ten *ryō* in silver. A bundle is to be made of the clothing and other effects. This is to be carried by Densuké. And the uncle: Mino presenting herself for the first time as wife, a present is to be brought. What should it be?" She talked away, already busy with piling clothes, quilts (*futon*), toilet articles onto a large *furoshiki* or square piece of cloth. Then she arrayed her person with greatest care, and in the soberest and richest fashion as the newly-wed wife. With time Densuké managed to get his breath amid this vortex of unexpected confusion into which he had been launched. " The uncle's teeth are bad. Soft *takuan* [1] is just the thing. For long he has eaten little else. Four or five stalks are sufficient." He went to the kitchen to secure this valued gift. Then he collected his own possessions. With the huge bundle of the *furoshiki* on his shoulders; with straw raincoat, sun hat, clogs for wet and dry weather, piled on the top, and the stalks of the *takuan* dangling down; " it was just as if they were running away from a fire." As Densuké departed O'Mino closely observed him. He was too subdued, too scared to give her anxiety. Later she left the house to join him at the Hanzō-bashi, far enough removed from Yotsuya. It was then Tenwa, 2d year, 11th month (December, 1682).

---

[1] The hard palatable pickled yellow *daikon* (radish). *Nukamiso-zuké* is a way station in its production by pickling in salt and bran. *Nukamisozuké* is better described than smelt.

CHAPTER II

KAWAI SAN OF KANDU KU

THIS uncle of Densuké, Kawai Kyūbei by name, was a rice dealer, with a shop in Matsudachō of the Kanda district. The distance to go was far. As with all ladies, O'Mino kept Densuké waiting long at the Hanzō-bashi. Indeed, there was much romance about this ugly, neglected, hard girl. She waited until the sound of O'Naka's clogs was heard. Then she halted at the corner of Teramachi untiĺ she could see her mother's figure in the dusk; see it disappear into the house. When she went down the street toward the Samégabashi she was crying. It was late therefore—after the hour of the pig (9 p. m.)—when the pair reached Kanda. The business of the day was long over in this business section of Edo. The houses were tightly closed. On reaching the entrance of Kyūbei's house said Densuké—"Ojōsan, condescend to wait here for a moment. The uncle is to be informed. Deign to have an eye to the *furoshiki*. Please don't let the dogs bite into or insult the *takuan*." He pounded on the door. Said a voice within—"Obasan (Auntie)! Obasan! Someone knocks. Please go and open for them." The more quavering and softer tones of an old woman made answer—"No, it is not my turn and time to go to the door. Get up; and first make inquiry before entrance is allowed. With little to lose, loss is much felt. Ah! Tamiya Dono in the Yotsuya has been sadly neglected." The scolding tones hummed on. Grumbling, the old man was lighting a rush. "'Tis agreed; 'tis agreed. Tomorrow without fail this Kyūbei visits Tamiya. Ah! It is no jest to go to that house. Not only is the distance great, but . . ." He had the door open, and his mouth too. "Densuké! Graceless fellow! But what are you doing here, and at this hour?

No; the luck is good. There is a big bundle with you, a huge bundle." He spied the *takuan* and his face broadened into a smile. "Ah! If dismissed, it has been with honour. Doubtless the *takuan* is for this Kyūbei. Thanks are felt. But is all this stuff Densuké's? He has not stolen it? Doubtless a woman is at the bottom of the affair. Never mind; an opportunity presents itself to offer you as *muko*—at the Tatsuya in Yokomachi. Of late a boy has been hoped for, but another girl presented herself. A *muko* now will be welcome. The wife is getting past child-bearing, and there is little hope of a son. The Tatsuya girl is just the thing. In a few months she will be fit to be a wife. She . . . "

Densuké edged a word into this stream. " The honoured uncle is right. The cause of Densuké's appearance is a woman." The old man made a face. Said he—" Well, in such a case it is good to be out of it. This Kyūbei has heard talk of Densuké—and of all things with the Ojōsan! That would be terrible indeed. But how is the Oni (demon)? What a sight she is! Bald, one-eyed, hairless, with a face like a dish and no nose—Kyūbei came suddenly on her at dusk in the Yotsuya. Iya! It was cold feet and chills for him for the space of seven days. It is that which keeps Kyūbei from Yotsuya, although a little aid would go far. The last dealings in rice notes were not favourable. Besides, account is soon to be rendered to Tamiya Dono. But though wicked of temper and ugly, O'Mino San is rich. Even for the demon in time a good match will be found. She will be the wife of an honoured *kenin* (vassal), and the husband will buy *geisha* and *jorō* with the money. Such is the expectation of Tamiya Dono. Don't allow any trifling there. Remember that she is the daughter of a *go-kenin*. They talk of Densuké in the Yotsuya. Of course it is all talk. Don't allow it to happen." Densuké found an opening. The words meant one thing; the expression another. " It is not *going* to happen." Kyūbei looked at him aghast as he took in the meaning. " What! With the demon?

Densuké has committed the carnal sin with the demon? Oh, you filthy scoundrel! Rash, inconsiderate boy! Obasan! Obasan! . . . What did she pay you for the deed? . . . This low fellow Densuké, this foolish rascal of a nephew, has been caught in fornication with the demon. . . . What a fool! How is it that death has been escaped? And you have run away. Doubtless a pregnancy has followed. After putting his daughter to death Tamiya Dono will surely hunt out Densuké. Or perhaps keep O'Mino San until he catches the interloper. Sinning together, both will die together. Ah! To cross the Sanzu no Kawa, to climb the Shide no Yama, with the demon as company: terrific! It is terrific! And what has become of her? Why fall into such a trap, with a woman old and ugly? Her riches are not for you. Caught here, the *tatami* of Kyūbei will be spoiled." [1] Densuké countered. He spoke in the old man's ear. " Refusing consent, she threatened to kill herself and haunt this Densuké as O'Baké (apparition). The Ojisan (uncle) has seen the Ojōsan. Would he be haunted by her, be seized and killed with torture? . . . And then—here she stands, just at the door." The old man spluttered, and gasped, and went on his nose in abject salutation—"Oh, the fool! . . . the Ojōsan is here in person . . . he would trifle with the devil! . . . the low rascal would seduce the honoured daughter of Tamiya . . . put ten hags in a row and pick out the worst . . . will the Ojōsan condescend to honour Kyūbei's place . . . Oh! She's a very O'Baké already. Pregnancy with a beautiful woman is bad enough. With this demon it makes her an apparition . . . condescend to enter; deign to enter." O'Mino slowly came for-

---

[1] Sanzu no Kawa—the river crossed by the dead; the Buddhist "Styx." Shide no Yama—the mountain to be crossed on the way to Hell, or to the judgment hall of its great king—Emma Dai-ō (Yama). All deserve, and get, some punishment in this nether world.

ward. That what had been said by the rash and unconscious Kyūbei had escaped her ear was unlikely. The humility of demeanor hardly veiled the offended dignity of her approach. " Densuké has spoken truth. We come as husband and wife. Condescend to give shelter for the time being, and become the intercessor with Tamiya Dono. Such is the prayer of this Mino." As she spoke she bowed low on the *tatami* (mats). Kyūbei caught the hint; for if she had heard the talk of Densuké, she had assuredly heard his still louder ejaculations and ill-timed wit. The Obasan was in a rage at him. Taking the conduct of affairs in her own hand—" Condescend to make this poor dwelling a home for as long as desired. Plainly the visitors have not come empty handed. Ma! Ma! 'Tis like an escape from a fire. Densuké is a strong lad to shoulder such a burden. But he always has been something of an ass. As for Matazaémon Dono, to-morrow the Ojisan shall attend to the affair, and see what is to be expected. Meanwhile, deign to be as in Samonchō itself." The kindly old woman pushed Kyūbei and his clumsy apologies out of the way. She busied herself about O'Mino. The two women understood each other. The varied contents of the *furoshiki* were quickly stowed away. A little supper was prepared for the hungry fugitives. Kyūbei sat by, his eyes dazzled by the wealth of goods displayed, and his nostrils shifting under the acrid perfume of the *takuan* and remembrance of his stupidity.

The next morning Kyūbei was up betimes. Matazaémon was no dawdler. It was best to catch him satisfied with the morning meal, and perhaps beset by the night's regret over the loss of his daughter. In no way was it a pleasant mission. Kyūbei's pace became a crawl as he approached the garden gate on Teramachi. He put in an appearance at the kitchen side. O'Naka was here established, engaged in her duties and surely awaiting him. At sight of him she burst into what was half laugh and half tears. " Ah! It is Kyūbei San. Doubtless he comes on the part of Mino and Densuké. It is kind of Kyūbei to befriend them. The Danna (master) is very angry indeed. An only daughter, and one on whom he depended for a *muko*, he is much upset. Please go in and talk with him. Show anger at the runaways. To agree with him may somewhat soothe his passion. Condescend so to act." Kyūbei winked. And turn some of this anger on himself? Well, agreement might rouse the spirit of contradiction in Tamiya Dono. It was a characteristic of this hide-bound official. Matazaémon was drinking the last sips of tea from his rice bowl when the *shōji* were gently pushed apart, and the head of Kyūbei inserted in the opening. At first he paid no attention. Then as one in haste—"Ah! Is it Kyūbei? He comes early to-day—and hardly to apply for anything. The rice notes are not yet due for some weeks." His tone was grim; the usual indifferent benevolence of demeanor toward a townsman was conspicuously absent. Kyūbei felt chilled. Densuké must not sacrifice his good uncle to his own folly.

Said Kyūbei—"Yet it is to seek the honoured benevolence of Tamiya Dono that Kyūbei comes." Matazaémon turned sharp around toward him. Frightened, the townsman continued—"Densuké has acted very wickedly. The low, lascivious rascal has dared to seduce the honoured daughter of the House. Both are now harboured at the house of this Kyūbei, who now makes report. Their lives are in the hand of Tamiya Dono. But Kyūbei would make earnest plea for delay. O'Mino San being pregnant, the child would be sent from darkness to darkness—a terrible fate. May it be condescended to show the honoured mercy and benevolence. Evil and unfilial though the action of the two has been, yet 'benevolence weighs the offence; justice possesses two qualities.' Such are the words of Kōshi (Confucius)." The eyes of Matazaémon twinkled. He had heard that Kyūbei was on the verge of shaving his head (turning priest). Truly the townsman was profitting by the exhortations of his teacher. After a time he said—"The memory of Kyūbei is excellent. Don't let it fail him on the present occasion. For such a deed as has been committed the punishment is death, meted out by the hand of this Matazaémon. The fact ascertained, it was intended to kill them both. The flight of Mino and Densuké has altered the complexion of the affair. It is no longer necessary to inflict the extreme penalty. O'Mino is disowned for seven births. Neither she nor Densuké is to appear before this Matazaémon. If the talk of the ward be true, in exchange for a loyal service Densuké has secured a beautiful bride. There can be no regrets." Then, taking a sprightly and jeering air, "But this Kyūbei has been the one to exercise benevolence. Matazaémon now learns that the two runaways have been received by him. Entertain them well; entertain them well. Thanks are due to Kyūbei San—from them. Doubtless he is much occupied with his guests. Less will be seen of him in Yotsuya. . . . But official duties press. This Matazaémon must leave. Don't be in haste. Stay and take some tea. . . . Naka! Naka! Tea for Kyūbei San; the *haori* (cloak) of Matazaémon . . . Sayonara . . . Ah! The rice notes this Matazaémon took up for Kyūbei San, they fall due with the passage of the weeks. But Kyūbei is one who always meets his obligations. As to that there is no anxiety." With this last fling the prostrate Kyūbei heard the sound of the clogs of Matazaémon on the flagged walk outside. A departing warning to O'Naka as to the tea, and steps were heard near-by. He raised his head, to confront the mistress of the house.

O'Naka spoke with tears in her eyes—a salve to the alarmed and wounded feelings of Kyūbei. "Don't be frightened. After all Matazaémon is a *samurai*. To press Kyūbei, or any tradesman, is beyond him. But this Naka cannot see her daughter! To add to his anger would bring disaster on her and the unborn child. Alas! Anyhow, give Mino this money; and these articles of value, properly her own. Her mirror has been forgotten in the hasty flight." O'Naka brought forth one of those elaborate polished silver surfaces, used by the ladies of Nippon in these later luxurious days of the Shōgunate. It was only now that it became the property of O'Mino. It was part of the wedding outfit of O'Naka herself. With this little fiction the mother continued—" When the child is born allow the grandmother at least a distant sight of it. Perhaps it will resemble Tamiya; be like its mother, and soften a father's heart." Now she wept bitterly; and Kyūbei wept with her—bitterly. " Like the mother! The Buddhas of Daienji [2] would indeed weep at the appearance of such a monster." This was his thought; not expressed with the humble gratitude, prostration, and promises, which he fully intended to keep. Kyūbei reverentially accepted the mirror, the goods, the money. Taking his leave of Yotsuya—a long one he feared—with sighs he set out for Kanda. Here he made his report. Said the old townsman with severity— " The will of the parent is not to be disobeyed. It is the duty of this Kyūbei to see to its performance." He had O'Naka more in mind than the master of Tamiya. O'Mino might yet be the goose to lay golden eggs. A goose of such plumage! Kyūbei made a wry face in the darkness of the corridor.

---

[2] Near Meguro: scores of quaint figures, seated in tiers and meditation.

CHAPTER III

TAKAHASHI DAIHACHIRŌ

SOME means of support had to be found. Employed in a *kenin's* house, and leaving it under such conditions, kindred occupation was out of the question. There was a sort of black list among these officials to cover all grades of their service. Time and the host of servants of some great House would get the lad back into the only occupation he understood. Trusting to some such accident of fortune, Kyūbei made Densuké his agent on commission. Densuké was no idler. Kyūbei managed to meet the Tamiya security for his loans, largely through the efforts of the younger man. The married couple at this time set up their establishment in Gorōbeichō of Kyōbashi Ku. Coming and going, often with no definite task in hand, Densuké to all appearance was an out-and-out idler. For the first time released from the trammels of her class, O'Mino could attend the theatres and farce shows of the capital. She delighted in acting this part of a tradesman's wife. Moreover she was very sure of not meeting with Matazaémon, of whom she was in great fear. Bound to the *formulæ* of his class, her father might feel bound to cut her down on sight.

One day Densuké was idling and hanging over the parapet of the Nihonbashi. Some fishermen were violently quarrelling in the fish market on the bank just below the bridge. As he looked on with interest a hand was laid on his shoulder. Turning, he saw a man, partly in the dress of a *chūgen*, partly in that of a menial attendant of one of the larger *yashiki* (nobleman's mansion). Scars of burns on his hands and arms, patches of rice flour and bran, showed that he was a cook. His eye was severe and his manner abrupt as he rebuked Densuké. "An idle fellow! This Tarōbei never fails to come across Densuké as an idler,

35

or on the way to Asakusa with the worthy wife. Is he fit for nothing?" Densuké was a mild man. To this man with a grievance his answer was soft. Besides he had no liking for the cook's knife stuck in the girdle, and handy to carve fish or flesh. He said—" Perchance the idleness is more in appearance than fact. Buying and selling on commission the task is an irregular one. It is true, however, that this Densuké has no settled labour. Alas! Former days in the service of a *samurai* are much to be regretted." —" Can you cook rice?" was the abrupt interruption. " This Densuké knows the " Sanryaku " fairly well. Is more needed?" The man looked at him dumbfounded. " The ' Sanryaku '— what's that?"—" Knowledge of the ' Sanryaku ' enables one to meet all the requirements of a *bushi* (knight).[1] At the school in Kazusa Tōgané the priest who taught this Densuké, at one time a *samurai*, was far more taken with the " Sanryaku " than with the *Sutra* (Scripture); the lessons taught applied more to Bushidō (the knight's way) than to Butsudō (the way of the Buddha). . . . But to the point; this Densuké for three years cooked the rice at Tamiya in Yotsuya. First there is the *toro-toro* of bubbling water; then the *biri-biri*, as what little remains passes as steam through the rice grains. Then the sharp whistling cry of a baby from the pot on the slow fire (*murashite*). The task is done, and the vessel is removed from the stove. " The man looked with respect on this learned cook. Said he—" Densuké is the man. Tarobei must leave the kitchen of Geishū Sama at once. The mother is ill in Aki province. A substitute is to be found. The salary—is next to nothing; but the perquisites are numerous, and the food ample to feed several Densuké and their wives. Deign to accept." Densuké did not hesitate—" The obligation lies with Densuké. But how secure the position? There is Tamiya . . ." The man laughed. " There are many Den-

---

[1] A famous Chinese book on military tactics. Prince Yoshitsuné, hero of the Gempei wars, served arduously for a glimpse of it. Cf: Life of Benkei, vol. i, pp. 311 reg. Densuké refers to the three (*san*) stages of rice cooking.

suké in Edo; and no connection between the yashiki of Matsudaira Aki no Kami and the house of a *dōshin* in Yotsuya. There
is small likelihood of meeting old acquaintances. Be sure to
remember that it is Densuké of Kyōbashi; not Densuké of Yotsuya. This pass will answer to the gate-man. Substitutes are
common. Whether it be Densuké or Tarobei who cooks the rice
makes no difference; provided the rice be well cooked. Tarōbei's
service lies elsewhere; to Densuké San deep his obligation." He
held out the pass, and Densuké took it.

With mutual salutation and joy in heart they parted. Densuké betook himself to the *yashiki* of Matsudaira Aki no Kami at
Kasumigaseki. No difficulties were encountered. Tarōbei was
not so superlative as a cook that the substitute could not be better
than the original. At this place Densuké acted the part of the
komatsukibatta. This is a narrow brown weevil, some three parts
of an inch in length, and which stands on its head making the
repeated movements of *o'jigi*, much as at a ceremonial encounter
in Nippon. Densuké was not long in becoming well liked. He
was ready to run errands for all, outside of the hours of his duties.
From those higher up in the *yashiki* these errands brought him
coin. Every month he could bring O'Mino twenty to thirty
mon in " cash "; apart from the ample rations of rice and *daikon*
bestowed on the kitchen staff. Nay: as cook at times fish could
not be allowed to spoil, and fell to the perquisites of Densuké.
Thus time passed; and with it the delivery of O'Mino, and the
crisis in the affairs of Densuké, approached. Now Geishū Sama [2]
was a fourth month *daimyō*. Hence with the iris blossoms he
took his departure from Edo to the government of his fief in
Aki province. The Sakuji Machibugyō, one Takahashi Daihachirō, plead illness on this occasion of the exodus. As unable
to accompany his lord he remained in Edo. On plea of con-

---

[2] Geishū-Aki province. For six months the *daimyō* left Edo to
govern their fief in person. Their wives and families remained in
Edo. The penalties at the barriers (Hakone, for instance) were severe
if the wife tried to get away (escape) from Edo.

venience he established himself in the abandoned quarters of the
ashigaru or common soldiers, situated right over Densuké's cooking stoves. Entirely removed from the bustle of the household,
except during Densuké's now rare attendance, he secured complete isolation and quiet. Densuké went on cooking for Takahashi Sama, just as if it had been for the whole military household. Daihachirō was a forbidding kind of man; and it was with
no amiable look that he greeted Densuké when the latter appeared
very late to prepare the meal. It being the 5th month 5th day
(the *sekku*) of Tenwa 3rd year (30th May, 1683), perhaps he
suspected Densuké of preparation for, and participation in, the
great festival which was in progress. " Densuké is very late. This
Daihachirō has made the trial; to find out that he is no cook.
Indeed the right hand has been severely burnt. A cook should be
on time—for the meal, not the *matsuri*." Densuké was all apology
—" Nay, Danna Sama; it is not the festival which has detained
Densuké. An infant was expected to-day by the wife. Hence
Densuké's neglect. Deign to pardon him."—" A baby being born
is no reason why Daihachirō should starve. Prepare the meal
in haste. The rice is to be soft; and please see that the fish also
is soft. Make the sauce not too sharp. It would give great
trouble to make the bath in the quarters. In Owarimachi, or
Kubomachi, good bath-houses are to be found." Densuké took the
hint. At once he recommended one he thought befitting the great
man's greatness. " Well: *Sayonara*. See that the meal is ready by
the return." Off stalked Takahashi Daihachirō, towel dangling
from his hand, and toothbrush and bran bag in his bosom.

Densuké gave a sigh of relief as he left the court. Daihachirō
often employed him on missions, and was never particularly generous even when the transaction was decidedly shady. Densuké
was dreadfully afraid of him. Somehow he felt as if Daihachirō
was Fate—his fate. Turning to his stoves, the pots and the pans,
the meal soon was in successful preparation. As Densuké lifted
the cover to inspect the rice—splash! A great red spot spread in
widening circle over the white mass. In fright Densuké clapped

on the lid of the pot. He looked upward, to locate this unusual
condiment to his provision. On his forehead he received in
person a second consignment. Applying his finger to his head,
and then to his nose—"Blood! Ah! O'Také's fierce cat has
caught a rat and is chewing it in the room above. How vexatious!
If the Danna should find out . . ." Hastily he tried to shove
his equipment to one side. This would not do. The massive stone
blocks forming the furnace were too heavy for Densuké to move
unaided. Somewhat helpless he looked around. The rice was
almost done; ready for the process of *murashité*, or simmering
over the slow fire. The fish, carefully prepared, as yet was to be
cooked. All was to be ready against the return of Daihachirō
Sama. Ah! Again the dropping began. As finding some channel
in the rough boarding of the ceiling it came fast. His kitchen
began to look like the place where the Eta (outcasts) slaughter
beasts. Densuké shuddered.

Circumstances, the results involved, make the timid brave.
Grasping a pole Densuké started up the ladder leading to the loft
and the quarters of the *ashigaru*. Arrived at the top his eyes took
in the poor apartment. The rafters and beams of a low-cast roof;
six wretched (Loo-choo) mats on the floor, for the men to sit,
and sleep, and live upon; such its bare equipment. In the middle
of the mats was a great red stain. Densuké was at once attracted
to it. "A cat would eat a rat; but it would not wipe up the
blood." His eyes were caught by the straw basket used to store
away the raincoats. This was all stained red at the bottom. Going
close up he found it was wet. Perhaps the cat was at work
inside. Densuké raised the cover and looked in. In alarm he
sprang back. On the trunk and limbs of a body was placed a
freshly severed head. Without replacing the cover, with pole
uplifted over his head in defence, Densuké backed toward the
ladder. His one idea was to flee this *yashiki*. As he reached the
top of the steps the voice of Daihachirō was heard below—"A
pest on such filthy bath-houses; and filthier patrons. . . .
What! No rice yet, Densuké? Ah! Where is the fellow?"

Densuké looked down, to meet the altered countenance of Daihachirō looking up. He retreated as the latter sprang up the
ladder. Daihachirō gave a rapid glance. He saw the raised cover
of the basket. The next moment the bosom of Densuké's dress
was harshly grasped, and he himself was forced down on the
floor. Gloomily Daihachirō regarded him—" Rash and curious
fellow! Why not keep to your pots and pans? Densuké loses his
life; and Daihachirō a fool for a cook." He had drawn his
sword to strike. Densuké clung to his knees in petition—" Pardon, master! Pardon! This Densuké is no idle gossip. The dripping blood threatened to spoil the meal. Thinking the cat was
eating a rat, fearing the anger of the Danna Sama if the meal had
to be re-cooked, Densuké came up here to chase the animal away.
Thus the crime was discovered . . ."—" Crime!" thundered
Daihachirō. " Ah! This intermeddler must certainly die. By
the word of a *samurai* . . ." In his terror Densuké almost
put his hand over the irrevocable sentence. He spoke with life
at stake. " Deign, master, to pardon Densuké. He has committed
no offence; knows of no offence in others. Densuké has seen
nothing. Life is a jewel, to be kept at any cost. Densuké is far
too insignificant to deserve the anger of Takahashi Sama." He
grovelled in the abject terror of his petition.

Takahashi Daihachirō hesitated. An idea seemed to occur to
him, at sight of the man's fear-struck state. He smiled grimly.
" Densuké saw the head? "—" 'Tis so," admitted Densuké. " But
to see a head means nothing." Daihachirō dragged him over to
the raincoat basket. Holding him down, he grasped the head
by the cue and lifted it out. " Look! " Densuké gave a cry of
surprise at sight of the features of a once neighbour. " It is the
head of Iséya Jusuké, the money lender of Hachōbori; a hard man.
Surely the Danna . . ."—" Just so," replied Daihachirō, carelessly throwing the mortuary relic back into the basket. " Borrow-
ing five *ryō*, in six months with the interest the sum now due is
twenty-five *ryō*. Pleading illness Daihachirō remained in Edo, to
try and soften the usurer. He threatened a report to my lord;
grew insolent beyond measure. The sword drawn, he was killed

forthwith. . . . Here Densuké finds his use and saves his life. This body is an awkward impediment. Densuké must take and cast it away. Otherwise, a second head is added to this first. With one already to dispose of a second gives no difficulty. Decide: is it agreed? Moreover there will be payment." He took out a money belt (*dōmaki*), that of Jusuké. Densuké recognized it. Daihachirō had robbed Jusuké, after killing him. Lovingly he ran the golden *ryō* through his fingers. Seventy of them Densuké counted. Daihachirō picked out three *ryō*. "Here is payment. Life is spared, and it is agreed to cast away the body." Stammered Densuké—"On the rubbish heap?" Daihachirō looked at him—"You fool! Why not proclaim that Densuké murdered Jusuké? Once the gate is passed—and this Daihachirō goes in company so far—it is Densuké who is the murderer of Jusuké. Remain in this place until night. Then off with the body; pitch it into the ditch of Kuroda Ke, or that of Saiō Dono. Daihachirō now takes his meal. There is nothing wrong with it?" He looked meaningly at Densuké. The latter, with eyes on the shining sword, at once denied all defilement. He now plumed himself on the care taken of the Danna's interests. Daihachirō descended; to feed at ease and keep watch over the unwilling Densuké.

In the 5th month (June) the days are long. Densuké was a coward; and for company had the corpse of the murdered Jusuké. To the poor cook the time passed was torture. He was continually going to the stair and calling down—"Danna Sama, has the time come? . . . Ah! The sky is light. The streets at night will be full of people with lanterns. Plainly O'Tentō Sama (the Sun) has forgotten to decline in the West. Alas! This Densuké is most unlucky." At last the hour of the dog was passing (7–9 P.M.). Daihachirō appeared. "Now for the corpse! Wrap it up in this matting. . . . Coward! Is Densuké afraid of a dead man?" He took the body and cut the tendons of arms and legs. Then he placed the head on the belly. Doubling the limbs over the body so as to hold the head he wrapped the matting around the whole. The outside he covered with some red raincoats—"in case of accidental stains." Then he strongly roped the whole together. He stood back to inspect a truly admirable job. Densuké wondered how many usurers Daihachirō had thus disposed of. His speculations were interrupted. Everything was ready. " Now! the loan of Densuké's back." Groaned Densuké— " Danna Sama, a request."—" What? " asked Daihachiro. " Condescend to put a board between the body of Densuké and that of Jusuké. The head might seize and bite me with its teeth." Daihachirō snorted with laughter, contempt, and anger mixed. " What a cowardly rascal you are! Off with it as it is." Said Densuké respectfully and firmly—" The task is that of Densuké. Condescend so far to favour him." His obvious terror threatened collapse even of the influence of Daihachirō. An old remnant of the back of a corselet was at hand. Said Daihachirō—" This is still better. It is metal. In it goes. Now off with you." Stalking along in the rear of the unfortunate cook, Daihachirō kept within easy distance of a sword blow. At the gate he said—· " Pray grant passage. Densuké takes washing of this Daihachiro —bed quilts and futon to be renovated."—" Respectfully heard and understood." The gate-man let fall the bar and stood aside. Densuké passed into the street. A little way off he looked around. Takahashi Daihachirō had disappeared. Now indeed it was an affair between Densuké and Jusuké.[3]

---

[3] The Japanese personal pronoun is used—in the first person only to obviate ambiguity in the sentence. Women use it more frequently than men. In the second person it is used to express emphasis, great familiarity, impertinence, or rebuke. The last two uses are frequent. Ordinarily the honorifics and the construction of the sentence take the place of these pronouns. Such at least seems to be the usage of the *kōdan* writers, and in the present book the example has been followed, as far as possible. In a few instances the use of a pronoun will relieve the strain of a lengthy sentence or involved circumlocution in the western tongue. At times the closer style can be abandoned—as in the direct narration of the Tale of the Baryufu Kwannon. So also with the translations of the *gidayu* and the *kōdan* attached. These are for recitation. In the original the pronoun is rarely written in. But the literal translation of the honorifics would appear stilted. To westerners these are appellations; to the native they are indications.

CHAPTER IV

THE APPEARANCE OF O'IWA SAN

SHOULDERING his pack Densuké made off down the broad space lined by the white walls of the *yashiki*. In this quarter of the *bushi* the highway was not crowded with citizens and their lanterns. Densuké had high hopes of an early disposition of the incubus. He approached the ditch which protected the wall of the *yashiki* of Prince Kuroda. When about to put down the bundle a hail reached him from the *samurai* on guard at the Kuroda gate. " Heigh there, rascal! Wait! " But Densuké did not wait. In terror he gave the load a shift on his shoulder and started off almost at a run. On doing so there was a movement within. The cold sweat stood out on the unhappy man's forehead. A moment, and would the teeth of Jusuké be fastened in his shoulder? " Ah! Jusuké San! Good neighbour! This Densuké is but the wretched agent. 'Tis Daihachirō Sama who killed Jusuké. Deign to pursue and haunt Takahashi Sama. Jusuké San! Jusuké San! " Fright gave him strength and boldness. The Tora no Mon (Tiger gate) of the castle should be the place of disposal. Here the ditch was deep and dark. But to its very edge swarmed the people with their lanterns on this night of festival in early summer. The moor of Kubomachi was his next goal. At this period it really was open ground. With a sigh of relief Densuké let the bundle slip from his now weary shoulders. Alive he would have laughed at the idea of carrying the portly Jusuké. Yet here the usurer bestrode him, far heavier weight than on other unfortunate clients. " Let's have a look at him; address him face to face." His hand was on the knot, when a woman's voice spoke in his ear. Densuké did not wait to ascertain the nature of her solicitation. He sped away into the darkness, toward the distant city. Without goal, he found himself at Shiodomé.[1] Crossing the Shim-bashi he entered on the crowded and lighted Owarichō. It was only the hour of the pig (9 P.M.), and the house lanterns as yet burned brightly. He hesitated, with the idea of turning toward Shiba, of trying his luck in this still rustic district; or on the seashore, not far off.

A man close by greeted him. "Iya! Densuké San at last is found. The honoured wife suffers great anxiety. Thinking that the festival might be the attraction this Goémon set out to find you. Deign to hasten at once to Gorōbeichō." Densuké shifted his burden away from the man. Did it not already somewhat taint the air? His nostrils were wide open in alarmed inquiry. He made excuses. With his heavy pack he would follow after slowly. He was overwhelmed by his neighbour's kindness. Goémon offered to share the work. Densuké did more than refuse. Unable to shake off his companion in stolid desperation he took his way to his home in the tenement (nagaya). "Tadaima" (just now—present), he called from the doorway. Entering the shabby room he put down the furoshiki in a distant corner. Going to the Butsudan, or house altar, at once he lit the lamps. O'Mino eyed him with astonishment. "What's that?" she asked, point-ing to the bundle—"Washing of Daihachirō Sama"—"But Mino is ill. So situated she cannot do washing. How negligent!"— "It makes no matter," replied Densuké recklessly. O'Mino did not like the tone of his voice. She eyed him sharply. Then more pressing matters urged. "Weary as you are it is to be regretted; but money must be in hand, for the midwife and other expenses. A few hours, and this Mino will be unable to leave her bed—for three turns (weeks). There is cooking and washing to be done. Please go to Kyūbei San and ask the loan of a ryō. Perhaps he will give half."—"He will give nothing," was the surly reply of Densuké. "Of loans he has grown tired of late. As the

---

[1] The old Shimbashi station and its yards cover this site. "Tide limit"—a suggestive name.

uncle is the only stay in dire necessity care must be taken not to offend. Moreover, the loan is unnecessary. Here are three *ryō*." He brought out the shining oblong pieces. O'Mino's eyes were bright with terror. "Ah! Has Densuké turned thief? How was this money secured? What has happened? Why so late in returning?" But Densuké was made confident and ready of tongue by the physical helplessness of O'Mino. "Don't be alarmed. Densuké is neither thief nor murderer. He is no Shirai Gompachi. Perhaps there is a corpse within, not washing. Would the Ojōsan see a head, arms, legs, freshly severed?" He laughed harshly as she turned her head from him to the bundle, then back again. "This money was given to Densuké by Takahashi Sama; in return for faithful service in an important matter. Don't be frightened. It has been honestly earned." Said O'Mino, almost to herself—"But Daihachirō Sama is not one to give such a sum as three *ryō*. He is always in debt. The wife of Jusuké San complains of his delays with her husband. However . . ." Confidence restored, she bade Densuké put the money in the drawer of the toilet stand. Then he was to prepare some food; for themselves, and for the neighbours ready to assist at the expected birth.

Densuké did so, his eyes shifting from O'Mino to the stove, from the stove to the deadly bundle. Finally he removed the *furoshiki* to their outer room, mumbling some excuse as to the foulness of a buck-basket. He returned to his cooking. Barely tasting some food O'Mino soon was sound asleep. Densuké observed her. "Ugly, rich, a very *o'baké* in appearance is the Ojōsan; and yet she takes as husband a spiritless creature, such as is this Densuké. Is it good or bad fortune? How grateful would be her advice." He went to bed himself in the outer room; to spend a hideous night of nightmare in company with the dead Jusuké, who now did taint the air with that indefinable pollution of even the freshest corpse. Wild visions floated through the brain of Densuké. The neighbours would assemble. The food was ready.

Ah! Here comes the wife of Jusuké San. She demands her husband. A moment, and Densuké was stealing from the house entrance into the darkness. The river? Ah! That was it. The canal of Hachōbori was close at hand to Jusuké's own home. It would float him to his very door. Densuké soon saw himself at the river bank. No one was at hand. Splash! In went the foul burden. There it was again. But now it was Jusuké in person. "Jusuké San! Jusuké San! Pardon! 'Twas not this Densuké who killed you. Seek vengeance of Daihachirō Sama. He is the murderer." In his terror he lost all fear of being heard. He shouted at the top of his lungs. But Jusuké laid a heavy hand on him. With one long drawn out groan Densuké—awoke.

O'Mino was leaning close over him, her face spectre-like with pain. Seeing that he was awake she took away her hand. "What is the matter with you? All night you have been shouting and mumbling in sleep. Just now it was 'Jusuké San! Jusuké San! Daihachirō Sama!' It is indeed a matter of Jusuké San. The time of Mino is at hand; the pains begin. Go at once to the house of Jusuké, and ask his wife O'Yoshi to condescend her aid." Densuké sprang up. An idea flashed into his mind. He would go to Hachōbori and make full confession. Which was the most important? O'Yoshi as confessor or as midwife? With his brain thus puzzled over an answer he started off. His last injunction to O'Mino was—"by no means meddle with the bundle of Daihachirō Sama." There could have been no more direct invitation to her to do so. For a short time O'Mino did nothing but eye the strange bundle. Then she was on her knees before it, examining it. "Rain coats as wrapping! And tied with rope: a queer kind of washing. What a strange odour! Pickled daikon (nukamisozuke)?" She shook it. Something inside went *gotsu-gotsu*. This was too much for her curiosity. Her old suspicion came back, that Densuké had turned robber. She poked a little hole in the straw wrapping. Some kind of cloth covering was within; a *kimono* without doubt. Through its tissue something shone white. The kitchen knife was close at hand on the brazier (*hibachi*). She reached out, and in a moment the rope was severed. " Oya! Oya!" Out rolled a head. An arm, two helpless flexible legs were extended before her. With a scream of horror O'Mino fell flat on her back. Lying stretched out she uttered one sharp cry after another. The neighbouring wives came hurrying in, a stream of humanity. " What is wrong? A young wife screams not without cause. Oya! Oya! O'Mino San has given birth to a baby and a head. Iya! Head, limbs, body— a monstrous parturition!." With the woman groaning in the pain of her delivery, the wives in confusion, children flying to summon the men folk, the whole district was in an uproar. In the midst of the confusion arrived Densuké and the wife of Jusuké. As yet he had not found courage to confess. He was still " deciding." A neighbour greeted him—" Densuké San! Strange things have happened to O'Mino San. She has given birth to a head and a baby at the same time. Hasten, Densuké San! Hasten!" Densuké did hasten; but it was to disappear down the nearest byway in headlong flight. Amazed and confounded the wife of Jusuké proceeded alone to the house; as the first thing to set eyes on the head of her husband, eyes still open and glaring in death. With a cry she precipitated herself upon it; took it in her arms. The midwife, summoned in haste, parted infant from mother. Thus did O'Iwa San come forth into the world.

The affair was grave. The *kenshi* (coroner) was soon on the scene. O'Mino with feeble voice told what she knew. " Deign to examine into the affair beyond the surface. My husband Densuké is not the man to commit this crime. Ask the neighbours, who know him. Last night he brought three *ryō*, given him by Takahashi Daihachirō Sama, the Sakuji Machibugyō of Geishū Kō. He said that it was for important service rendered. There is no doubt that Takahashi San is the murderer. Deign to examine well; show benevolence. . . . Ah! This Mino shall have vengeance. For seven lives Daihachirō shall be pursued. . . ."

Her eyes became injected with blood. Her breast heaved painfully in the attempt to get air. The women around her gave cries of alarm. O'Mino sank back in a pool of blood. She had died in the midst of her curse. Said one present—" This Tōkichi would not be the honoured Sakuji Sama; nay, not for the full seven existences in human form." The others felt as he did. Even the *kenshi* drew up his shoulders a little at the frightful mask of the dead woman's face. He could learn but little. Kyūbei, soon at hand, petitioned for the dead body of O'Mino and the custody of the infant. The neighbours corroborated the story of O'Mino; but Densuké had disappeared. Daihachirō never had confidence in his agent. His preparations for flight had been made before Densuké's discovery, and almost together with Densuké he had passed out the gate of Geishū Sama, with the seventy *ryō* provided by Jusuké. Report being made to the Machibugyō a " grass dividing " search was made, without result. No trace of either man was found. As for the child born under these auspicious conditions, Kyūbei went at once to Tamiya Matazaémon and made report. With bowed head the old man awaited the decision. Said Matazaémon—" The name giving is to take place on the seventh night. Kyūbei will not fail to be present." He did not speak further. Thus the offence of the parents was pardoned in O'Iwa the infant; the grandchild of a man and woman passing the period of middle age.[2]

---

[2] A *sakuji bugyo* was the official who had charge of the maintenance and construction of public works within the daimyō's fief.

CHAPTER V

THE AFFAIR OF THE SHIBA KIRIDŌSHI [1]

IT was Genroku 8th year (1695). O'Iwa, a girl of twelve years, could understand what came to her ears. In dealing with each other the Nipponese are very exact and exacting. The New Year must start with a clean balance sheet for the tradesman—all bills paid and collected. The last night of the dying year, and its last few hours; this time is the busiest and most anxious. Zensuké, the *bantō* (clerk) of the Shimaya dry goods shop, accompanied by one Jugorō, was passing the Shiba Kiridōshi. It was the hour of the tiger (3 A.M.). Of the two, Jugorō was the fighting man. Jurōzaemon of the Shimaya had provided him with a short sword and sent him as guard to Zensuké, who would have more than three hundred *ryō* in gold. Said Jugorō—" Bantō San, whither now? The hour is late."—" It is never late on the *ōmisoka* (31st of the 12th month)," replied Zensuké tersely. " However, there remains but one account to collect; at Nishikubo. We will hasten."—" Go on ahead," said Jugorō. "A moment here for a necessity." Thus the two men became separated by nearly a *chō* (100 yards). The district was one of *yashiki* and temples. The white walls of the former blended with the white carpet of snow on the ground. At any hour it was no busy place; now it was desolate. The high banks of the cutting crowned by woods and approached through the trees, made it an ideal place for a hold-up. Zensuké hesitated. He slowed his pace to allow his companion to join him. He thought he saw something move in

---

[1] A deep cutting through the hill. They are common features in Nippon. Many valleys are only accessible by a climb, unless mitigated by a *kiridōshi*, or obviated by a tunnel. Kamakura, for instance, is accessible by land in no other way. Asahina kiridōshi: there are several others.

the darkness close by. From behind a tree just before him came
a *samurai*. Two others followed this man from the shadows.
The heads of all three men were covered by *zukin* (hoods). They
wore vizors. "Wait!" Zensuké stopped in fright. "What
suspicious rascal is this, travelling the quarter at this hour?
Probably some clerk making off with his master's funds. Come
now! Give them into better keeping. Low fellow! You are fairly
trapped." Zensuké began to retreat, but two of the men were now
behind him. He began to shout for Jugorō. The latter came
up at a run—"Honoured Sirs! This is the Bantō San of the
Shimaya of Honjō Itchōme. He is collecting the house bills.
Deign not to disturb him."—"Shut up!" was the reply of the
leader. "Another fellow of the same kidney. Look to him."
Roughly he thrust his hand into Zensuké's bosom and began to
hustle and fumble the clerk. When Jugorō would interfere the
two other men prevented him. With fright he saw the money
belt of the *Bantō* dangling from the man's hand. The nature
of the affair was plain. "Heigh! Jokes don't go, honoured sirs.
We are not suspicious fellows. Condescend to pardon us." As
he spoke he took advantage of the negligence of his opponents,
their interest in the struggle of Zensuké and their leader, to
wrench himself free. At once his sword was out. Jugorō was
of no mean skill. None of his wardsmen could face him. One
man received severe wounds in scalp and face. The other lost
part of his hand. But Jugorō was no match for the odds of two
trained soldiers. He was soon cut down. Meanwhile Zensuké
was shouting lustily for aid. At this period there was a guard
called the *tsujiban* (cross-roads watch). It was mostly composed
of oldish men not fit for active service. Such regulations as there
were they observed. These were very severe; but, as with the
present day police, kept them to their post. They rarely troubled
themselves to patrol their district. From these men there could be
little hope of aid. Just then, however, the train of some lord came
in sight. With one hand the leader held Zensuké by the bosom

of his robe. The hand holding the money belt was already thrust in his own bosom. In a moment it would be free. Then Zensuké would go in company with Jugorō to the Yellow Fountain (in Hell). His captor gave a startled cry. " The train of Geishū Sama! Lose no time!" As he wrenched himself away Zensuké sank his teeth deep into the man's hand. With a howl of pain the fellow made off, exchanging a little finger for the three hundred and twenty-five *ryō* in Zensuké's *dōmaki*.

The *bantō* crouched in conventional attitude by the roadside. His distress was plain; the prostrate body of a man evidence of some unusual condition. A *samurai* left the passing train and came up to investigate. " Ah! Robbery and murder: follow behind to the *tsujiban*. It is their affair." With moans and groans Zensuké made his report. He was indignant at the luxury of these watchmen, toasting at their fire. They noted it; looked at each other and out into the snowy night, and laughed with contempt. For a tradesman's money belt were they to disturb themselves? They questioned him harshly, in such way as to excuse any further effort on their part. Surely the thieves by this time were at the other end of Edo. Two of them, however, did accompany Zensuké to the scene of the hold-up. Casting an eye over Jugorō's mangled corpse, said one—" A good fight: the occasion has been missed. As perhaps the criminal this man is to be bound. Probably his intent was to run away with the master's funds." Roughly they seized him, hustled him back to the guardhouse. Trussed up Zensuké had to spend the hours in alarm and fear. Luckily the *kenshi* soon appeared. It was the *ōmisoka*. No official business would be performed during the three days following. Jugorō could hardly exercise patience and remain as he was for that space of time. So the examination was duly held. The Shimaya soon secured the body of Jugorō and the release of Zensuke. The latter's evidence was put on record; none too satisfactory, as the concealing *zukin* prevented any recognition or description of the features of the assailants. He only knew of the cries of impatience at wounds received, and knew that he had left his mark on his own opponent. How then were they to be run down? The *kenshi* showed some impatience. Said he to the captain of the *tsujiban*—" Why truss up this man, even though a tradesman? He has all his own fingers, and the corpse lacks none." He touched the severed finger with his baton. With this all were dismissed, and to all seeming the affair was forgotten.

The Tokugawa had their plain-clothes police. One of the most noted was Magomé Yaémon of Hachōbori. His great grandfather had captured Marubashi Chuya, of note in the rebellion of Yui Shosetsu at the time of the fourth Shogun Iyetsuna Kō. One day this Magomé Dono, in company with a *yakunin* (constable) named Kuma, was rummaging the poorer districts of Shitaya Hirokōji. The two men were disguised as charcoal burners, and attracted little attention. All the legitimate profession in the way of medicine and pharmacy had been ransacked by the magistrate (machibugyō) of the south district. Yaémon felt sure that there were still some by-ways. " Who's that fellow? he asked Kuma. The constable laughed. He's a *sunékiri* (shin-cutter). The rascals can be told by their tough dark blue cotton socks, the coarse straw sandals, and the banded leggings. Deign to note the long staff he carries. They peddle plasters—shin plasters, guaranteed to cure any wound, to stop any flow of blood. A man's arm hangs but by a strip of skin; the blood flows in torrents. Apply the plaster and the flow ceases at once, the arm heals. They drive a roaring trade, even among the *bushi* (*samurai*) ; selling a shell here, two there. As for their real usefulness. . . ." He laughed.[2] They followed after the man and

---

[2] " The description is curious. Writing fifty years ago Ryuō tells us these men no longer practised. His book is not readily met with and the passage in the original is worth preserving—" *Kono sunegiri yatsu to iu wa tadaima de wa arimasen ga; makurajima no tabi ni asaura wo haki, sankeigyō no kyahan de, nagai no wo ippon sashi. Eh! Tō de o*

soon came to a guard house. Said Magomé San—"Detain that man yonder. He is to be examined." The ward officer was a little surprised—"Respectfully heard and understood. It is old Yamabayashi Yōgen." Soon the man entered the guard house. Said the official drily—"Magomé Dono is here to talk with Yōgen. What has he been up to?" But the old fellow was confident. "Thanks are felt." With the ease of the righteous and prosperous he passed into the presence of Yaémon. The latter greeted him with a non-official genial smile. "Ah! This is Yamabayashi Yōgen, the head of the *Sunékiri*. And business?" —"Truly this Yōgen is grateful. Man was born with teeth. Men and women still seek each other's company. So long as such endures Yōgen finds profit."—"And plasters?"—"They are the affair of Tōkichi. Would his worship deign to examine him. . . . condescend dismissal. At once he presents himself."

Thus in short order the straight haired, unshaven, low browed Tōkichi stuck his head into the Sanbashi guard house. "Deign to pardon this Tōkichi. The honoured benevolence. . . ." The ward officer eyed him knowingly and quizzically. "Shut up! Magomé Dono has questions to ask about clients. Wait until the questions deal with the doings of Tōkichi. That will be well. Then it will be time enough to lie. Meanwhile, be sure and tell the truth." With this disinterested advice Tōkichi was passed to the presence. Once more conscience spoke louder than caution.

---

isogi de nai. Okata wa watakushi no mosu koyaku no kōnō wo kiite o motome nasai. Nukeba tamachiru nagai no yaiba da nure kami de mo kayo ni kireru, tadaima yatsu ga wo kiri chi wo tomete goran ni ireru; to maru de kiru yō desu ga ha (yaiba) no aru tokoro wa madzu no kata bakari de, moto no kata wa yaiba ga hiite aru yue, sono ha hiku no tokoro wo ude he ataru to suji ga tsuku bakari de kire washimasen ga, tanka ga kireru kara, chiwa taki-tsu se no gotoku nagareru. Chi ni wa sakarawazu ikusa naka ko wo mochiireba, sokuza ni todomaru nani mae kara todotteru no desu ga, hagyū da kara maru de chi ga tomaru yō ni micru kara, kono ho he hitotsu gai, kono ho he futatsu gai, to uremasu."
—"Yotsuya Kwaidan," pp. 31-32.

The honoured benevolence, the honoured pity; condescend the honoured examination into the innocence of Tōkichi." Yaémon laughed. "Fortunately it is not a matter of Tōkichi, but of his plasters. Who bought these at this year's Shōgwatsu (New Year)? Be careful in answer. The case is a bad one." Tōkichi considered. "The first day of the New Year a man came. His purchase of salve was large. In the course of the past three months he has been many times to buy. His visits now are wider spaced, and he praises the goods—as he ought. No hand ever had a worse poisoned wound. He . . . "—"Age and appearance?" interrupted Yaémon, now all attention. He had struck a trail. "Perhaps fifty years; fair of complexion, tall, and stout. By his lordly manner he must at least be a *go-kenin,* or a charlatan." Who was this man? Yaémon felt sure that he was about to learn something of interest. Kuma was given his instructions. "Go daily to the shop of this man and receive his report. As to the *samurai* in question be circumspect. Evidently he is no ordinary person. A *samurai* is to be summoned, not disgraced by arrest— if he is a *samurai.*" So Kuma with several aids established himself in the rear of Tōkichi's shop. The man not having put in an appearance for several weeks, the wait, if uncertain, was soon rewarded. On the 25th day of the 3rd month (May) he presented himself. Kuma recognized him at once by the description; sooner than Tōkichi, who was engaged in filling his little shells with the marvellous salve. The officer's decision was prompt. At a call Tōkichi turned from his drugs. "Ah! the honoured Sir. And the arm, does it honourably progress?"—"Progress could not be better. This is probably the last visit." In replying the man eyed Tōkichi with some astonishment. The latter made his bows, first to the new-comer, then to the indefinite rear of the establishment. "Indeed the drug is all that is claimed for it. The wound being poisoned, at one time it looked as if the hand, nay arm, must go. These House doctors are notoriously good for nothing. Just as nothing can surpass your product, good leech.

Here is money for two shells of its virtues." He held out a silver
bu.[3] Busied with his preparations Tōkichi looked in vain toward
the rear apartment. After as long delay as he could contrive
he passed the shells and a heap of copper change over to the customer. As soon as the latter had left the shop Tōkichi bolted for
the rear. Kuma was gone. His aids were calmly smoking their
pipes and drinking the poor tea (*bancha*) of Tōkichi.

Kuma had little trouble in following his man to Okachimachi
in Shitaya. He found near by a shop for the sale of everything, from tobacco to *daikon* (radish), both odoriferous, yet
lacking perfume. Said Kuma—"A question or so: this tall
samurai, an oldish man, who lives close by; who is he?" The
woman in charge hesitated. Then dislike overcame discretion.
"Ah! With the hand wrapped in a bandage; his name is Sakarai
Kichirō Tayu. Truly he is a bad man. That he should quarrel
with his own class is no great matter. Maimed as he is, thrice
report has been made to the guard house, but in each case he
has escaped further process. He is a dreadful fellow; one who
never pays a debt, yet to whom it is dangerous to refuse credit.
Already nearly a *ryō* is due to this Echigoya. It has been the
bad luck to support him and his family during the past six
months." Said Kuma—"Thus maimed, to hold his own in
quarrels he must be a notable fencer as well as brawler. Was
the wound so received?"—"Iya! That is not known. Some
quarrel at the New Year's festivities probably was the cause.
Before that time he was sound enough." She laughed. "He
has two friends; Kahei San and Miemon San. They are birds
of a feather; and all partly plucked. Perhaps they quarrelled
in company, but if so have made it up. Sakurai San is a match
for the two others." She looked at Kuma, to see if he had more

---

[3] One-fourth of a *ryō* = 15 silver mommé = 872 grains Troy. Money
had much greater purchasing value at that time as compared with the
present days; perhaps 20 times, but adulteration of the coinage caused
great variations.

to say. Indifferent he picked out a strand of tobacco. "He shouldered this Gōbei into the ditch close by here. Fortunate is it to have escaped worse injury." Satisfied with his inquiries he took his way in haste to his master. The eyes of Yaémon and his aid shone with enjoyment. Surely they had the men of the Shiba Kiridōshi.

Magomé Yaémon at once sought out the machibugyō's office. His lordship heard the report. "Different disorders require different treatment. Of two of these men this Gemba knows something. The other man is hard to place, and evidently not so easy to deal with." Two *dōshin* and *yakunin* were sent at once to the addresses indicated. To capture Nakagawa Miemon and Imai Kahei was an easy task. The *dōshin* and *yakunin* sent to the house of Sakurai formed a band of twenty men. The house surrounded, without ceremony the officer and an aid entered. "On the lord's mission: Sakurai San is wanted at the office of Matsuda Dono. If resistance be made it will be necessary to use the rope. Pray accompany me." Sakurai Kichirō divined the object of the arrest. "The affair at the Kiridōshi has been scented out. The manner of that rascally drug seller was strange to-day." The officer had planted himself right before the sword rack. Sakurai could neither kill anybody, nor cut belly. He turned to his wife. "There is a matter on hand to be explained. Absence will probably be prolonged. Already the day is far advanced. . . . Ah! Is it Kichitarō?" A boy of seven years had rushed into the room. "Pretty fellow! . . . . Honoured Sir, be patient. The separation is no short one. No resistance is made. We go the same road. . . . Tarō; rude fellow! Salute the gentleman." The boy obeyed, with grave ceremony and a hostility which divined an unpleasant mission. "Your father leaves you. It is now the time to obey the mother in all she says. Remember well, or the end will be a bad one." Wife and child clung to him, frightened and now weeping. It was an arrest; their mainstay was being taken from them. In the last caresses he had time to bend

down and whisper to O'Ren—" In the toilet box is a scroll sealed
up. All is there explained. Read and destroy it. In later days
at discretion let our son know." Roughly he pushed woman and
boy aside. With rapid stride he reached the entrance. The
yakunin confronted him. He laughed and waved a hand. " There
is no resistance. We go the same road." The _dōshin_ permitted
the laxity of discipline. He had his orders.

Meanwhile the examination of the other two men was in
progress at the office of the _machibugyō_. As the biggest fool
of the two, Nakagawa Miemon was the first summoned to the
presence of Matsuda Dono. Said the Judge ⁴—" Nakagawa Uji,
there is a slight inquiry to make. How were those scars on the
face come by? These are marks of wounds not long since received. Consider well and remember." The tone of menace staggered Miemon. He had anticipated some rebuke for slight in-
fraction of the peace, not unusual with these men. " Naruhodo!
Has the Shiba Kiridōshi matter cropped up? " He hesitated—
" The story is a long one, and a foolish one. To weary the
honoured ears . . ." Matsuda Gemba caught him up with
impatient gesture. " Answer the question, and truly. , Nakagawa Miemon is noted neither for judgment nor sobriety." The
man caught up the last phrase as a cue. Eagerly he spoke, the
doors of the jail opening wide for exit—" So it is indeed. Wine
never benefited man; much less a _samurai_. Hence, with Kahei
and Sakurai Uji, it was decided to forswear wine forever. It
was determined to make a pilgrimage to Kompira San. There
the vow of abstinence was to be taken; on its holy ground. All
went well. We met at Nihonbashi. Alas! At the Kyōbashi the
perfume of a grog shop reached our noses. The vow had not
yet been taken. The ground was not holy. Just one last drink

---

⁴ The Machibugyō was judge and prosecutor (procurator or district attorney); the two offices being held by the same man. A court
trial included both functions. _Tengu_, used below, is the long-nosed
wood bogey. There is a note in Benkei, i, 260.

before setting out. But the Buddha was unfavourable. Once begun, the drinking was adjourned to a cook shop. There the bout continued all day. Wine lent us the wings of *tengu*. We travelled the road to Kompira San in a dream. In the progress Kahei and this Miemon quarrelled. Swords were drawn, and we cut each other. These wounds on head and face were the portion of this Miemon. Kahei had his hand nearly severed. Sakarai San, who was asleep, aroused by the noise, sprang up to part us. He is a man to be feared; but in my rage I sank my teeth in his hand. The bite of man or beast is poison. His wound was worse than that of either of us.

Gemba Dono was in conversation with his chamberlain. He let Miemon talk away. He was not one to say too little. As barely having listened he asked—" When was this fight? The day of the vow and journey to Kompira? Truly the result has been the vengeance of offended deity."—" The twelfth month tenth day," naturally replied Miemon. Gemba forced him to repeat the answer. Several times he put the query in different forms. Miemon, fool that he was, stuck to the date. Then said the magistrate—" Miemon, you are a liar. Moreover, you are a murderer. On the 13th day, on going up to the castle, this Gemba had converse with your lord. At that time Nakagawa Miemon was summoned to carry out a mission. As a man of whom report had been made you were noted well. At that time you had no wound. . . . Tie him up, and take him away." The *yakunin* fell on him from all sides. In a trice he was trussed up and removed.

Then appeared Imai Kahei. Kahei was cunning, but also a coward. To the questions of the *Machibugyō* he procrastinated in his answers, confused them all he could. What had Miemon said? " He spoke of the eloquence of Imai San; of Kahei Uji as the clever man, the one to tell the tale properly. Now let us have the true statement of the case." Such was Gemba's reply. It was flattering. Unable to help himself Kahei set sail on his sea of lies. "We all like wine . . ."—"Ah! After all you are agreed." Gemba smiled pleasantly. Kahei took courage—"But wine costs money. Together we went to Kuraya Jibei, a money-lender living at Kuramae no Saka, as is well known." Gemba nodded assent. "Of him two *ryō* were borrowed, on agreement to repay ten *ryō* as interest within a month. The nearest grog shop was sought, and it was the hour of the rat (11 P.M.) before the return was started. At the Teobashi a band of drunkards was encountered. Without cause these men forced a quarrel on us. Thus was the hand of Kahei nearly severed. This is the truth."—"And what was the date of this money bond?" Imai hesitated. He had caught a glimpse of the drug seller Tōkichi on being brought into the place. Without doubt the Kiridōshi affair was in question. He must antedate his wound. "Kahei does not remember with certainty. Perhaps it was the seventeenth day; before the Kwannon festival of the eighteenth day." He mumbled, and was frightened. Said Gemba sharply—"Speak distinctly; the seventeenth day?"—"Hei! Hei! Some time in the last decade of the month; the nineteenth or twentieth day—not later; not later." Matsuda Gemba almost leaped at him. "Oh, you liar! On the last day of the year you came, in person, to this Gemba to anticipate the New Year's gift (*sebo*). At that time you had no wound. Yet the drug seller sees you next day with maimed hand. It was not at Teobashi, but at Shiba Kiridōshi, that the wound was received. . . . Tie him up, and away with him." The *yakunin* came forward. Imai made a spasmodic attempt to rise. They threw him down, and in a moment he was keeping company with Nakagawa Miemon.

Gemba Dono braced himself for the more serious task. So did his *yakunin*. A glance showed the magistrate that he had mistaken his man. Sakarai Kichirō came forward with calm and dignity. Making his ceremonial salutation to the judge he came at once to the point. "What lies Miemon and Kahei have told, this Kichirō knows not. The fact is that we three plotted together

to rob the fatly supplied purses of the *bantō* making their rounds
in settlement of accounts at the close of the year. Hence the
bantō of the Shimaya, Zensuké, lost his money belt, and a man
of the same stamp, one Jugorō, was killed. All three of us are
guilty of the murder. . . ." As he would proceed Gemba held
up his hand. " Bring in the other two men. Continue, Kichirō."
Said Sakarai—" Miemon was badly cut about the head and face.
Kahei nearly lost his hand. This Kichiro would have killed the
clerk, but the procession of Geishū Sama came in sight, and
recognition was feared. Of the three hundred and twenty-five
ryō secured. . . ." The eyes of Nakagawa and Imai stood
out. Aghast they had followed the confession of Sakarai Kichirō,
with full intention to deny its truth. Now they were in a fury.
" What! Three hundred and twenty-five *ryō!* And we had but ten
ryō apiece. You jest, Sakarai Uji. . . . Oh! The low fellow! The villain! A very beast! A swine!"

Gemba Dono could ask for nothing more. With smiling face
and courtesy he turned to Sakurai Kichirō. Why did Kichirō
take the three hundred *ryō,* giving to these fellows such a paltry
sum?" Answered Kichirō—" As deserving no more. They are
paltry fellows; little better than common soldiers (*ashigaru*).
But there is more to tell, now the end is reached. The true name
of Sakarai Kichirō is Takahashi Daihachirō, at one time a retainer of Matsudaira Aki no Kami. Pressed by the money lender
Jusuké, I killed him and had the body disposed of by one Densuké,
the cook at the soldiers' quarters of the *yashiki.* This was in
Tenwa 3rd year 5th month (June 1683). Fleeing to avoid arrest
the occupation of writing teacher was taken up at Yūki in Shimosa.
Densuké, too, had fled, and hither he came as a wandering beggar.
Fearing his tongue I killed him; and mutilating the corpse, threw
it into the castle moat close by. A beggar found dead, no inquiry
was made."—" When did this take place?" asked Gemba. " Just
one year later—Jōkyō 1st year 5th month." He made a little
movement. Nakagawa and Imai broke out into protest at the

completeness of this confession, but Sakarai turned fiercely on them. " Shut up! To undergo public trial would bring shame on all *kerai* throughout the land; would cause people to fear our caste. We three planned the deed and secured the money." He put his arms behind his back. The *yakunin*, stepping softly, roped him up almost with respect. A wave of Gemba's hand and the guilty men were removed. Unable to help themselves, Nakagawa and Imai made confession to avoid the torture in what was now a hopeless case. Later the sentences of condemnation were issued. Degraded from their status the three men were taken to the execution ground of Shinagawa, and there decapitated.

The wife of Takahashi Daihachirō did not wait these proceedings. The confession of her husband was in her hands before he himself told everything to Matsuda Gemba. Before night she had decamped with her son. At eight years of age Kichitarō was placed as disciple (*deshi*) at the Jōshinji of Fukagawa. Receiving the name of Myōshin he became the favourite of the rector (*jūshoku*) of the temple. The mother now became reduced to the greatest penury. For a time she was bawd in the Honjō Warigesui district. Subsequently she was promoted to the position of favourite sultana (wife) of her master Tōeman, local head of his profession. Her name now was O'Matsu. When Myōshin was thirteen years old in some way he was told that she was dead. Henceforth he had no stay in the world but the worthy priest, who became a second and better father to him. This treatment found its usual and virtuous reward. At eighteen years, now a priest and learned in priestly ways, he took to himself the contents of the temple strong box. Fifty *ryō* soon disappeared in the company of the harlots of Fukagawa Yagura-Shita. A prolonged absence of Myōshin aroused the inquiries of the other monks, and the eyes of the rector were soon opened as to his unworthy proselyte, the blighted issue of a miserable stock.[5]

---

[5] The *tawara* equals two-fifths of a *koku*. At present-day figures the stipend of Tamiya can be put at about 2000 yen; that of Itō Kwaiba,

mentioned later, at 13,000 yen. The great *daimyō* with incomes running into the hundreds of thousands of *koku* were princes administering part of the public domain, with armies and an elaborate civil service to support. Even a *hatamoto* (minor *daimyō*, immediate vassals of the shōgun) of 10,000 *koku*, such as Yagyū Tajima no Kami had a large train at his Edo *yashiki* and at his fief. The Daté House of Sendai, or the Maeda of Kaga, Etchū, and Echizen, are examples of the greater Tōzama, or lords independent in the administration of their fiefs. Labour, it is to be added, was cheap compared to food values. Taxes were heavy—ranging from 30 to 70 per cent. The middleman took his high fee. Yet sumptuary laws were necessary to prevent extravagance among the farming class. Some of them were rich men, especially in the better administered Tokugawa fiefs. The public works required of the *daimyō* —especially the Tōzama—prevented a dangerous accumulation of resources, and sometimes almost ruined his subjects. Accurate measurements of income are not available. The *koku* of daimyō income has been placed as high as ten bushels. The present-day *koku* equals 5.13 bushels. The price of rice ranges between 15–20 yen per *koku*.

CHAPTER VI

NEGOTIATIONS: THE BUSINESS OF A MARRIAGE BROKER (NAKŌDO)

THE presence of O'Iwa created an upheaval in the Samonchō household. The wet nurse required brought with her a train of servants. With the child's growth this was maintained, even increased. The young lady (Ojōsan) found herself graduated into one with a *status* to maintain. All the niggardly habits of Matazaémon were thrown to the winds with the advent of this grandchild. The affection never shown outwardly to the mother, was lavished on her daughter. At seven years of age O'Iwa underwent the common enough infliction of smallpox. It showed itself on the anniversary day of O'Mino's death, and the child's sickness afforded but mutilated rites for the memorial service of the mother. Matazaémon would have abandoned all his duties, himself to nurse the child. O'Naka loved O'Iwa for self and daughter. She had sense enough to drive the old man into a corner of the room, then out of it; and further expostulations sent him to his duties. Who, in those iron days, would accept such excuse for absence? The child worried through, not unscathed. Her grandmother's qualifications as nurse have been mentioned. O'Iwa was a plain girl. She had the flat plate-like face of her mother. The eyes were small, disappearing behind the swollen eyelids, the hair was scanty, the disease added its black pock marks which stood thick and conspicuous on a fair skin. Otherwise she was spared by its ravages, except—

Whatever her looks O'Iwa compensated for all by her disposition. She had one of those balanced even temperaments, with clear judgment, added to a rare amiability. Moreover she possessed all the accomplishments and discipline of a lady. At eleven

63

years Matazaémon unwillingly had sought and found a place for her in attendance on her ladyship of the great Hosokawa House. O'Iwa's absence made no difference in his household. The train of servants was maintained, to be disciplined for her return, to be ready on this return. Perhaps it was a pleasing fiction to the fond mind of the aging man that she would return, soon, to-morrow. O'Naka acquiesced in the useless expense and change in her habits. She always acquiesced; yet her own idea would have been to make a good housekeeper of O'Iwa—like herself, to sew, cook, wash, clean—a second O'Mino. She could not understand the new turn of Matazaémon's mind. As for O'Iwa, she grew to girlhood in the Hosokawa House, learned all the accomplishments of her own house and what the larger scale of her new position could teach her; everything in the way of etiquette and the polite arts, as well as the plainer tasks of housekeeping, she was likely ever to be called on to perform. The plain child grew into the plain woman; perhaps fortunately for her. The okugata (her ladyship) was a jealous woman. Her spouse was mad on women. Every nubile maid (koshimoto) in the yashiki was a candidate for concubinage. His wife countered by as hideous a collection of females as her own House and her lord's retainers could furnish. O'Iwa attracted from the first by her lack of all physical attraction. His lordship tried to get used to her with the passage of years—and failed. He could not stomach the necessary advances. But the girl's admirable temper and even judgment secured the esteem of all. These latter qualities captivated the whole household. It was O'Iwa who performed all duties for her ladyship, took them in charge as her substitute. For the first time in his life Oki no Kami found something in a woman apart from her sex. When the time came for O'Iwa to depart, the regret of lord and lady was substantially expressed in their gifts. But his lordship had to admit failure. Not a retainer could be found willing to take the daughter of Tamiya as wife. So far O'Iwa's mission at the yashiki had failed.

O'Naka knew this. Matazaémon never gave it thought; so glad he was to get her back. He received the honoured words and presents with humble and delighted thanks. O'Iwa reëntered her home, a recovered jewel. She was the Ojōsan, the lady daughter. A first step of her's was gradually to get rid of a good part of the superfluous train. O'Iwa was a very practical girl. Matazaémon was now old and ill. He was nearing his seventieth year. The one idea in his head was the *muko*, the son to be adopted as husband of the heir of the House; the mate to be secured for O'Iwa, and the posterity to be secured for his House. As a little girl O'Iwa had been much courted—in fun. Watanabé Juzō, Natsumé Kyuzō, Imaizumi Jinzaémon, many others the growing " sparks " of Samonchō and roundabout, could not forbear this amusement with the little " Bakémono " (apparition). Of their ill intent O'Iwa knew nothing. Indeed a short experience with O'Iwa disarmed derision. Most of the unseemly lovers came genuinely to like the girl, unless inherent malice and ugliness of disposition, as with Natsumé and Akiyama Chōzaémon, made their sport more than mere pastime. But as grown men they could not face the results of the final step, and no parent was harsh enough to graft his unwilling stock on O'Iwa's persimmon trees. The girl was clever enough to know this. It was Hōei 6th year (1709) and she was now twenty-six years old. It was indirectly at her suggestion that Matazaémon sought the aid of Kondō Rokurōbei. This man lived just behind the large inclosure of the Sainenji, on the hill slope which dips steeply down to the Samégabashi. The relationship was very distant at best; but with nearer relatives in general, and with Yoémon his brother in particular, the master of Tamiya had deadly feud. To them he would not turn to find a husband for O'Iwa.

Thus it happened that one day in the seventh month (August) Rokurōbei was awaiting the appearance of Yamada Chōbei. He really knew little about the man, but Chōbei at one time had been resident in the ward. He had undergone vicissitudes, and now

5

was a dealer in metals and a kind of broker in everything under the sign of Musashiya. He had a wide acquaintance over Edo in his different businesses, and was the easy and slip-shod means by which Rokurōbei would avoid the more arduous part of the task laid on him by Matazaémon. Chōbei was not long in putting in an appearance. All affairs were gifts of the gods to a man who lived on wind. Kazaguruma Chōbei—Windmill Chōbei —he was called. His flittings were so noiseless and erratic, just like the little paper windmills made for children, that the nickname applied exactly fitted him. The maid in announcing him showed no particular politeness. " Wait here a moment . . . Danna Sama (master), Chōbei San, the metal dealer, requests an interview."—" Ah! Pass him here at once. . . . Is it Chōbei? Please sit down." Chōbei had followed almost on the girl's footsteps. She drew aside to make room for him, then flirted out in haste. Poverty and dislike had no influence in Yotsuya in those days. She seemed to scent the man.

Chōbei looked with envy at the comfortable Rokurōbei. The day was hot. The thin *kimono* fallen about his loins, the latter's garb was a pair of drawers and a thin shirt. He sat looking out on the garden, with its shade of large trees, its shrubbery and rock work. Everything was dripping with the water industriously splashed to this side and to that by the serving man. The tea was brought and Kondō at last remembered that he had a guest. As he turned—" It is a long time since a visit has been paid. Deign to pardon the intrusion." Chōbei sighed in making this remark. The irony was lost on his fat host. As Rokurōbei seemed unwilling, or hardly to know how to impart the subject concerning which he had summoned him, Chōbei continued— " And the honoured health, is it good? The honoured business, is it on some matter of moment that Chōbei is summoned? " Rokurōbei woke up under the direct question. He, too, sighed. Chōbei was noted for a greed which inspired fear. For money he would do anything. " Blindman Chōbei " had been his nickname of old days in the ward. Kondō remembered this. He liked money, too. It brought in so much comfort. He hated to part with comfort. It was to be a question between himself and Chōbei how much of his hard-earned commission was to be parted with. This last thought completely aroused him. " It is a matter of securing a *muko*. This Rokurōbei is the one charged with the task. As a son-in-law outside the ward is desired, no one has wider circulation and better opportunities than Chōbei San. Hence the desire for a consultation." Chōbei whistled inwardly. Outside the ward! What was wrong with the case. Here was coin to be turned up by the circumspect. " Surely there are young fellows enough in Samonchō, fit to be *muko*. Of course with impediments . . ."—" It is the daughter of Tamiya; O'Iwa San. Matazaémon Dono has commissioned this Rokurōbei to secure a *muko*." Chōbei whistled outwardly. " For O'Iwa San! . . ."—" She is no beauty, as Chōbei evidently knows. Wealth compensates for other deficiencies. At all events his aid is desired."—" For how much? " Chōbei spoke bluntly. If Rokurōbei had forgotten Chōbei, Chōbei had not forgotten Rokurōbei. He went on—" To get a price for damaged goods is no sinecure. Fortunately she is only out of repair on the surface. . . . Say ten *ryō?* " Kondō laughed scornfully—" And they call Chōbei ' the Blind-man '! Rather is it vision magnified. The entertainment should be the reward; with what Chōbei collects from the happy bridegroom." Chōbei replied gravely—" With such a wealthy connection the future of Kondō Dono is to be envied. Chōbei has to realize his future at once. Not a *ryō* less can he afford." Plainly he was in earnest, as was the long conversation which followed. Finally Chōbei emerged with partial success, and half the sum named as stipend for his labours.

He began them at once. The next day he was at the metal market in Kanda. In course of chaffering over wares he never bought—" You fellows always have some *rōnin* in train; a fine, handsome fellow for whom a wife is needed. Application is made.

Jinzaémon, you have a candidate."—"Not for the kind of wife Chōbei San provides." Those present laughed loudly at the sally. Chōbei did not wink. He explained. "No bad provision is this one. Rich, with an income of thirty *tawara*, a fine property in reversion, and but twenty-five years old. The man therefore must be fit to pose as a *samurai;* able to read and write, to perform official duty, he must be neither a boy nor a man so old as to be incapable. Come now! Does no one come forward? *Rōnin* are to be had. A *ryō* for aid to this Chōbei."—"Too cheap as an offer," was Jinzaémon's retort. "A *rōnin* is one to be handled with care. Those favoured with acquaintance of the honoured *bushi* often part with life and company at the same date. Those without lords are equally testy as those in quarters." He spoke with the bluntness of the true Edokko, the peculiar product of the capital; men who were neither farmers nor provincials, but true descendants of the men of the guild of Bandzuin Chōbei. He jested, but the subject interested the crowd. Said one—"Does Chōbei San get the *ryō* out of groom or bride? She is a bold wench, unmarried at that age; and none too chaste eh, Chōbei San? She will provide the husband with wife and child to hand, or in the making. Or, are matters the other way? Has she been tried and found wanting? Is she impotent, or deformed; or is Chōbei making fools of us?" Answered Chōbei slowly—"No; she is a little ugly. The face round and flat, shining, with black pock marks, making it look like speckled pumice, rouses suspicion of leprosy. This, however, is not the case. At all events she is a woman." All were now roaring with laughter—"A very beauty indeed! Just the one for Chōbei's trade! Too honied was his speech. He would market anything. But in this market it is a matter of hard cash; without credit. This is a bit of goods too wilted. Even Chōbei cannot sell it."— "You lie!" said Chōbei in a towering passion. "At the first hint of ill-fortune threatening wine supply or pleasure, there is not one of you who would not turn to Chōbei to find the money needed.

Sisters, daughters, wives, aunts . . . mothers are for sale."
He was choking with rage. " Sell her? Chōbei can and will."
Angered by the final item on his family list, a man nearby gave
him a sharp poke in the back. Others voiced resentment, perhaps
would have given it material form. The canal was spoken of.
Chōbei took the hint. He did not wait for a ducking. At a sharp
pace he trotted off toward his tenement at Asakusa Hanagawadō.
For a while he would avoid the metal market. He regretted his
display of temper. It was in the necessities of other trades that
he found the material of his own, and flourished.

In plain terms Kazaguruma Chōbei was a pimp for the Yoshiwara and kindred quarters. His other occupations were mere
channels accessory to this main business. Hence his seasons of
increase and decline. Just now he was in a period of decline. His
eagerness in this Tamiya affair was sharpened. Pushing his way
through the Kuramae of Asakusa suddenly a hopeful light came
into his eye. Abruptly he made his way to the side of the roadway. Here boarding covered the ditch, removing the occupant of
a booth erected thereon, and would-be clients, from the passing
stream of humanity. There was a table in the booth, and on it
were several books, a vessel containing water, brushes (*fudé*),
scrolls for writing, and a box containing divining sticks. It was
the stand of a strolling fortune-teller. At the time the occupant
was engaged in gathering together his professional apparatus, with
the evident purpose to decamp. Chōbei did not delay in accosting
him. " Ah! The Sensei; [1] Kazuma Uji finds the day too hot to
pry into the future. Does the Sensei leave his clients to their fate,
or have the clients abandoned the Sensei? Deign to come along
with Chōbei. Perhaps he, too, can tell fortunes. At all events
the wife has been forewarned; the bath is ready. It will put life

---

[1] The title for all men of learning and professional attainments.
The great medical doctor is " Sensei," the doctor of literature is
" Sensei "—and the charlatan who peddles charms by the highway is
" Sensei "-teacher.

into both of us." The young man laughed and hastened his operations, nodding assent—"Thanks are felt, Chōbei San. Indeed
this Kazuma has but to continue the art of prophecy if he would
foretell his own fate. No one will buy the future when money
is so needed for the present. Besides this is a pleasure ground.
Men have no hankering to learn of possible worse luck than being
here. All the fools have died—except their prophet." He shouldered his scanty apparatus, and with rapid stride the two men
pushed their way up the crowded street toward the great gate of
the temple. In his haste Chōbei yet had time to eye, from time to
time, his companion, always gaining encouragement from the pal-
pable seediness made more plain by a handsome person. The
two were neighbours in a house-row (nagaya) of the Hanagawadō, that poverty-stricken district along the river close to the
great amusement ground, and furnishing those who perform its
baser tasks. On arrival Chōbei called out—"O'Taki! O'Taki!
The bath, is it ready? The Sensei, Kazuma San, honours us with
his company. Make all ready for his reception. . . . Sensei,
condescend to enter; please come up."

Yanagibara Kazuma dropped his clogs in the vestibule. As he
entered the room—"Pray pardon the intrusion. This Kazuma
feels much in the way. He is continually putting his neighbours
of the nagaya to inconvenience; too great the kindness of Chōbei
San and wife." O'Taki laughed deprecatingly. Truly this was
a handsome young man. In this 6th year of Hōei (1709) Yanagibara Kazuma was twenty-one years of age. O'Taki was thirty
odd. She appreciated masculine beauty all the more. Chōbei
grunted from heat and the merest trace of discomfiture. He
had his limit, even in his business. Quickly he shook off his
kimono, and fan in hand squatted in his loin cloth. "Ah! 'Tis
hot beyond endurance. Business is bad—from Yoshiwara to
Yotsuya." O'Taki looked up at the last word. He continued—
"The Sensei takes precedence. Kazuma Uji, deign to enter the
bath. All is ready?" His wife nodded assent. Kazuma fol-

lowed the example of Chōbei. In a trice he was naked as his mother bore him. Chōbei burst out into phrases of admiration—" What a splendid fellow! Ah! Waste of material! If a woman Kazuma San would be a fortune to himself and to Chōbei. . . . Taki, note the skin of the Sensei. It has the texture of the finest paper. How regrettable!" He drew back for the better inspection of the sum total of his subject's charms. O'Taki drew closer for the same purpose. Chōbei sighed—" It is plain enough that Kazuma San is not a woman. An error of Nature! Somehow the age at which a woman becomes of use, is that at which a boy becomes a mere burden. He is fit for nothing but to be a story-teller. . . . And you, Taki, what are you about? The lady of his affections was far advanced in the process of disrobing. She protested. "Does not the Sensei need aid in the bath? How cleanse the back, the shoulders. This Taki would aid him."— " Immodest wench!" bellowed Chōbei. " The Sensei needs no such aid. "Why! You . . . Taki . . . one would take you for a charcoal ball (*tadon*), so dark your skin. Nay! For two of them, for a cluster piled in a box, so round the buttocks and belly. The Sensei wants no aid from such an ugly jade. This Chōbei can do what is needed; with as much skill and better purpose than a woman." Kazuma modestly interposed in this incipient quarrel between husband and wife. " Nay, the matter is of no importance. Kazuma is grateful for such kindness, but aid is not needed. His arm is long." He held it out, almost simian in proportion and slenderness, the one proportional defect of this handsome body. The quarrel of Chōbei and O'Taki lapsed before his pleasant smile.

Seated over tea said Chōbei—" This Chōbei, too, has claimed to be a diviner. Don't deny it. The Sensei at one time has been a priest." Kazuma looked at him with surprise, even misgiving. Explained Chōbei—" The manner in which the Sensei takes up the cup betrays him; in both hands, with a little waving of the vessel and shake of the head. The rust of the priest's garb clings close." Said Kazuma—"Chōbei San is a clever fellow. It is true. At one time I was priest."—"Whereabouts?" asked Chōbei. "At the Reigan of Fukagawa," replied the prophet—"Ah! Reiganji; and later would return to the life of a *Samurai*. Such pose and manner possessed by the Sensei are only gained in good company. He would reassume the status. This Chōbei was not always as he is. Wine, women, gambling, have brought him to pimping. The buying of *geisha* and *jorō* cost the more as they imply the other two vices. Wife, status, fortune; all are gone. Such has been Chōbei's fate."—"Not the only case of the kind," grumbled his partner in concubinage. "And the wife, what has become of her?"—"None of Taki's affair, as she is no longer an issue. Would the jade be jealous?" He glowered at her. "But Kazuma San, this Chōbei is not only diviner, to tell fortunes. He can make them." Kazuma laughed. "Don't joke. Chōbei San's line of business has already cost this Kazuma fortune and position."—"To secure a better one. Kazuma San is a *rōnin* (without lord), a man of education, and of fine appearance. He is just the one to become a *muko*.—"In some tradesman's family?" The *samurai* spoke with disdain. Said Chōbei eagerly—"No: Chōbei prophesied the return of Kazuma Uji to his own caste."—"At what cost?" said Kazuma coolly. "The honour of a *samurai* cannot stand open taint. Kazuma has no desire to cut belly at too early a date, to save the situation for others. Has the woman erred, and is the father's sword dulled?" —"It is no such case," answered Chōbei. The parents, rather grandparents, are fools in pride. The girl is twenty-five years old, rich, and, one must admit, not too good looking. It is by a mere chance, a former connection, that the affair comes into Chōbei's hands. As Kazuma Uji knows, it is not much in his line. Let us share the good luck together."—"Is she a monster; one of those long-necked, pop-eyed *rokurokubi?*"—"That can be determined at the meeting," said the cautious Chōbei. "She is somewhat pock-marked, as with others. It is a matter of luck.

Chōbei's position forces him to fall back on Kazuma San as the only likely man to recommend. Deign not to refuse to come to his aid."—" Rich, and granddaughter of people old in years." He eyed Chōbei quizzically. The latter nodded agreement. " No matter what her looks, this Kazuma accepts with thanks—unless this be a jest of Chōbei San." Chōbei slightly coughed—" There is a commission. . . ."—" Ah! Then the foundation is rock. As to commission, assuredly; Kazuma is not rich, nor in funds." —" But will be. At ten *ryō* it is a cheap affair."—" Agreed," replied the diviner carelessly. " The money will be paid."—" With the delivery of the goods." Chōbei now was all gaiety—" Of the Rokurokubi, the monster with sextuple lengthed neck," laughed Kazuma Sensei as he took his leave. He was engaged to meet Chōbei the next day at the house of Kondō Rokurōbei in Yotsuya.

CHAPTER VII

IÉMON APPEARS

IN his difficult mission Kondō Rokurōbei had hopes of Chōbei; but not much more. It was with no small pleasure that he heard the announcement of his visit the next morning. The maid was a shade more civil—" Please wait." Kondō was decidedly so. He greeted Chōbei with an effusion which Chōbei noted. The tea brought, the two men faced each other over the cups. To Kondō's inquiring look—" Honoured master the task is a difficult one." He retailed his experience at the Kanda market. Kondō was somewhat discomfited. He had put a different interpretation on the early visit of Chōbei. Continued the latter—" A difficult task, but not hopeless. Surely five *ryō* is very small remuneration." Kondō's eye lit up. Chōbei had his man. " It is all this Kondō is qualified to give. Chōbei knows Tamiya Dono. After all it is he who pays, and Chōbei can claim but his share. However, the matter is not urgent. A bad turn with Matazaémon, and O'Naka will be much easier to deal with . . . unless it be Yoémon who interposes." He made a wry face; joined in by Chōbei. Kondō went on—" It is matter of regret to have troubled you. The parents of Natsume Kyuzō show signs of breaking off present negotiations and coming round to us. This is a matter of yesterday, and on hearing that the affair of O'Iwa San was definitely in the hands of Rokurōbei." Chōbei was frightened. Was this the cause of Kondō's joy? Had he misinterpreted on his entrance? He put out a hand, as if to stop the talk of his host. " Deign to allow the money question to stand as agreed. Such step would put this Chōbei in an awkward position. The man is found, and soon will be here. Probably even Kondō Dono will be satisfied."—" Who is he? " asked Kondō.—" One Yanagi-bara Kazuma. He has practised divination at Asakusa . . ."

—"A charlatan! A quack doctor! Chōbei, are you mad?"
Rokurōbei pushed back his cushion and his cue in horror. Not a
word did he say of Natsume Kyuzō. Chōbei smiled. He had been
trapped; but he had detected Kondō. "Don't be alarmed. The
man is a *rōnin*, his divination of small account and due to temporary stress. Kondō Dono will soon judge of the man by his
appearance. Let the subject of Kazuma San be dropped—with
that of Natsume San. Our bargain has been made firm." Kondō
looked down. He felt a little injured. Continued Chōbei—"For
his man Chōbei cannot answer if all be known. Pray follow my
plan, and precede us to the house of Matazaémon. He must not
see O'Iwa at this juncture. Tamiya Dono is ill and not visible.
The O'Basan is wise enough to do as she is told. Years have
drilled that into her. O'Iwa has taken cold. Her hair is loose
and she cannot think of appearing. Make this known when the
time comes to serve the wine. Meanwhile send her off on some
mission; to the house of Akiyama, or that of the newly-wed
Imaizumi."—"But the man must see the girl," protested Kondō.
Answered Chōbei—"He must see the property. It is with that
Chōbei intends he shall become enamoured. He is not to see
the girl until she is his wife. To keep the estate he will cleave to
the woman. Trust Chōbei for a knowledge of men's hearts
. . . at least that of Yanagibara Kazuma." Perhaps he spoke
a little too plainly. Rokurōbei had a last touch of conscience—
"Chōbei, what manner of man is this one you bring? What is
his real nature? Tamiya is upright as the walls of the Honmaru
(castle). And Yanagibara Kazuma . ." Chōbei's brow
wrinkled. He was spared an answer. Said the maid—"Yanagibara Sama would see the master."—"Show him in at once," said
Rokurōbei.

He rose, as much in amazement as in courtesy. Kazuma was
a striking figure as he entered the room. His dress of white
Satsuma was of finest quality, and perfectly aligned. The *haori*
(cloak) was of the corrugated Akashi crape. In his girdle he

wore the narrow swords then coming into fashion, with finely lacquered scabbards. In person he was tall, fair, with high forehead and big nose. Slender and sinewy every movement was lithe as that of a cat. Kondō gasped as he made the accustomed salutations. " This man for O'Iwa! Bah! A fox has stolen a jewel." All his compunction and discretion vanished before this unusual presence. Kazuma gracefully apologized for his intrusion, thus uninvited. Kondō stammered protests and his delight at the opportunity of meeting Yanagibara Dono. Chōbei smiled inward and outward delight at thus summarily removing any too pointed objections of Kondō. For absolute self-possession in this awkward situation the younger man easily carried the palm. Kazuma acted as would a man double his years. Chōbei was not only delighted, but astonished. " Whence had the Sensei produced all this wondrous get-up? Was he in real fact a magician? Kazuma knew, but he was not one to enlighten Chōbei or anyone else. After talk on general matters the affair of the meeting was broached. Said Kondō Rokurōbei—" Thus to trouble Yanagibara Dono requires apology, but the affair is not without advantage. The lady is the daughter of Tamiya, a *dōshin* and favoured by the Hosokawa House. This Kondō is honoured in presenting Kazuma Dono in Yotsuya."—" Nay, fear enters.[1] The honour of this meeting with Kondō Dono is as great as the intrusion has been unseemly. Deign to pardon the precipitancy of this Kazuma." Kondō protested in his turn. Said Chōbei—" The presentation made, doubtless the matter is as good as concluded. But Tamiya Dono is ill; this visit is unexpected. If Kondō Dono would deign to precede, and ascertain how matters are at Tamiya,

---

[1] A technical social expression = " I trouble you " or " with highest respect and consideration." Satuma = Satsuma-Jōfu, the grass cloth of fine quality woven and dyed in Loo-choo; narrow swords; all this (Momogawa) is an example of the earnest study the kōdan lecturers make of their subject. These delightful little expositions of dress and manner are frequent.

it would be well." To this Kondō assented. Making his excuses
he set out for Samonchō, bubbling over with excitement, and
praying that the matter would have certain issue; and thus estab-
lish him for life on the shoulders of the wealthy Tamiya. Prayers?
Indeed he did stop on the road, one lined with the ecclesiastical
structures. Kondō had too much at stake, not to invoke all
likely aid.

With his departure Chōbei began to go into the externals of
the House of Tamiya. As they walked along—" Congenial surroundings." This was with a grin and a wave of the hand toward
the long line of temple buildings and graveyards they were passing.
" Not much savour of present lodging in Hanagawadō. Eh!
Kazuma Uji, even Chōbei notes the difference." He stopped
opposite the Gwanshōji and looked across the way. The fruit
was already formed on the trees of Matazaémon's garden.
" Persimmons of a hundred momme (375 grammes) each; twenty
cartloads for the profit of the house at the fall of the year." As
they passed in the entrance on Samonchō he pointed to a store-
house. " Stuffed with rice, from the farms of Tamiya in Kazusa.
No husks to be found in it."—" Who said there were?" said
Kazuma testily. His eyes were taking in the wide proportions of
the garden, the spreading roof and eaves of a stately mansion.
As they passed along the *rōka* to a sitting room Chōbei called his
attention to the fret work (*rama-shōji*) between the rooms, the
panelled ceilings, the polished and rare woodwork of *tokonoma*
(alcoves). A *kakémono* of the severe Kanō school was hung in the
sitting room alcove, a beautifully arranged vase of flowers stood
beneath it. Matazaémon could not use his legs, but his hands were
yet active. Of his visitors he knew nothing; least of all of
Chōbei. Kondō Rokurōbei appeared. With him was an old lady.
O'Naka bowed to the ground before the proposed son-in-law.
She was in a flutter over the beautiful man destined for O'Iwa.
The admirable courtesy of his manners, the tender softness of
voice, robbed her of what little judgment she had. Her only fear

was that the candidate for honours and the Tamiya would escape. Said Chōbei—" Asakusa is a long distance; the occasion exceptional. Cannot the Ojōsan favour us by pouring the wine?" The old woman hummed and hawed. Kondō, too, seemed put out. " As a matter of fact O'Iwa is not presentable. She has taken cold, and just now is in bed. Perhaps the O'Basan will urge her further, now that Yanagibara Uji is present." O'Naka at once rose, like to an automaton, the spring of which has been pressed. She disappeared, to return and repeat her lesson. " Wilful as a child! One would suppose her such. Illness she would disregard, but her hair is not made up. She cannot think of appearing before company. Truly she is vexing."—" Not so," defended Chōbei. " She could not show higher regard than by refusing to appear before a future husband in careless attire. It is a guarantee of conduct when married. She is much to be commended for such respect. All women like to appear well. A man in the neighbourhood, and rice powder and rouge are at once applied. How neglect such an elaborate structure as the hair? Trust Chōbei's judgment as to women."

O'Naka thought that he spoke well, but like most men with great conceit. Kazuma looked out towards the beautiful garden. He took the chance to smile, for he had soon ascertained that Kondō knew little about his agent; was in fact a precipitate, testy man. However, he was a little put out at not seeing the would-be bride. At an opportunity he stepped out, to see more of the house and its surroundings. Chōbei came up to him as he stood on the *rōka*. His voice was coaxing and pleading. " Is it not a fine prospect—for Kazuma Dono?" His voice hung on the ' Dono.' " Nay, don't let escape this splendid piece of luck. Long has Chōbei interested himself in his neighbour. Such a beautiful exterior should have a proper setting. Marry O'Iwa San and Kazuma Dono is master of Tamiya. Is it agreed?" Kazuma looked down in thought. At his age there are ideals of the other sex, hard to put aside. Said he—" Not to see the lady.

... Is she so horrible?" Chōbei protested. "Not so! The lady is a mere item, well fitted to go with this fine house, this beautiful garden, these store-houses filled with goods. Look: Tamiya Dono is a man of double rations. The property has *nagaya* for attendants. For long this has not been used. Tamiya will not rent it out. It will be so much revenue added to the stipend of the House, and will replace the old man's uncertain income from his accomplishments as master of *hanaike* and *cha-no-yu*." Kazuma looked around, following the pointing finger of Chōbei. He was in sad straits. His only future was this position of a *muko*. No matter what the woman might be, there was compensation. To Chōbei's direct question he made answer—"Yes."

The affair of the marriage suffered no delays. Chōbei had struck home. Kazuma was so impressed with the surroundings, especially after a return to his own miserable quarters, that the matter of the interview took a minor place to the inspection of his future property. Within the week he had removed to the house of Kondō Rokurōbei. The latter introduced him to his future associates in the ward by a succession of fish and wine dinners dear to the heart of the men of Nippon. These neighbours were astonished at the future son-in-law of the Tamiya. This man was to be the husband of the O'Baké? Was he mad, or drunk? Perhaps the latter, for neither themselves nor Kazuma had the opportunity to be particularly sober during this period of festivity. Of course there was an introduction to Matazaémon, the other principal involved. As Kondō carefully explained, no set date could be made for this interview. Tamiya Dono was ill, and to be seen at a favourable time. As ill luck would have it, on the very day the interview was permitted O'Iwa San received an urgent summons from the Okugata of the Hosokawa House. This could not be disregarded, and her absence on the second occasion was easily explained and condoned. Kondō certainly made no effort, and Kazuma no suggestion, for a meeting in the three days intervening before the formal marriage.

At evening the guests met in the reception rooms of Tamiya. In a private apartment were Kondō Rokurōbei and his wife, O'Iwa, and Iémon. The latter name had been assumed by Kazuma on his formal registration in the Tamiya House. It was Chōbei who had purchased the *wataboshi*, or wadded hood, of floss silk worn by the bride on this great occasion of her life. Iémon could see but little within its depths, except the shining light of her countenance. Joy perhaps? At least this curiosity was soon to be satisfied. Nine times—three times three—were the *saké* cups drained. Kondō Rokurōbei joined the hands of the train, exhorting them to mutual forbearance, O'Iwa to unquestioning obedience to the husband. He pattered over the maxims of the Dōjikun of Kaibara Yekken in this strange case, as he had done twenty times before with favourable results. Yekken's book was comparatively recent, only a few decades old, and the woman's guide. Truly the position of the *nakōdo* was no easy one, if it was to bring him at odds with either House involved. He felt complacent. This pair at least presented less complications in that line than usual. What there was of doubtful issue came now to the test. At this crisis he cast an eye to the *rōka* (verandah) to see that Chōbei really was at hand as promised. Then the strings of the *wataboshi* were loosed. The hood concealing the face of O'Iwa was removed.

Iémon rose to his feet as if impelled by springs; then hurriedly he sat again with some mumbled excuse and trembling hands. He could not take his eyes from the shining white of the face before him, the glazed smooth surface left in many places between the black of the pock marks. The removal of the hood had somewhat disarrayed the hair, leaving the broad expanse of forehead more prominent, the puffed heavy eyelids in the face more conspicuous. In the depths shone two tiny points, the eyes. Indeed, as Chōbei afterwards described it, eyelids and eyes had the appearance of *kuzumanju*, the dumplings of white rice paste with the black dots of dark brown bean paste sunk deep in the centre. Never had O'Iwa appeared to such disadvantage. She was now engaged in removing the white garment, to appear in her proper array as bride and wife. Iémon took advantage of this absence to step to the *rōka*. In leaving the room Kondō had given a wink to Chōbei. Iémon almost ran into him. He seized him by the arm. The young man's voice was excited. He spoke in a whisper, as one who could barely find speech. With satisfaction Chōbei noted that he was frightened, not angered. "What is that? Who is that creature?" were the first words of Iémon. Replied Chōbei coldly—"That is the wife of Tamiya Iémon; O'Iwa San, daughter of Matazaémon Dono; your wife to eight thousand generations." Then roughly—"Deign, Iémon San, not to be a fool. In the purchase of cow or horse, what does the buyer know of the animal? Its real qualities remain to be ascertained. O'Iwa San is ugly. That much Chōbei will admit. She is pock-marked, perhaps stoops a little. But if the daughter of the rich Tamiya, a man with this splendid property, had been a great beauty, this Iémon would not have become the *muko* of Tamiya, the future master of its wealth. What qualification had he for such a position—a diviner, a man whose pedigree perhaps would not stand too much search." He looked keenly at Iémon, and noted with satisfaction how the last thrust had gone home. Chōbei must know more of Iémon, ex-Kazuma. He determined on that for the future.

He continued—"Withdrawal at this juncture would merely create scandal. Matazaémon is not so bereft of friends that such a step would not cause serious displeasure in high quarters. The insult would find an avenger. Then consider please: the old man is kept alive by the anxiety to see his granddaughter established in life, the line of the Tamiya assured. He will die within the month. If the old woman hangs on too long"—he halted speech for a moment, then coldly—"give her lizard to eat. A diviner, doubtless Iémon San knows Kondō Rokurōbei by this time. He will never prejudice the man who holds in his hands the purse

6

of the Tamiya. Iémon San and O'Iwa San are left alone. Good luck to you, honoured Sir, in the encounter. In this Chōbei a counsellor and friend always is to be found; and one by no means lacking experience of the world. As for the woman, she is your wife; one to take charge of the house and affairs of Iémon Dono is to hand. No other *rusu* [2] could be found so earnest in duty and so cheap, as O'Iwa San. Take a concubine. This Chōbei will purchase one for you; such a one as will be the object of envy and desire to the whole of young Edo. His opportunities in that line are exceptional. Come! To turn on the lights. On our part at least there is nothing to conceal." Iémon did not pay attention to the hint. The one thought harassing him must out— " lop-sided and—a leper!" He spoke with despair and conviction, eyes fastened on Chōbei, and such a frightened look that even Chōbei had pity. One foot in the room he turned back. " That is not so—absolutely." Iémon could not disbelieve the earnest testimony. Said Chōbei—" The wounds of smallpox were no trivial ones. In healing the scars were such in places as form over burns. Hence the shining surface. Positively there is no leprous taint in Tamiya." He was gratified by the sigh which came from Iémon, sign of the immense weight lifted off the young man's mind. " Bah! leave things to the future, and—enjoy the present. O'Iwa cannot grow ugly with age. So much is gained. What difference will her looks make to Iémon thirty years hence? She is a woman. Make a child on her. Then you are free to turn elsewhere."

At once he began to place lights everywhere, as a sign to Kondō that all was well. This worthy came forward with other guests, to congratulate the Tamiya House on being once more in young and vigorous hands. It was Iémon himself who gave the signal to retire. How matters went alone with his bride has reference to one of those occasions over which the world draws

---

[2] *Rusu* or *rusuban* = caretaker in the owner's absence. As often as not the wife is so regarded by the Japanese husband.

the veil of decency. In the morning O'Iwa arose early to attend to the matutinal needs of her spouse. The ablutions performed, Iémon sat down to tea, as exquisite and exquisitely served as in any dream in literature of how such ceremony of the opening day should be performed. Then the morning meal was brought, under the same supervision of this woman, as expert in all the technique of her craft as she was ugly in feature; and that was saying much. Iémon watched her movements in the room with curiosity, mixed with a little pain and admiration. He was quick to note the skill with which she concealed the slight limp, due to the shrinking of the sinews of one leg and causing an unevenness of gait. It was a blemish in the little quick movements of a woman of surpassing grace; who by art had conquered disease and an ungainly figure.

O'Iwa had left the room for a moment to get flowers to place in the vases, offering to the *hotoké* (Spirits of the departed) in the Butsudan. On his return Iémon held the *ihai* (memorial tablets) in his hands. A priest, these had at once attracted his notice. "Kangetsu Shinshi; Kangetsu Shimmyō; O'Iwa San, these people have died on the same day of the month—and the year?"—"Is on the back of the *ihai*," replied O'Iwa. "No; it is not a case of suicide together." Then seeing his evident curiosity she motioned him to sit as she poured tea, ready for a long story. With its progress voice and manner grew more strained and earnest. She never took her eyes from the *tatami* (mats). "The tablets are those of the father and mother of this Iwa. My mother's name was Mino. Daughter of Tamiya she acted badly with my father Densuké, a mere servant in the house. This Densuké was a good man, but his status of *chūgen* made my grandfather very angry. He drove the twain from the house. Thus deprived of means to live, my father took a position as cook in the *yashiki* of a great noble. Here he was frightened into becoming the tool of a very wicked man. Having killed an usurer this man forced my father to dispose of the body under penalty of death if he refused. The body being placed in a cloth, my father had carried it to his house. During his short absence my mother's curiosity led her into untying the bundle. Her screams aroused the neighbourhood. As they entered she was seized with convulsions, and gave birth to this Iwa, thus brought into the world together with the exposure of the crime. My father, doubtless warned by the crowd, fled from Edo. My mother had but time to tell her story to the *kenshi*. Then she died. A year later to the day my father's dead body was found floating in the castle moat, near the town of Yūki in Shimosa. A beggar man, but little inquiry was made into the crime. For long the cause and the criminal were unknown. Then a *bantō* was robbed in the Shiba Kiridōshi; his companion was killed. The criminals were traced, and on confession were put to death. The leader and most wicked of them also confessed to the murder of the usurer Jusuké and to that of my father Densuké. My father had met him again in Yūki town, and had aroused in him fear of denunciation of past crimes. He spoke of 'this Densuké' as a superstitious, haunted fool; thus in his wickedness regarding my father's remorse and desire to clear up the strange affair. The execution of this man removed all chance of my avenging the deaths of father and mother on himself. But he has left behind a son. The one wish of this Iwa is to meet with Kichitarō; to avenge on him the wickedness of his father Takahashi Daihachirō." Iémon at first had followed in idle mood her story. With the development of the details he showed an attention which grew in intensity at every stage. With the mention of the name of Takahashi Daihachirō he gave a violent start. Yanagibara Kazuma, Iémon Tamiya— what were these but names to cover this Kichitarō, the one-time priest Myōshin of the Jōshinji at Reigan Fukagawa, and son of Daihachirō.

Strange was this retributory fate which had brought these two into the most intimate relations of husband and wife. When Iémon could control his voice he said—" That O'Iwa San should have this feeling in reference to the wicked Daihachirō can be understood. But why such hatred toward this Kichitarō? Surely the boy is not to be held guilty of the father's offence!"—"That is a man's way of reasoning," answered O'Iwa. "A woman, ignorant and foolish, has but her feelings to consult. To seven births this Iwa will clutch and chew the wicked son of a wicked father. Against Kichitarō is the vow made." She raised her head. Iémon turned away shuddering. She had aged into a hag. The shining face, the marks like black spots in pumice standing out, the mere dots of eyes in their puffy bed, the spreading mouth with its large shining teeth—all turned the plain gentle girl into a very demon. The certainty, the intensity, of a malignant hate was driven into Iémon. He was so frightened that he even nodded assent to her last words. The gentle voice of O'Iwa added— "Iwa is ugly; perhaps annoys by the tale. Leave the affair to her and to the enemy. To Iémon she is bound for two existences. Deign to drop all formality; call her Iwa, and condescend to regard her with affection." And Iémon covenanted with himself so to do. The present should compensate for the past. But in the days which followed O'Iwa sat on him as a nightmare. He felt the impress of her teeth at his throat, and would wake up gasping. Time made the situation familiar. He carefully lulled her into a blind admiration and belief in her husband Iémon. There seemed no likelihood of O'Iwa learning the truth; or believing it, if she did.[3]

---

[3] Reiganji, the great temple giving the name to the Reigan district of Fukagawa, is one of the many temples there found. The Jōshinji is close by.

CHAPTER VIII

IF OLD ACQUAINTANCE BE FORGOT

MATAZAÉMON's illness justified all the predictions of Chōbei. In the course of the month it was plain that his last hold on life was rapidly weakening. In that time Iémon had won golden opinions from household and neighbours. His face was beautiful, and this they saw. His heart was rotten to the core, and this he kept carefully concealed. The incentive of his fear of O'Iwa kept up the outward signs of good-will. He found this easier with the passage of the days. Plain as she was in face and figure, no one could help being attracted by the goodness of O'Iwa's disposition. Iémon, in his peculiar situation, placed great hopes on this, even if discovery did take place. Day following day he began to discount this latter contingency. To a feeling of half liking, half repugnance, was added a tinge of contempt for one so wrapped in her immediate surroundings, whose attention was so wholly taken up with the matter in hand. She easily could be kept in ignorance, easily be beguiled.

One day Iémon was summoned to the old man's bedside. He was shocked at the change which had taken place in a few hours. Propped upon pillows Matazaémon would speak a few last words. With a shade of his old impertinent official smile and manner— "The Tamiya is to be congratulated on its great good fortune in the entrance of one so well qualified by appearance and manners to uphold its reputation. Deign, honoured Muko San, to accept the thanks of this Matazaémon. All else has been placed in the hands of Iémon—goods, reputation, granddaughter." Iémon bowed flat in acknowledgment and protest at the good-will expressed. Continued Matazaémon—"There is one matter close to the old man's heart. Concerning that he would make his last

86

request to the admirable heart of Iémon. Iwa is a plain girl. The end of time for man, and the carping comment of neighbours come to his ears, have opened the eyes of Matazaémon to the truth. Great has been the favour in disregarding this plainness and taking her to wife. Everything is in the hands of Iémon San. Consider her happiness and deign to use her well. Abstain if possible from taking a concubine. At all events conceal the fact from Iwa, if it be deigned to keep such company. Plainness and jealousy go together. Faithful and upright, such a disposition as hers is not to be strained on that point. She would be very unhappy. Better the light women of Shinjuku Nakachō, than one who takes the place of the wife. Condescend to remember this last request of Tamiya Matazaémon." He clasped the hand of Iémon, and tears were in his eyes as he spoke. Iémon, too, was affected. It almost frightened him to be left alone with O'Iwa. "Deign not to consider such unlikely contingency. The amiability of O'Iwa is compensation for the greatest beauty. Who could think of injuring her in any way? Perhaps a child soon will be the issue. With this in mind condescend to put aside all gloomy thoughts. Concentrate the honoured will on life, and complete recovery to health will follow. Such, indeed, is the daily prayer of this Iémon at the Myōgyōji."

Matazaémon smiled faintly—with gratification or grimness? Perhaps death unseals the vision. Often indeed did Iémon present himself at the family temple; he the substitute for the Master of Tamiya. But as often did his feet return by the diametrically opposite direction, running the gauntlet of the charms of the frail beauties of Nakachō. Iémon held on to the hand of Matazaémon, swearing and forswearing himself with the greatest earnestness and the best of intentions. Suddenly he raised his head. The emotion aroused by the interview had been too much for the old man's fluttering heart. His head had slipped down sideways on the pillow. A little stream of dark bitter refuse flowed from the mouth and choked him. He was dead.

Great was the grief of wife and grandchild; great was the importance of Iémon, now in very fact Master of Tamiya. Whether or not he followed the advice of Chōbei, and gave the old woman *tokagé* (lizard) ; whether her constant small journeys to the houses of neighbours, reciting a litany of praise of this wondrous son-in-law; whether the loss of the companion of so many years wore out the feeble frame; it is fact that O'Naka followed her lord before the maple leaf turned red. Again the Tamiya was the scene of the funereal chanting of the priest. The corpse removed with the provision for the guests and watchers at the wake, the seventh night of the death observed, with this removal of the deceased spirit from the scenes of its former activities Iémon could turn himself without impediment to the life of the future. Outward change there was none. He was the same kind and affectionate husband as of former days. Neighbours, anticipating some change of manner, were still louder in their praises. One day there appeared at Tamiya two intimates, Natsumé Kyuzō and Imaizumi Jinzaémon. "Iémon Uji, a matter of importance presses. We are on our way to the ward head, Itō Kwaiba Dono. Deign to go in company. You are known to be an expert at *go*,[1] a game at which the old man prides himself for skill. He chafes at the presence of this unknown rival, heard of but not yet tested. A dinner and wine are at stake. Without Iémon Uji we do not dare to present ourselves. Condescend to go in company. To know the great man of the ward, the wealthy Itō Kwaiba, is of advantage even to Tamiya." Iémon laughed and assented. He was soon dressed for the greater ceremony of a first visit. All three climbed down into their clogs, and set out for the house of the Kumi-gashira near Saméga-bashi.

If Iémon had been impressed by the wealth of Tamiya, he felt insignificant before that of the head of Yotsuya. Itō Kwaiba was a man of sixty-four years, retaining much of the vigour of his youth. For the past ten years he had added *go* to his twin passions

---

[1] A complicated checkers-chess like game.

for wine and women, neither of which seemed to have made any impression on a keenness of sight which could read the finest print by the scanty light of an *andon*, teeth which could chew the hard and tough dried *mochi* (rice paste) as if bean confection, and an activity of movement never to be suspected from his somewhat heavy frame. At the name of Tamiya he looked up with much curiosity, and Iémon thought his greeting rather brusque. He saluted with great respect—" Truly fear is inspired. For long no visit has been paid to the honoured head. Coming thus without invitation is very rude. Intrusion is feared."—"Nay! Nay!" replied Kwaiba, apparently attracted by the splendid externals of Iémon. "The failure to visit is reciprocal. In fact, Tamiya and this Kwaiba have been at odds these many years. Visits had altogether ceased. This, however, is no matter for the younger generation. But Iémon San is indeed a fine fellow. So Kwaiba had heard from all he met. Ah! A fellow to put all the girls in a flutter. He is the very image of this Kwaiba in younger years. The husbands were little troubled when he was around. The fair ones were attracted. Well, well: they all had their turn at Kwaiba; and Kwaiba has stood the pace. He is as good to-day as ever; in some ways. . . . And it is a man like Iémon San who has married the—lady of Tamiya." Iémon knew the term " O'Baké " had nearly slipped out. Knowing O'Iwa's attractiveness of temperament, feeling touched in his own conceit, this astonished and satirical reception he met with on every side nettled him more than a little. Perhaps Kwaiba noted it. With greatest unction he urged a cushion and at once changed the subject. " Iémon San is noted as a *go* player. This Kwaiba is a mere amateur. It is for him to ask odds in making request for a game. . . . Ho! Heigh! The *go* board and stones! "

Kwaiba and Iémon were the antagonists. Natsumé and Imaizumi sat at the sides of the board. Kwaiba, confident in his powers, readily accepted the deprecatory answer of Iémon at its face value. The game was to be on even terms. Iémon really was an expert of the sixth grade; certainly of several grades superiority to Kwaiba.[2] The latter's brows knit as his position rapidly became imperilled. Natsumé was in a ferment. Fish or wine? If Iémon sought Kwaiba's favour by a preliminary sound thrashing at his favourite game, the prospects of either were small. He dropped his tobacco pipe. In picking it up he gave the buttocks of Iémon a direct and severe pinch. Iémon was too astonished to cry out. His ready mind sought a motive for this unexpected assault and pain. The face of Natsumé was unmoved, that of Imaizumi anxious. A glance at Kwaiba's attitude enlightened him. Politeness and a dinner were at stake. Even Natsumé and Imaizumi wondered and admired at what followed. The blunder of Iémon was a stroke of genius, the inspiration of an expert player. It was a slight blunder, not obvious to the crudeness of Kwaiba; but it opened up the whole of Iémon's position and put the game in his antagonist's hands. Kwaiba promptly seized the advantage. His triumphant glance shifted continually from Iémon to the onlookers, as the former struggled bravely with a desperate position. Kwaiba won this first game somewhat easily. A second he lost by a bare margin. In the third he scored success in a manner to make evident his superiority over a really expert player. Confident in his championship of the ward, he was all geniality as at the end he sorted and swept back the go stones into their polished boxes. " Go-ishi of Shingu; soft as a woman's hands. But never mind the sex. Now for fish and wine. . . . However, Hana can serve the liquor for us." To the servant—" Heigh! Some refreshments for the honoured guests; and convey the request of Kwaiba to O'Hana San, to be present."

With the wine appeared O'Hana San. She was a beautiful girl. Of not more than twenty years, on the graceful sloping shoulders was daintily set a head which attracted attention and admiration. The face was a pure oval—of the uri or melon, as

---

[3] There are nine of these stages of skill.

the Nipponese class it—with high brow, and was framed in long hair gathered below the waist and reaching nearly to her ankles with its heavy luxuriant mass. She was dressed for the hot season of the year in a light coloured Akashi crape, set off by an *obi* or broad sash of peach colour in which were woven indistinct and delicate wavy designs. The sleeves, drawn a little back, showed the arms well up to the shoulder. Glimpses of a beautifully moulded neck and bosom appeared from time to time as she moved here and there in her preparation of the service of the wine utensils. The delicate tissue of the dress seemed to caress the somewhat narrow hips of a girlish figure. Every movement was studied and graceful. This O'Hana had belonged to the Fukadaya at Yagura no Shita of Fukagawa. She had been what is known as an *obitsuké* harlot, wearing the *obi* in the usual form, without the loose overrobe or *shikaké* of the common women. " In the period of Tempō (1830–1843) all Fukagawa harlots were dressed in this manner." Attracted by her beauty old Kwaiba had ransomed her and made her his concubine. For nearly two years she had held this position in his house. In serving the wine she came to the front and knelt before Iémon as first to receive it. In handing him the tray with the cup she looked into his face. The start on the part of both was obvious. Some of the wine was spilled.

Said Kwaiba—" Then Iémon Uji, you know this woman? " His tone was hard and truculent. It conveyed the suspicion of the jealous old male. Iémon's former profession stood him in good stead. He had a glib tongue, and no intention to deny what had been made perfectly obvious—" It is fact, and nothing to be ashamed of on the part of Iémon; except as to attendant conditions beyond control. I was a diviner on the public highway."—" So 'twas heard," grumbled Kwaiba. " Without customers, and with no use for the diviner's lens but to charr the rafters of the garret in which you lived." Iémon did not care to notice the attack. He merely said—" Deign not to find amusement in what really is a serious matter to one who has to suffer poverty. While seated at the diviner's stand attention was drawn by a girl coming down the Kuramaé. Slouching along close by her was a drunken *samurai*. From time to time he lurched entirely too close to her. Turning unexpectedly her sunshade caught in his *haori* (cloak), which thereby was slightly torn. At once he flew into a great rage. Laying hands on her he showed no disposition to accept her excuses. "Careless wench! You have torn my dress. How very impudent of you. Unless you at once accompany me to the tea house close by, to serve the wine and please me, pardon, there is none; be sure of that." The people had gathered like a black mountain. Nothing was to be seen but heads. O'Hana San was in the greatest embarrassment, unable to free herself from the insults and importunities of the drunken fellow. The *samurai* was hid under the diviner's garb. Stepping from the stand I interposed in the girl's behalf, making apology, and pointing out the rudeness of his behaviour to the drunkard. Instead of becoming calm he raised his fist and struck me in the face. His condition gave the advantage without use of arms. Locking a leg in his tottering supports I threw him down into the ditch. Then with a word to O'Hana San to flee at once, we disappeared in different directions. The *samurai* Iémon again became the diviner. That part of his rôle this Iémon regrets; but a weapon he could not draw in the quarrel. Later on meeting O'Hana San at the Kwannon temple of Asakusa thanks were received, for what was a very trivial service."—"And again renewed," said the beauty, raising her downcast face to look direct into that of Iémon. Said Kwaiba—"Ah! That's the tale, is it? A fortunate encounter, and a strange reunion; but the world is full of such. O'Hana, it comes in most befitting that opportunity is afforded to favour the rescuer with something of greater value than thanks. Pray serve him with wine." Then did Kwaiba take the matter as a man of the world. But he was no fool, "this old *tanuki* (badger) of a thousand autumns' experience on hill and in dale." He understood very well that between Iémon and O'Hana there had been a closer connection than that of mere accident.

CHAPTER IX

LOVE KNOTS

MANY were the visits paid by Iémon to contest at *go* with Itō Kwaiba. Rapid was the progress of the love affair between a young man and a young woman, both inspired with a consuming passion for each other. In former days—something more than two years before—when Iémon was priest in the Jōshinji of the Reigan district of Fukagawa, and was spending the money of the *ōshō* so freely, he had met O'Hana at the Fukagawa of Yagura no Shita. Just entering on her career, she at once captivated him with a permanent passion. It was in her company that the funds of the temple had been cast to the four winds of heaven. His love had been fully reciprocated by O'Hana. The one purpose was to ransom the lady, and then to live together as husband and wife. Such was the engagement plighted between them. However, the ransom figure was large. Iémon—or Kazuma at that time, he dropped his priestly name when out of bounds—had already planned a larger raid than usual on the ecclesiastical treasury. Warned by O'Hana that his operations had been discovered, he had sought safety in flight; not without a last tearful parting with his mistress, and assurance that fate somehow would bring them again together. The engagement thus entered on was to flourish under the new conditions.

As to this pursuit of O'Hana, in which the maiden was coy and willing, the lover circumspect and eager, or at least thought he was, those around the pair were soon well informed; that is, with the exception of the most interested—O'Iwa and Kwaiba. The marked neglect which now ensued O'Iwa took in wifely fashion; and attributing it to some passing attraction of Shinjuku Nakachō, she did not take it to heart as she would have done if a concubine

93

had been at issue. As for Kwaiba, the usually astute and prying old man was so immersed in his *go* as to be struck blind, deaf, and dumb. The matter coming to the ears of Kondō Rokurōbei, the worthy gentleman was seriously alarmed. If true, the old man had indeed reached a parting of the ways, at which he had to satisfy Iémon, Master of Tamiya, O'Iwa, his ward, and Itō Kwaiba, the powerful influence in the daily life of all of them. That night there was a meeting at the house of Kwaiba, a competition in *gidayu* recitation, dancing, and poetry (*uta*) making. He presented himself in season at the door of the Tamiya. "Ah! O'Iwa San; and to-night does Iémon join the company at the house of the *kumi-gashira?* Rokurōbei comes from Kawagoé, and perhaps is not too late to find company on the road."—"Oya! Is it Kondō Sama? Iya! the Danna has but begun his preparations. . . . Iémon! The Danna of Yotsuyazaka has come; for company on the way to Itō Sama's house. . . . Deign to enter. In a short time Iémon will be ready." Kondō looked at her quizzically. There was no sign of distress or misgivings in this quarter. He felt encouraged. Probably the rumour was false or exaggerated; perhaps it was wholly due to the malice of Akiyama Chōzaémon, from whom that day he had heard it.

He turned to greet Iémon, who emerged ready for the street. At the entrance they halted. Said Iémon—"It will be a long drawn-out affair. Deign to retire, and not await the return." Replied O'Iwa—"A small matter. The sound of the Danna's footstep will arouse Iwa to receive him." Iémon laughed. "How so? How distinguish my steps from those of Akiyama San or other constant callers?" Said O'Iwa gravely—"When the wife can no longer distinguish the husband's footstep, then affection has departed. O'Iwa will be ready to receive Iémon, no matter what the hour."—"And, indeed, a late one," put in Kondō. "The party consists mainly of young men. After it they will adjourn to Nakachō. Is it allowed to Iémon Dono to accompany them?" O'Iwa winced a little. "The Master is always master, within

and without the house. He will do as he pleases."—"Gently
said; like a true wife. Truly such a married pair are rarely to be
encountered. They are the mandarin duck and drake of Morokoshi transplanted to Yotsuya. Rokurōbei feels proud of his
guardianship." As he and Iémon took their way along the Teramachi, he said—"Iémon is indeed a wonderful man. He is handsome and pursued by the women. O'Iwa undeniably is ugly; yet
never is there failure to show her respect and consideration, in
private as well as public. One's life here in Yotsuya is open to
all the neighbours, and these speak well of Iémon." Said the
younger man, in matter of fact tone—"Who could fail toward
Iwa? She is amiability itself. Plain, perhaps, but gentleness is
the compensating quality, a truer source of household wealth than
beauty."—"Well spoken! Deign to keep it in heart, for the
neighbours' tongues wag as to Iémon and O'Hana. Malice can
cause as much unhappiness as downright wickedness. Besides,
Kwaiba is no man to trifle with." Iémon was a little put out and
alarmed at the directness of Kondō's reference. "Be sure there
is nothing in such talk. A slight service, rendered in earlier days,
makes O'Hana San more cordial to one otherwise a stranger.
The excess shown is perhaps to be discouraged. But Itō Dono is
good company and has good wine; and besides really is a good *go*
player. It would be loss to shun his house."

Kondō noted a first symptom on their arrival. He spoke
sharply to the maid—"Middle age in company with youth plainly
finds a poor reception. Is that the master's order? The clogs of
Tamiya are not the only ones. Is Rokurōbei to shift for himself?"
The girl, all confusion, made profuse apology as she hastened to
repair the neglect. Kondō was easily mollified. "Bah! No wonder. Bring Tamiya near a woman, and all is confusion. . . .
But Itō Dono?"—"This way, honoured Sirs: the Danna awaits
the guests." They entered the sitting room, to find Kwaiba in a
high state of anger and sulks. For some reason, error in trans-
mission or date or other ambiguity, not a man of the guests had

appeared. "The supper prepared is next to useless. We four can do but little in its dispatch. Not so with the wine; let every man do double duty here." He hustled around and gave his orders with some excitement; more than cordial with the guests who had not failed him. There was present one Kibei. Iémon had noted with curiosity his first appearance on this ground. What effect was this factor going to have on O'Hana's position in the household. He had been reassured on the physical point. Kibei was exceedingly ugly, a regular mask, and O'Hana was a woman to make much of physical beauty, as well as strength and ruggedness. He was a younger son of Inagaki Shōgen, a *hatamoto* with a *yashiki* in Honjō and an income of three thousand *koku*.[1] It was almost certain that Kwaiba would adopt Kibei. The negotiations had been long continued, and there was some hitch in the matter that Iémon could not make out. What he did realize was Kibei's hostility to himself. A noted fencer, making some sort of a living as teacher of the art, he was the last man with whom Iémon had any desire for a quarrel. Iémon was a coward, and the cold eye of Kibei sent a chill down his spine. Himself, he was always excessively polite in their intercourse.

Limited as to number the party tried to make up for the missing guests by liveliness. There was a dance by Kibei, drinking as substitutes of the absent, and competition in *uta* (poetry). Handing in his own effort—no mean one—Iémon left the room for a moment. As he came out on the corridor, and was about to return to the guest room, he found the maid O'Moto awaiting him with water and towel. A slight puckering frown came over Iémon's face at this imprudence. Said the girl pleadingly—"Danna Sama, deign to exercise patience. That of the mistress is sorely tried. The absence of the other guests, the pursuit of Kibei Dono, who only seeks to compromise her and secure her expulsion from the house, or even death at the hand of Kwaiba Dono, has driven her well nigh mad. A moment—in this room." Iémon drew back.

---

[1] 5.13 bushel. Income of the *samurai* classes were so measured.

—" A room apart, and in darkness! The age of seven years once passed, and boy and girl are never to be allowed alone together." He would have refused, but a sudden push and he was within. The *shōji* closed at once. Kwaiba's voice called loudly—" Hana! Hana! What has become of the girl? There is no one to serve the wine. If the ugliness of Kibei drives her to cover, Tamiya's beauty should lure her out. Hana! Hana!" O'Hana slipped hastily from the arms of Iémon. Passing through the garden she entered the kitchen and snatched up a *saké* bottle from the stove. She did not notice that the fire had gone entirely out. She and Iémon entered the sitting room together, from different sides. Rokurōbei looked sharply at Iémon. Kibei was engaged in hot talk with Kwaiba. Said Kondō—" Where have you been? Pressed by necessity? For such a lapse of time! nonsense! Is rice powder found in such a place? ' Plaster '? It does not leave the mark of a cheek on the sleeve." He laid a warning hand on Iémon, skilfully removing the telltale mark in so doing. " What has happened is clear enough. Fortunately Kwaiba and Kibei have got into a dispute over the merits of Heinai and Shōsetsu as fencing masters; both of them dead as the long ago quarrels of the Toyotomi and Tokugawa Houses. Heinai was loyal, and Shōsetsu a traitor; but Kibei tries the old man and officer by supporting the prowess of the latter. Besides the *saké* is cold and Kwaiba at start was in a very bad temper. He has thought for naught but his drink and disappointment. Cajole him by agreeing with him, but don't get into a quarrel with Kibei. He is expert with the sword, has a temper as ugly as his face, and would willingly engage in one. He don't like you. . . ." He stopped. Kwaiba was speaking sharply. He had just taken the fresh bottle. " Cold as a stone! How careless you are."—" Not so," said O'Hana in some surprise. " It has just come off the stove." Kwaiba put the bottle in her hand, to her confusion. " O'Hana must have been asleep; or much engaged, not to note the difference." For

7

the first time he looked sharply at her, then at Iémon. O'Hana often executed great freedom with him—"Asleep! Just so; and no wonder. Without guests the evening has been stupid enough. If Tamiya Sama had brought his wife with him it would have been complete." Kwaiba, Kibei, Kondō smiled at the sally. Iémon took the cue, and chose to resent the words. He said coldly—" O'Iwa certainly brings spice into everything she engages in. Her intelligence is unusual." O'Hana looked at him; then smiled a little, reassured. Passing behind him she stumbled. " Forgotten "—Iémon felt a letter thrust into his hand, which he passed quickly to his sleeve. Then he and Kondō rose to take their leave. The usual salutations followed. As if to compensate for the failure of the entertainment all joined in seeing them depart. Kwaiba was still grumbling and half quarrelling with O'Hana. O'Moto was engaged with Kondō Rokurōbei. Kibei insisted on aiding Iémon; and Iémon did not dare to refuse his services in donning the *haori*. As he adjusted the awkward efforts of Kibei on one side, this amateur valet made a mess of it on the other. Besides, neither of them was any too steady on his feet. Then Kondō and Iémon set out in the rain. " Sayonara! Sayonara! "

CHAPTER X

THE PLOT AGAINST O'IWA

THE following morning Iémon sat brooding, mind and tongue clouded by the drinking bout of the previous night. O'Iwa silently busied herself with his renovation. Rokurōbei had delivered him over to her, decidedly the worse for wine and wear. He was somewhat astonished at the young man's easy discomfiture. Middle age with the Nipponese usually means the seasoned and steady toper. Regarding the matter as partly due to her own fault, and reassured by Kondō as to the events of the evening, O'Iwa heated the *saké* with all the greater care, serving it herself, chatting on the indifferent gossip of the neighbourhood. She spoke of the talk current as to Itō Kwaiba's adoption of an heir. " This man Kibei, his disposition appears to be as ugly as his face." With a little smile she added, " for the latter compensation is to be found in the first-named quality; a truth which he seems to disregard. What will become of O'Hana San?" For the first time since the night before the thought of the letter flashed into Iémon's mind. He put down the renovating morning draft, and on some excuse arose. His *kimono* lay neatly folded in the *hirabuta* (flat tray). Hastily he searched the sleeves. There was not a sign of the missive. With clouded brow he returned to the sitting room. A glance at O'Iwa made him feel ashamed. It had never come into her hands. He knew her well enough to be assured that he would have found it, scrupulously laid together with the tobacco pouch, nose wipe (*hanagami*), and divers other minor articles of daily use carried on the person. The whole affair perhaps was a dream. The more he considered, the more he became so convinced. His transports with O'Hana, their surprise, Kondō's rebuke—so far the evening was tolerably clear. It was only as to the final cups, the rising to depart, the standing

99

in the cold night air, that the exact course of events became clouded. " Ah! It was all a vision. O'Hana never would have been so imprudent." There was a trace of doubt in his mind. He would clear it up at the fountain source—at Kwaiba's house and by the lips of O'Hana. ·

Kwaiba greeted him with almost boisterous cheerfulness. " Ah! Tamiya comes early; a flattering acknowledgment of last night's reception." To Iémon's deprecatory speech and apology— " Don't talk folly, after the manner of a country boor. Iémon San is a man of the world; and will give this Kwaiba credit for being the same. What does it amount to? A matter of a little too much wine. . . . Hana! Hana! The Master of Tamiya is present. Cut some bean paste, and bring tea. Heat the wine. Matazaémon was so sober an old dog that it is doubtful whether O'Iwa knows aught about the best remedy for past drinking." As Kibei entered—" There is the inventory of the Shimosa farms. Condescend to take a glance at the report of the *nanushi* (bailiff). Hana will aid." Thus dismissed, the two left the room. Kwaiba turned to Iémon—" A draught: no? Then Kwaiba will drink for both. For Him it is a day of rejoicing. The coming of Tamiya is opportune. It was intended to send for him. Deign to aid this Kwaiba with counsel. The adoption of Kibei has finally been settled." The old man's exultation influenced even the indifference of Iémon's aching head. With well-simulated interest he said—" Naruhodo! Kibei Dono is indeed to be congratulated. As to our chief, since everything is to his satisfaction, Iémon is but too glad to speak his pleasure, to offer his congratulations."— " Nay! A little more than that, Iémon Uji. This Kwaiba would seek his aid in another matter of importance. Kwaiba is old. A woman no longer is an object to him. He cannot make a child. If O'Hana should give birth to a child great would be the discomfiture, knowing the truth. What is to be done in such a case?" He now was looking with direct inquiry into the face of Iémon. The latter was much confused. He stammered—" Just so: so indeed. O'Hana San is truly an embarrassment. Doubtless she is also an obstacle to Kibei Dono. She . . ." Sneered Kwaiba—" Tamiya, though young, is wise. He grasps the situation at once. Deign, Iémon San, to take O'Hana yourself." Kwaiba raised his voice a little. Kibei brought O'Hana with him from the next room. She seemed alarmed and embarrassed. Said Kwaiba—" What have you there; the inventory? Ah! A letter: and there is no one to read a letter like Iémon San. Deign, Sir, to favour us. Iémon San alone can give the contents the proper inflection. He handed it to Iémon. A glance showed the latter that it was a letter from O'Hana, probably that of the previous night. His pocket had been neatly picked by Kibei. It was plain. He had been trapped. The pretended entertainment had been a plot in which the passion of O'Hana had been given full chance to range. Even the disinterested witness, the old fool Kondō, had been provided. He caught a curious, mocking smile on the face of the girl O'Moto, just then passing along the rōka.

Kwaiba allowed the silence to become oppressive. He seemed to await an incriminating outburst on the part of O'Hana, plainly on the verge of tears. However, the girl caught herself up. Instead she turned a calm, inquiring look toward the three men. Iémon alone looked down, his gaze on the letter the characters of which danced and waved before his eyes. Sharp as he ordinarily was, before this vigorous and astute old man, backed by the ruffianly prospective son with impertinent smile, the cowardice of Iémon deprived him of all spirit. His faculties were numbed. Kwaiba leaned over and removed the letter from his hands. " Since Iémon San will not read the letter, Kwaiba will try to do so; a poor substitute for the accomplished cleric." The old fellow seemed to know everything, as the tone of contempt indicated. He ran the scroll out in his hands—" Naruhodo! Ma! Ma! What's this? From some woman: a lascivious jade indeed! . . . Eh! Kibei Dono, apology is due your ears. This Kwaiba laughed at your suspicions." He threw down the scroll, as in a fury. Kibei picked it up. He began to read:

"Night is the source of pleasure, but greater that pleasure at sight of Iémon. The day comes when Iémon and Hana will be husband and wife, in fact if not in form. 'Ah! Day and night to be at the service of Iémon.' Thus does Hana pray gods and Buddhas. When distant from his side, even though the time be short, painful is its passage. Place this letter next to your very person. May that night come quickly, when the coming of Iémon is awaited. The connection with O'Iwa San is the punishment for sin committed in a previous existence. Condescend to dismiss her from your mind. View the matter wholly in this light. The spiteful brush (pen) refuses further service. Hard, hard, is the lot of this Hana. The honoured Master comes; the heartfelt wish is accomplished.

With compliments,

To Iémon Sama."   HANA.

Kwaiba's rage grew and grew with the reading. At Iémon's name he sprang up and made a movement toward the stand on which reposed his swords. Laying a hand on the larger weapon he turned with a scowl—"Ah! This Kwaiba is old, but in vigour he is young. It is for Kwaiba to sport with the women. They are not to make a fool of him." Kibei sharply interposed. "Does Kwaiba Dono gain satisfaction by such a vengeance? To Kibei it seems a poor one. A matter so easily to be settled is not to be made a scandal in the ward. Deign, honoured Sir, so to regard it. To punish both at once with death is proper. But is it expedient? Condescend to hear the words of Kibei."

Kwaiba pulled himself up. It was as if some one had dragged him back. His rage departed. A cold malice took its place. He smiled blandly—"One does not quarrel over a harlot. Kwaiba spares their lives. Iémon shall take Hana home—as wife."— "As wife!" Iémon broke through his fear. "Surely the honoured *Kashira* is unreasonable. This Iémon is but the *muko* of Tamiya. To demand that O'Iwa San be discarded is going too, far. Positively in this matter, though there have been love passages, the most intimate relation has never followed—now or in previous relations."—"You lie!" said Kwaiba coldly. "Furthermore 'tis a matter not passing the period of last night.

But that is not to the point. Against Matazaémon this Kwaiba has a grudge—as yet unsatisfied. Through O'Iwa San this shall be paid. With Iémon no harsh measures are adopted. Nay; Kwaiba comes to his aid. You, too, Kibei, shall assist. . . . Ah! For the ready consent, thanks. Ma! A delicious revenge is that gathered by Kwaiba. O'Hana the harlot takes the place of the Ojōsan. And she loves Iémon! In our feasts Natsumé and Imaizumi get the skin of the omelet; Iémon the centre. Then O'Iwa is to be driven out. To that Tamiya cannot object. He substitutes honey for garlic;[1] O'Hana the flower for the ugly toad O'Iwa. Splendid! Splendid! But how? Ah! Here's Kondō, just in the nick of time. Rokurōbei, aid us with your experience and influence. Aid us with Iémon, who would cleave to the O'Baké."

Put in possession of the facts Kondō was aghast. He had come to the parting of the ways; and under conditions which assured his participation in the plot. At first he turned on Iémon with bitter recrimination. "Oh! A virtuous fellow, who would drink a man's wine, lie with his woman, and then preach morality to a household! But the mischief is done. If not the paramour of O'Hana San, everybody believes it to be so . . ." Kwaiba held up his hands in well-simulated anger. Kibei and Rokurōbei interfered. Iémon's last resistance was broken down. To talk? That is the business of a priest. Soon he was as eagerly engaged in the plot as if he had left the house in Samonchō for that purpose. Said Rokurōbei—"What difficulty does the matter present? Set on Watanabé Gorō to tempt and make love to O'Iwa. He is badly in debt. The handsome man of the ward everyone would suspect her fall. Surprised by Iémon, O'Iwa is driven out as unchaste. This Kondō stipulates that matters go no fur-

---

[1] *Kyara* = nut gall, in Momogawa's *kōdan*. From the marriage to the expulsion of O'Iwa his treatment of the story is mainly followed. Ryuō slurs the marriage, but describes the persecution with great effect. The lines of treatment only diverge subsequently. Ryuō is to be preferred.

ther. After all O'Iwa is innocent of offence. The husband's full rights are not to be excused. Neither she, nor Watanabé is to suffer injury." Kibei laughed outright at the idea of a drawn sword in Iémon's hand. Iémon turned the contempt on to Kondō. Sneering, he replied—"The plan is worthless. O'Iwa is chastity itself. In the absence of this Iémon no man is allowed entrance to the house." Kwaiba knitted his brows—"Kakusuké! Kakusuké!" As the *chūgen* appeared—"Go yonder to the house of Akiyama Chōzaémon San. Say that the Kumigashira would speak with Akiyama San." As the man departed—"Chōzaémon is the man. For gossip and malice he is a very woman. Rejoice and he weeps; weep and he rejoices. If Akiyama cannot concoct some plan to get rid of O'Iwa, then no one can. . . . Alas! O'Hana and Iémon must die by the hand of this Kwaiba. Kibei will give his aid." The old man and Kibei got much enjoyment out of the cowardice of Iémon and the fright of O'Hana. But not for long. Akiyama Chōzaémon, the one-time boy lover of O'Iwa; a long, lean, hungry-looking man, with long, cadaverous face and a decidedly bad eye, appeared with the *chūgen* Nakusuké close behind. The latter seemed a sort of policeman attending the none-too-willing Chōzaémon. The latter's brow lightened at sight of the company. He owed Kwaiba money. Sending away the servant, Kwaiba unfolded the situation. Said Chōzaémon—"Heigh! Tamiya takes the cast off leman of Itō Dono. Fair exchange is no robbery; Kibei Uji against O'Hana San. Iémon San goes into the matter with eyes wide open. The lady is an old intimate, it is said." This manner of approaching the subject was Chōzaémon's way. He cared nothing for the scowls of Kibei nor the wrath of Kwaiba. He was needed, or they would not have called him to counsel. As for Iémon, he was grateful to Chōzaémon; as neighbour, and for the insult to Kibei and Kwaiba.

Continued the mediator—"The obstacle of course is the O'Baké. O'Iwa is to be driven out. And Watanabé won't answer? Maa! Chastity in an O'Baké! It is a thing unheard of. 'Tis such, once of womankind, who seduce living men. Tamiya is now head of the House. O'Iwa once driven out, the property remains in his hands as its representative. She must be forced to leave of her own will. Good; very good. What is it worth to Kwaiba Dono? "—" Look to Iémon for commission," said Kwaiba roughly. "Nay! Nay!" mouthed Chōzaémon. "Kwaiba is Kwaiba; Iémon is Iémon. The two are to be settled with separately. If Kwaiba Dono had gone to extremes at the start no question would have been raised. To do so now, with all present and after discussion, is out of the question. Kwaiba Dono wishes to adopt Kibei Uji; to get rid of O'Hana San. Iémon San has been neatly trapped. He must consent. O'Hana is a woman. She has no voice in the matter. All this is clear. But as to Chōzaémon's labour in the affair; that it is which interests this Akiyama." He gave a sour reprimanding look at Kibei. Then he looked impertinently from Kwaiba to Iémon, and from Iémon to Kwaiba. Iémon in delight nodded assent. Chōzaémon promptly turned his back on him and faced Kwaiba. At first the old man was very angry at the acuteness of Chōzaémon. The sharp, free exposure did not please him. Then the idea of countering on this acuteness made him good tempered. He grumbled—"The ten *ryō* owing to Kwaiba at the New Year—principal and interest; such is the fee for a successful issue." Chōzaémon held up his hands in pretended horror—"Pay back borrowed money! Is that expected by the Kumigashira?"—"Not ' expected,'" put in Kwaiba promptly. "With the seal of Akiyama San the return is assured." Chōzaémon became thoughtful—"It is true. The last loan was under seal. . . . Too bad. . . . Well! Well! The conditions are hard. Submission is necessary. The debt will be forgiven?"—"Kibei and Iémon stand as witnesses," replied Kwaiba—"Then how is this?" said Chōzaémon. All put their heads together. Akiyama Chōzaémon went into details. Kwaiba pushed back his cushion; slapped his thighs. "Chōzaémon, you are cheap at double the money. Just the thing! Eh, Iémon, Uji? Eh, Muko San?" All grinned a raptured assent.

CHAPTER XI

THE PLOT DEVELOPS

For two days Iémon was maturing the preliminaries. He seemed unwell and out of sorts. The third day he did not get up at all. O'Iwa was properly anxious. Said she—"The change in the year is a sickly season. Condescend to take some drug. Allow Suian Sensei to be summoned." Iémon grumbled a dissent. She went on in her enthusiasm—"He is the very prince of doctors. See: here is a salve he recommends; for skin and nerves. O'Hana San, the beautiful concubine of Itō Sama, uses nothing else. He guarantees it on her praise, as means to remove blemishes of any kind or source." Iémon looked up quickly. The connection puzzled and did not please him. Perhaps he noted a puffiness about O'Iwa's face, remembered a repulsion toward marital usages. The women should leave the men to play their own game. He said gruffly—"Suian! A dealer in cosmetics and charms. Have naught to do with his plasters and potions; as cheats or something worse. As for O'Iwa, she is black as a farm hand from Ryūkyū (Loo-choo). O'Hana is fair as the white *kiku*. Can the pastes of Suian Sensei change black to white?" Startled, O'Iwa looked round from the glass into which she was peering. She was taken by surprise. In their personal relations Iémon had always been more than considerate. For some weeks in secret she had been using this drug of Suian Sensei. In childhood O'Iwa had shown something of an epileptic tendency. This had worn off with time. Of late the recurrence had alarmed her. The drug of Suian, at the time anyhow, made her less conscious of the alarmed critical feeling which heralded the inception of the attacks.

Iémon gave her but time to catch the meaning of his insult. He went on—"Probably it is but a cold. Some eggs, with plenty of hot wine, will obviate ill effects. Deign to see that they are prepared." The channel of O'Iwa's thoughts changed. At once she was the housekeeper and nurse, and all solicitude to make him at ease. In the course of the meal of eggs with *saké* in came Natsumé Kyuzō and Imaizumi Jinzaémon. "Ah! Iémon, pardon the intrusion. Probably the engagement of yesterday with Kwaiba Sama was forgotten. . . . In bed! A cold? But such is no treatment for the complaint. There should be a cheerful, lively atmosphere. . . . Ah! Here is the dice box. One can shake dice as well lying down as sitting. Deign to refresh the spirits with play as well as wine." Iémon saw to it that both were available. With surprise at first, misgiving afterwards, O'Iwa heated bottle after bottle of *saké*. The men did not pay the slightest attention to her presence. Absorbed in their game, there was but a rough call from time to time for wine, addressed to the air, a servant, anybody. At the end of the play Natsumé rose to leave in high spirits. Imaizumi and Tamiya were correspondingly depressed. This was but a first day's procedure. Day after day, for the space of half the month, the play was repeated. Iémon had long since recovered. One day he stood with his hands shoved into the folds of his sash. He was very sober and sour. "Iwa, is there money in the house?" She looked at him in surprise. "Matters have not turned out at all well with Kyuzō and Jinzaémon. This Iémon is a hundred *ryō* to the bad. With spare cash at hand an attempt can be made to repair the loss."

O'Iwa prostrated herself before him. "May the Danna deign to consider. To Iwa this pastime of gambling seems a very ill one, particularly in a man of official rank. It is fraught with peril; and the offence once known rarely is pardoned. Condescend to hear and forgive the warning of this Iwa." She stopped a little frightened. Iémon was looking at her in greatest wrath and astonishment. "What! Is there argument from wife to husband? This insolence of behaviour crowns the insult of refusal. The very sight of your face is enough to make one sick at the stomach. Boors and *bakémono* are shut out at the Hakoné barrier. But you—the guards have been put to sleep, and you have slipped

through. Shut up! Get the money, or . . ." O'Iwa crouched
at the *shōji*, in terror and surprise. The insulting words heaped
on her pained and tortured. Now she felt the sharp sting of a
hand forcibly applied to her cheek. Without a word she left the
room. Returning she brought thirty *ryō* in gold on a salver.
Timidly prostrate she presented it to Iémon. " Condescend to pardon Iwa. That she is ugly and incompetent she knows. Did not
Iémon accept her?" The man stuffed the gold in his girdle. In
reply—" No: Iémon was cheated by Kondō and Chōbei. A plain
woman—perhaps; but a monster, a worse than *rokuro-kubi*, was
never thought of even in a dream. Compensation is to be found.
Iémon likes gambling. He will gamble. Have a care to supply
the needed funds; and don't interfere." Roughly he shoved her
out of the way, and left the house.

For long O'Iwa saw nothing of Iémon; but she heard from
him. In fact he was living in semi-secrecy at the house of
Rokurōbei. Now this messenger, then that, would come to O'Iwa.
" If there is no money—sell something. The bearer will indicate.
A supply must be found." Thus one thing after another left the
house—to be stored in the godown of Kondō Rokurōbei, to whose
clever suggestion was due this way of stripping O'Iwa of all she
possessed. With goods and clothes went the servants. In the
course of a few weeks O'Iwa was living in one room, furnished
with three *tatami* in lieu of the usual twelve in number. Hibachi,
andon (night lamp), the single garment she wore, this was all she
possessed in the house. Then at last she saw him. The light
dawned on a cold snowy morning of early March. O'Iwa rose,
opened the amado, and started her day. About the fourth hour
(9 A.M.) the *shōji* were pushed aside and Iémon entered. He
looked as if fresh from a night's debauch. His garments were
dirty and disordered. His face was sallow, the eyes deep set and
weary, his manner listless. O'Iwa gave him the only cushion in
the room. Seated before the *hibachi* (brazier) after some time
he said—" A million pardons: the luck has been very bad. . . .
Ah! The place here seems in disorder. It is not fit for a man

to live in." He looked around as one waking from a dream.
" No wonder: yet all can be restored. Iémon has surprised you?"
Said O'Iwa timidly—" Matters are a little at odds and ends.
O'Iwa needs but little; a stalk of *daikon* (radish) and a handful
of wheat (*mugi*). Does the Danna remain here? If so . . ."
There was a painful hitch in her voice, a puzzled look on her face.
She had one *bu* in cash. In fact she was hoping for the monthly
visit of Yosuké the farmer; if there was a farm any longer. She
did not know.
" For the night," replied Iémon. " Sleep and food are the
essentials of good play. All has been lost in the gambling houses
of Shinjuku and Shinagawa, at the Nakanochō. Is there no
money in the house? . . . Evidently not. Deign to secure
some, no matter how." He took the silver *bu* she presented to
him. " At least a bath and tobacco can be had. See to it that
a meal is ready at even; not much, sashimi (sliced raw fish) and
wine. Iémon would play, not eat." With this he rose. O'Iwa
heard the sound of the closing gate. Long she remained, her
face buried in her knees. In this gloomy situation what was she
to do? She looked around. There was not a thing to sell; not
even herself. Who would buy the ugly O'Iwa? An idea came
into her head. In a moment she was in the street. Soon she
stood at the door of her uncle, Yoémon. With this uncle and
aunt she had but little to do. Matazaémon had been at daggers
drawn with his brother, whom he accused of being a wretched
miser, one acquiring wealth by very questionable means for a
samurai. In old days Chōbei had been a hired agent of Yoémon.
The principal had escaped; the second had to leave Yotsuya and
its neighbourhood. The Obasan (aunt) came out at O'Iwa's
call. She greeted her niece with surprise. " Oya! Oya! Iwa is
a stranger to this house. It has been heard that a splendid
muko was received at Tamiya." The old woman looked at O'Iwa
shrewdly, and not without kindness. O'Iwa took heart. She
made answer—" It is true; of late matters have not gone well.
Just now Iwa would ask the loan of a *shō* ($^1/_5$ peck) of rice,

together with a *bu* to buy eels or sashimi.[1] It is very rude indeed
. . ."—"Very rude indeed!" said a harsh voice close by.
O'Iwa shrank to the outer part of the doorway. The aunt fled
to the inner part of the house. Continued Yoémon—" And what
is Iwa doing at the house of Yoémon? That there is relationship between them this Yoémon does not recognize. Yoémon
never exchanged look or word with his brother Matazaémon,
nor does he desire to do so with the issue. Let the Tamiya of
Samonchō look out for itself. A *muko* was taken without aid
or advice of Yoémon. A stranger, one practising wayside divination, this fine fellow turns out a gambler and a debauched man,
to the ruin of the House. Iwa can look to him; ignorant and
foolish woman that she is. This Yoémon would contribute to
the needs of a beggar before granting even a single *mon* to Iwa."
     The grating rattled sharply as the angry old man pushed it
to and let fall the bar. O'Iwa looked into the dark recess with
pained and startled eyes. So much of a recluse she was learning
that Iémon had long been the talk of the ward. She turned,
and slowly took her way back to Samonchō. Here the reaction
came. Strong was the inclination to laugh and weep; too strong
for self-control. In alarm she ran to take from the closet the
potion of Suian. Its effect was the opposite of what she expected—or perhaps it was taken too late. For an hour O'Iwa
writhed, screamed, laughed in her agony. Then she sank into
slumber. On awakening the sun was already well past the zenith.
She sprang up in alarm. This meal to prepare—the duty of the
wife—and not a step taken. It could not be helped. Just as she
was, twisting a towel around her disordered hair, she started out
to the place of one Kuraya Jibei of the Asakusa Kuramaé no
Saka. This man was a lender on the notes from the rice pensions
of the *samurai*—a *fudasashi* dealer, as these men were called.

---

[1] The monetary *bu* was one-fourth the *ryō*; the *shu* was one-fourth
the value of the *bu*. A hundred *mon* = one *sen*. To-day there are
blind shampooers (and for massage) at 500 *mon* = 5 *sen*.

The distance was great. O'Iwa was tired out on her arrival. At the entrance the kozō or "boy" hailed her sharply. He waved her off. "No! No! Old girl, it won't do. Nothing is to be had here. Please come back the day before yesterday." He barred the way. Said O'Iwa, shrinking back—"Nothing is wanted of the honoured house. An interview with Jibei San, an inquiry to make. Such the request." Something about tone or manner, certainly not pity, made the fellow hesitate—"Jibei San! A beggar woman wants an interview with Jibei San! How about it?" —"Nothing to be had," answered the bantō's voice. "Tell her to read the white tablet hung before the entrance. It is all the house has to give." In speaking he edged around a little. O'Iwa raised the towel from her face. At once he was on his feet. "Ah! For long the honoured lady of Tamiya has not been seen. Many and profitable the dealings with Matazaémon Dono. Condescend to pardon this senseless fellow. He outrivals his companions in lack of brains. Deign to enter." The kozō was all apology—"Condescend wholly to pardon. Deign to have pity on the ignorance shown. With fear and respect . . ." Looking into O'Iwa's face he was overcome by his feelings. Bursting with laughter he fled to the front of the shop to stuff the dust rag into his mouth in mistake for a towel. This slight error restored his equanimity. The bantō looked after him with some fellow feeling and much anger. "He is half idiot. Condescend to disregard his rude speech and manner. After all he is but a kozō. . . . What can this Jibei do for the lady of Tamiya?"

"Knowing that the House has dealings with Jibei San, and there being necessity for three shō of rice, it is ventured to ask the loan." Thus spoke O'Iwa. Money, actual coin, was on the end of her tongue, but somehow she could not get the words out. Jibei was not particularly astonished. Since Iémon had taken charge of the affairs of Tamiya, its income was usually discounted well beforehand. Moreover, the rumour of Iémon's gambling was spreading among his connections. Neither Kwaiba nor Akiyama, nor the others engaged, were men to lose sight of the likelihood of fine pickings from the Tamiya. Jibei made prompt answer. "Respectfully heard and understood. It shall be sent . . . Ah! It is required now? Matsu! Matsu! Put up three *shō* of rice for the lady of Tamiya. Its conveyance is to be provided. Place a *bu* in the parcel. The distance to Yotsuya is great. The *kago* (litter) men are exacting." O'Iwa's heart leaped with gratitude at the perspicacity of Jibei. He watched her departing figure as far as he could see it. Then he took out a ledger; and against the name of Tamiya he placed a question mark.

It was dusk when O'Iwa entered the house at Samonchō. She gave a start on finding Iémon glumly seated before the fireless brazier. " A fine hour for a woman to be gadding the street. And the meal! Unprepared: excellent habits in a wife! ——" To the Danna apology is due. This Iwa is much in the wrong. But for the meal money had first to be secured . . ." —" Then there is money, or means to procure it? Where is it? How much?"—" Nay, the rice is here. This *bu* is enough to secure eels, *sashimi,* some delicacy . . ." She hesitated before Iémon's doubting glare. He was eyeing rice and money. The mark on the bag caught his eye. " Whence was this rice had? And this money? From Jibei, the *fudasashi* dealer? A visit paid in such garb? Truly the House is disgraced, not only by your ugliness, but by ill conduct. Who could remain in such a den? " O'Iwa threw herself in his way as he rose to leave the room. Clinging to his sleeve she pleaded for pardon, as only a woman can do who has done no wrong. There was an ugly look on Iémon's face as he turned on her. Frightened, she would have fled. Instead she could only crouch like a dog under the blows he showered on her. Then with a violent kick in the groin he rolled her over, and departed.

O'Iwa heard footsteps. Had Iémon returned? Despite the pain, she half sat up in her dread. Kondō Rokurōbei appeared. The portly man held up his hands in horror and benevolence at what he saw. " But O'Iwa—what has occurred? Ah! Kondō has heard rumours of what is going on. The *tatami* (mats), screens, drawers (*tansu*), clothes-baskets—the house is completely stripped to satisfy the thirst for the money of others. Now he has descended to blows! Truly he is a miserable fellow." Kondō's voice grew loud in his wrath. "This must not go on. Rokurōbei is responsible to Tamiya, to the ancestors. To be subject to a fellow like this will never do. A divorce is to be secured. Let him depart with his plunder. Let him have everything; only to get rid of him. He is husband, and head of Tamiya. But Kondō will be too much for him. A divorce shall be secured. Itō Dono, the ward chief, is to be interested in the affair. Pressure shall be put on Iémon to grant the letter of divorce." Indignation choked the worthy man. O'Iwa spoke slowly, with pain and effort. "Be in no such haste, Kondō Sama. Iémon has not been a good man. Much is known to this Iwa. He buys women at Nakachō. He buys *geisha*. He gambles. These are a man's vices. As to these Iwa has nothing to say. She is the wife, for two lives to maintain the house in good and ill fortune. A good wife does not look to divorce to rectify mistakes. With such remedy Iwa has nothing to do. But is not Kondō Sama the *nakōdo*? Was he not the mediator in the marriage between Iémon and Iwa? Deign to speak as *nakōdo*. Rebuke Iémon. Cause this gambling to be brought to an end." Rokurōbei could hardly hear her to the end. His testy impatience was in evidence. He broke into protest—"This is complete madness; utter folly. You allow this fellow to ruin the House. He will dispose of the pension."—"The goods, the House, Iwa, all belong to Iémon; to do with as he pleases. Iwa is the wife. She must submit . . . Ah! You refuse. Kondō Sama is no longer the friend of Iwa, to act as *nakōdo*." What had come into the soul of this gentle woman? Kondō in fright shrank back from the look she gave him—"A very demon! The mother, O'Mino, has returned to life. Oni! Oni! You are not human. Kondō assuredly will have nothing to do with O'Iwa, or O'Iwa's affairs." He left her helpless in the middle of her fit. Forgetting in his fright even his clogs, barefooted, he fled from the house in Samonchō.

8

CHAPTER XII

KWAIBA'S REVENGE

KONDŌ ROKURŌBEI went direct to the council of the conspirators. He found them assembled in the house of Itō. Kwaiba, Iémon, O'Hana, Chōzaemon, Kibei, were drinking *saké*. Kwaiba as usual was bragging over his prowess in youth extended into age. O'Hana was laughing at him behind his back. Kibei was surly; yet his share of income was assured. Kwaiba roundly berated Iémon for lack of energy. "O'Iwa has been allowed to get the upper hand. Iémon is far too soft to deal with a woman who has been spoiled all her life." Iémon listened in silence, with a rather doubtful smile of acquiescence or contempt. In fact, knowing O'Iwa as he did, he had little confidence in Kwaiba or Chōzaémon, or the methods they proposed. His own plan was maturing. Meanwhile in part it ran parallel. On this assembly burst the discomfited Rokurōbei—"Ah! What an experience! The woman is a very fiend. A new pair of *geta*, bought but yesterday, and left at your house, Iémon Uji." Iémon looked at Kondō's frightened face and bare feet. Then he burst into a roar of laughter. Kwaiba was indignant. "Is the fright of Kondō San any license to bring his dirty feet on the *tatami*. Deign, good sir, to accept water for the cleansing. O'Hana San now is inmate of the house of Kondō; yet condescend for the moment to act the mistress here." This was part of the arrangement. With the goods of O'Iwa the person of O'Hana had been transferred to the charge of the honest Rokurōbei. There Iémon had easy and decent access to the use of both.

Said Iémon—"What happened after this Iémon left Samonchō? Kondō Dono has been frightened." Kondō puffed and fumed as he cleansed his feet at the mounting step. He groaned—

114

" Iémon Dono, you are certainly done for. Was it ' three years,' she said? Her face was frightful. This Rokurōbei has no more to do with the affair. He goes no more to Samonchō. Alas! He will never sleep again. Oh! Oh! To be haunted in the next existence by such a rotten O'Baké." Said Kwaiba—" Did Iémon really beat her? He says he did." Answered Kondō—" She could barely move a limb. Of love for Iémon not a spark is left; but she clings to the honour of Tamiya, to the wife's duty to the House. There is no moving her. Rokurōbei is suspect, as not doing his duty as *nakōdo*. Look to yourselves. If she ever gets suspicious of the real facts, has an inkling of the truth— look out for yourselves."

Kwaiba was thoughtful; Iémon was indifferent. None of them could think of aught but the venture already engaged in. A week, ten days, passed. In that time every effort was made to move O'Iwa to consent to a divorce. As *Kumi-gashira,* Kwaiba summoned her to his house. Before his kindly sympathy O'Iwa melted into tears. The scandalous treatment of Iémon had reached his ears. Why had he not heard of it before it reached such extremes? He looked indignation at his messenger, the one who had brought O'Iwa to his presence, Akiyama Chōzaémon the neighbour of Tamiya, living not far off near the Ten-ō. Said the ward head—" Kwaiba always took this Iémon, or Kazuma, for a scoundrel. A stranger, why bring him into the ward? But now he is master of Tamiya. In the place of the excellent, if obstinate, Matazaémon. Alas! The pension of the House is said to be hypothecated for five years. And the household goods; and separate properties of Tamiya—all gone?" O'Iwa nodded assent, and Kwaiba threw up his hands at such wickedness. At all events he counselled her to consider matters, to accept his aid. He would place her somewhere; in the country and far off from the ward in which Iémon as master of Tamiya in its degradation would always be an unpleasant sight and influence in her life; at least until Iémon could be expelled. With the fellow's past career doubtless this would happen before long. Meanwhile O'Iwa was to pass into one of the wretched, overworked, exhausted drudges on one of Kwaiba's Shimosa farms. From his chief's expressed views Chōzaémon dissented. This was the one man O'Iwa distrusted. He had always shown dislike to her. In defense of her conduct Chōzaémon was too clever to show any warmth. He was the subordinate making exact report to his chief. O'Iwa was completely taken in. This friendly neutrality aroused her every grateful feeling. Said Chōzaémon—"Iémon is a coward. A *samurai* beats neither woman nor dog. If either are unfaithful to him, he kills the offender. Iémon's conduct has been thoroughly bad. Before the reproaches of O'Iwa San, beaten in argument he has retaliated by beating her to a jelly. Her face bears the marks of his violence. As to her body, my wife answers for it that it is a mass of bruises."—"Is that so?" said Kwaiba in deep sympathy. O'Iwa burst into tears. Kwaiba fumed with rage—"Truly Iémon is not a human being. He has the horns of a demon."

Then the priest Myōzen, of the family temple, the Myōgyōji of Samégabashi,[1] appeared at the Samonchō house. To him O'Iwa looked for ghostly consolation against the ills of this world. Instead he merely chanted the old refrain, harped on the scandal brought on Samonchō by the continued bickering of the married pair. Husband and wife had mutual duty toward each other; but also there was a duty toward their neighbours. Iémon was irreclaimable. . . . This stranger! O'Iwa San should deign to take the active part herself; not afford this ill spectacle and example to the ward. Like most parsons he was convinced by the noise of his own voice, and spoke with the intense conviction of long rehearsal. O'Iwa heard him out with a curious chill at

---

[1] Of the Nichiren sect. The characters of the "Yotsuya Kwaidan" move within the circle of this Presbyterian cult: *i.e.,* Presbyterian in its stiff attitude of hostility and superiority to all other sects. There is another Myōgyōji, neighbour to the Ten-ō shrine.

heart. The graves of her beloved *hotoké* (departed ones) were in the cemetery of Myōgyōji. The temple had been one of the few generous features, almost extravagances, of Matazaémon. It had profited greatly by his donations. It was the honour of the House against the argument of the priest and the convenience of the neighbours; and all because a bad man had been brought into it. " What the revered *ōshō* (prebend) has said reaches to the heart of this Iwa. Submission is to be an inspiration from the revered *hotoké*. Iwa will seek their counsel." Baffled, the priest left the house; veiled censure was on his lips; open disobedience and contempt on the part of O'Iwa.

Said Kwaiba—" Chōzaémon has failed. At least this Kwaiba has saved his ten *ryō*—and gained one object. Kondō Dono, thanks for your kind hospitality to O'Hana San. Do you propose to adopt her?" Kondō made an emphatic gesture of protest and dissent. He said—" At least Kondō has the security of goods and money for his generous expenditures."—" Both of them belonging to O'Iwa San; just as Kwaiba holds the acknowledgment of Akiyama San." Chōzaémon made a wry face. The prospect of pressure put on him, with all the added accumulation of the months of interest, was not a cheerful one. Said Kwaiba angrily —" Ah! Whoever would have suspected such obstinacy in the O'Baké; she who always was so yielding within her home and outside of it. She seemed to be such an easy mark. It was merely a matter of ordering her out. And now she baffles this Kwaiba of his revenge!" Iémon laughed outright. Kwaiba looked at him with surprise. Was this charlatan playing a double game? Said Iémon—" Fear enters at the words of the honoured chief. Pray condescend to be easy in mind. As yet Chōzaémon has not failed. At least the question can be argued with the *Kumi-gashira*. It is left to these principals. Iémon is of better counsel." Then after a silence during which Kwaiba intently eyed him—" To-morrow O'Iwa San leaves Yotsuya. Kwaiba Dono gets his revenge on the late master of Tamiya. Pray re-

member it, in favour of the present incumbent of the House."
Said Kwaiba fervently—"Iémon would be a son to Kwaiba!
Is it really true—that the O'Baké will be expelled the ward, in
disgrace?" Iémon nodded assent.

On the following day O'Iwa had completed her ablutions.
She arrayed herself in freshly washed robes. Then she took her
place before the Butsudan. It was memorial day of the decease
of the *hotoké*. Earnestly she prayed—"Deign, honoured *hotoké*,
to have regard to this Iwa. The year has not lapsed since the
hand of Iwa was placed in that of Iémon. Now the House is
brought to ruin. No heir appears to console this Iwa and to
continue its worship, to inherit its revenues. 'Take these in hand.
Life lies before Iémon for their enjoyment. His revenue will be
ample. Deign but to have the honour of the House in mind, the
continuance of its line as object.' Such were the words of the
honoured Matazaémon when in life. Unworthy has been the
conduct of this trust by Iémon. But divorce is a scandal, always
to be avoided by a woman. Return the love of Iémon to this Iwa.
Deign, honoured *hotoké*, to influence his wandering passions
toward this child of the House. Cause the husband to return
to Tamiya, once more to uphold its rights and influence. Such is
the prayer of this Iwa." She rose, placed the offerings, and
struck the little bell with the hammer. As she did so a noise
was heard at the entrance. Iémon, carrying fishing rod and
basket, and followed by Natsumé Kyuzō and Imaizumi Jinzaémon, burst into the room. All three were more or less drunk.
Dumfounded O'Iwa looked from one to the other. Imaizumi
carried a tub. Kyuzō knocked it from his shoulders. Then
tumbled clumsily down on the cask. None of them had removed
the dirty *waraji* (straw sandals) they wore. "Why do so in such
a barn?" hiccoughed Kyuzō. "And this *saké*; Kyuzō found it
without, at the kitchen door. Jinzaémon shouldered it. Whence
does it come, Iémon San? Faugh! It smells as if the cask had
been placed for the convenience of passers-by on the wayside.

It stinks. That's what it does." He gave the cask a kick, knocking out the bung. The filthy liquid poured out on the floor. Iémon appropriated the tub. He seated himself on it." 'Tis the fine liquor of Tamiya. All the house possesses. Iémon is hungry." Opening his basket he took out an eel. He began to skin it. A cry from O'Iwa arrested him. His wife sank down before him in attitude of prayer. "Importunate jade! What would you now? Further advice to a husband who wants but to get rid of the sight of an ugly face? Bah! This lump of a wench is neither good for child-bearing nor for house-keeping; she is not even a good *rusu* (care-taker). His knife made a rip in the skin of the squirming animal. O'Iwa laid a hand on his sleeve. With a voice in which sobs mingled with the petition— "To-day is a memorial day of the honoured *Hotoké Sama;*. Deign to refrain from taking life in the house; nay, before the very *ihai* in the Butsudan. Such deed will cause pain to the *Hotoké Sama;* bring disaster on the House, perhaps on this Iwa and Iémon San." Iémon fairly roared as he sprang up from the tub—"What! You noisy slut! Is this Iémon to go without food because the *hotoké* dislikes the smell of eels? . . . Jinzaémon, can you cook eels?" Imaizumi had sought the *rōka.* His round featureless face showed his fright and indecision before this critical quarrel of husband and wife. Of all involved in the plot he was the most unwilling in performance of his rôle. But he answered according to rote—"Iya! Iémon Uji, the office of cook is a special one. Jinzaémon is no cook. He leaves that office to his wife. Moreover the cooking of eels is an art in itself." —"And the artist is here," chimed in the malignancy of Kyuzō. "O'Iwa San is noted for her skill."—"Right!" said Iémon. "Kyuzō and Jinzaémon have heard the refusal of O'Iwa. Cook this eel—or else Iémon pronounces the formula of divorce against the disobedient wife."

In silence O'Iwa rose. She went to the portable stove. With the bellows she stirred up the fire therein. She did not dare even for a moment to pray at the Butsudan. The skillet was on the fire. The eels were sizzling in the hot liquor. Suddenly Iémon made an exclamation. Taking a towel he grasped the handle of the vessel. The next moment he had forced down the hot pan and its contents on the head of O'Iwa. "Kiya!" With the single cry she fell over backwards, writhing in pain under the infliction of the scalding mess streaming over face, neck, and bosom. Imaizumi fled in dismay. Even Natsumé Kyuzō protested. Seizing the arm of Iémon—" Iémon Uji, you go too far. Don't kill her." "Kill the O'Baké? It's impossible." Iémon spoke coldly. He was the one person of collected wits in the room.

Groaning with agony O'Iwa came to her senses. A man was leaning over her. Half blind as she was, she could recognize Chōbei. His look was grave. His voice was reticent and confused. "What has been going on here, O'Iwa Dono? Ah! Chōbei comes at a bad season. Ma! Ma! The house, too; stripped bare to the very boards, and the season still wintry. Truly this Iémon is a beast—a very brute (*chikushō*). What is Chōbei to do? There is this matter of the honour of Tamiya." He wrung his hands as in great perplexity, glancing sideways toward O'Iwa. The first part of his speech she disregarded. Such talk and consolation were growing stale. That all should pity her caused no surprise. Her situation was not unusual. It was the last words which caught her ear. "The honour of Tamiya: Chōbei San?" Chōbei turned away; to put some peppermint in his eyes. Tears stood in them as he turned again to her. O'Iwa was alarmed. "What has happened?" She caught his sleeve, drew close to him. He answered—"Chōbei cannot speak: To find O'Iwa San in such dreadful state renders it impossible to explain. Iémon San has gone too far." So he had, from Chōbei's point of view and for his purposes. These young fellows never can keep within bounds; even in abuse of a woman. His resentment was extreme. O'Iwa insisted. Finally the resistance of Chōbei was overcome. Iémon's name was posted at the

Kuramaé of Asakusa. He was in debt on every side. As the
final blow, he had stolen the seal of Itō Kwaiba and forged an
acknowledgment for twenty *ryō*. Kwaiba's enmity to Matazaémon was well known. He liked Iémon no better, and would pursue him to the end, force him to cut belly, and accomplish the
official degradation and extinction of the Tamiya House (*kaieki*).
" What is to be done? " He turned squarely to O'Iwa. She said—
" Itō Dono has been kind to O'Iwa. Perhaps if request be
made . . ." Chōbei laughed. " Itō Kwaiba is always kind
to a woman. It is not O'Iwa San whom he hates. But this is
an affair between men. He secures vengeance on Matazaémon
through Iémon and this official extinction of Tamiya. It is too
tempting. He is not to be trusted. No hint of the deed must
reach him. Is there no money at the command of O'Iwa San?
The sum is but twenty *ryō*. Iémon brought this news to Chōbei
last night. He leaves Edo, to go in hiding, after . . . after
. . . punishing the . . . Well! Well! He is a wicked
man. Chōbei never suspected such wickedness. But Iémon is
not the issue. He represents and can disgrace the Tamiya. There
lies the issue. Has O'Iwa San no means, nothing in coin? "—
" Less than a *bu,* sixty mon." She held out the coppers to Chōbei.
    Said Chōbei with decision—" There is one resource left. There
is the person of O'Iwa San. Deign to go into service at the
pleasure quarter. Chōbei is skilful. In seven days these wounds
can be healed. Twenty *ryō* secured, the paper is taken up, the
robbery of the seal is never discovered. We can laugh at Kwaiba's
anger. All is for the Tamiya." He noted that O'Iwa was hesitating—" It is but as a pledge. The money is advanced on the
person of O'Iwa San. A week, ten days, and other sources of
loan will be discovered. This is the only measure Chōbei can
suggest. He has no means of his own to meet this debt." He
smiled as at a thought—" Perhaps Kwaiba himself will pay his
own debt! " He chuckled at the idea. " Why not make appeal
at once? " repeated O'Iwa, grasping at any straw of safety from

this resource, so horrible to the *samurai* woman. Said Chōbei promptly—"Itō Sama knows perfectly well the state of Samon-chō. Asakusa, Honjō, are far removed. An appeal for twenty *ryō* as surety money in applying for a situation would appeal to him; the other would not. Besides, thus far away he could not investigate closely, if he would. He could but say ' yes ' or ' no.' " O'Iwa remembered what Kwaiba had said—the necessity of removing to a distance. The words and actions of these rascals dove-tailed admirably. A long silence followed. With exultation at heart Chōbei saw her rise. She put out the fire, gathered together the few personal articles she still possessed. On seeing her struggle with the heavy rain doors he came to her aid. " For the time being accept the hospitality of Chōbei's poor quarters. These wounds are to be healed." With full heart O'Iwa gratefully accepted. She took his hand as if to kiss it. Chōbei hastily snatched it away. In his sleeve, the ink not twenty-four hours old, was the paper of the sale of O'Iwa to Chōbei; her passing over to his guardianship, to dispose of as a street harlot, a night-hawk. The consideration? Five *ryō:* payment duly acknowledged, and of course nominal. The paper of transfer was in thoroughly correct form. Chōbei had drawn it himself.

CHAPTER XIII

THE YŌTAKA (NIGHT-HAWKS) OF HONJŌ

O'IWA's stay of nearly seven days at Chōbei's house was one of the golden periods of her life. O'Taki received the Ojōsan with humble joy. Iémon could not drop Chōbei out of his life of prosperity. O'Iwa was soon brought in contact with the humble pair in adversity. Her's was a generous heart, and O'Taki could not look around her house without some indication of this kindness. Her sympathy with the wronged wife was great. A husband—thriftless, a gambler, inconsiderate—of such a one she had some experience. By the same means this lady was brought to her present pass. It roused her indignation. As to brutality; that was another matter. She squared her stout shoulders and looked derisively at the loose angularity of Chōbei, his rickety physique. But the storm would pass. Itō Sama, Kondō Sama, Myōzen Oshō, all these were agreed. The Ojōsan now out of his reach, without a home to go to, and only hostile faces met with in the ward, Iémon Sama would soon come to terms. Would the Ojōsan deign to honour their humble home as long as she liked. She at once suppressed O'Iwa's rather futile attempts to aid in her rough household work. It had been the lady's part to direct her maids in their more repugnant tasks, and now brought right under her hand in this plebeian household. O'Iwa never had undergone the harsher lot of her mother O'Mino.

Chōbei in his way was as kind as his wife. At once he devoted himself to the repair of his property. When O'Iwa produced the paste and lotion of Suian Sensei, as sovereign for the complexion, Chōbei took them, smelled and carefully tasted, and finally put some of the paste on the end of the *hashi* or sticks to arrange the charcoal in the *hibachi*. A smell of garlic pervaded

123

the room. He noted the puffy face of O'Iwa, the unnatural, almost ghastly, white of the skin where the wide pockmarks permitted it to be seen. Within the circles of these scars there was a curious striated effect, only seen at times in the efforts of artists to depict the supernatural, or of savages to frighten their foes. It gave a drawn cadaverous look to the lower part of the face. "There is more in it than *that*," mused Chōbei. During her stay O'Iwa had one of her attacks—of nerves—in fact a true epileptic seizure. Chōbei put an embargo at once on all remedies but his own. Cynically, he added—"But elsewhere there will be no Chōbei. If the Okusama deigns to apply the drugs of Suian Sensei where she now goes, doubtless she will find early relief. At present they spoil Chōbei's efforts." The clever rascal at once recognized his fellow in Suian, bribed to render O'Iwa more hideous than Nature had made her, to take away her womanhood and hope of an heir to the Tamiya. To poison her? That he doubted; although the ignorance of leech and victim might readily lead to such result.

Within the seven days O'Iwa San once more could show herself in public. It was now Chōbei's part to carry the plot to completion. Iémon, at the proposition, had said—"Sell her as a nighthawk! An ugly woman like that no one will approach."— "'Tis Chōbei's trade," said the pimp coolly. "In Yoshidamachi they have noses—over night. Between dark and dawn the member melts, becomes distorted, and has to be made. It has served its purpose. This is Chōbei's affair. Provided that O'Iwa never again troubles the presence of Iémon Sama the object is attained." —"That is true. Do what you please. Kill her, if desired. O'Iwa in the Yotsuya; and Chōbei feels the wrath of Itō Dono, of this Iémon." Unwillingly he signed the contract required by Chōbei. He gave the latter a fee of ten *ryō* for the excision of this excrescence, and with a sigh of joy learned of the disappearance in company of the pimp and O'Iwa. Within three days carpenters and other workmen swarmed over the Tamiya in Samonchō. The master made ready for his return.

O'Taki had gone forth on a mission for Chōbei. This would insure her absence for the greater part of the day. Said Chōbei— "Deign, Okusama, to allow Chōbei to prove his art. All his accomplishments have not been displayed." To pass off the ugly woman at night could be done. He was compelled to act by daylight; though relying somewhat on the dusky interior of Toémon's entrance and reception room. This Toémon was the chief of the guild which bought and controlled these unfortunate streetwalkers, lowest of their class. Chōbei sat down before O'Iwa. As if in an actor's room he was surrounded with a battery of brushes and spatulas, pastes, paints of all shades of greys, flesh colour, pinks—even reds. Under his skilful hands O'Iwa was transformed. To make her beautiful was impossible. He made her passable. The weather was cold, though spring was now close at hand. Chōbei hesitated. The walk was a long one. His handiwork might fade or melt under the sweating induced by effort. Besides he had no desire for conversation. There were to be as few answers to curious questions as possible. In his house he had left the two women to themselves, and saw O'Iwa only when O'Taki was present. So he called a *kago* and gave the necessary directions. As the coolies moved off with their fair burden he trotted along in the rear, his project occupying his busy mind.

The place of Toémon was at Yoshidachō Nichōme, in the centre of the Warigesui district. To the north was the canal of that name. To the south a second canal ditto; the second stream was the larger, fairer, and more pretentious South Warigesui. An equal distance to the east was the Hōonji Bashi, with the great temple of that name just across the bounding river or canal of the district. As the *kago* bearers ambled down the bank of the North Warigesui, O'Iwa thought she had never seen a more filthy stream than this back-water with its stale current. The bearers put them down at the canal. Chōbei had some directions to give during the

short walk of a couple of hundred yards to their destination.
Said he—"For a *samurai* woman to engage in this business is a
serious offence. After all the matter is mere form; a pledge to
secure the return of the sealed paper forged by the husband.
The wife performs her highest duty in saving the honour of
the House. Is not that true?" There was a little sob in O'Iwa's
voice as she gave assent. She felt different now that she was
close at hand to the scene and crisis of her trial. Continued
Chōbei—"The agreement has been made out as with O'Iwa,
daughter of Kanémon, the younger brother of this Chōbei and
green-grocer of Abegawachō of Asakusa. Deign to remember
that the twenty *ryō* is needed to save a father in peril of default
and imprisonment."—"The cases are not so different," whispered O'Iwa. "Just so," said Chōbei. "Here is the place. Condescend to wait a moment, here at the entrance." Briskly he
entered the house. "A request to make!"—"Ah! Is it Chōbei
San? The Danna Sama is absent for the day, at the office of the
ward magistrate. Some drunkard considers that he has been
robbed. The girl he accused was punished—perhaps unjustly.
All the women of this house are honest."—"Beyond repair,"
laughed Chōbei. "However, the other matter has been agreed on.
The girl is here. An uncontrollable jade! The master has deigned
to aid Chōbei. Thanks are felt. Since she will run with the men,
it is as well for Kanémon to get the profit of the business. If she
breaks out—put a ring in her nose, and treat her as the farmers
treat their cattle. Don't let her again bother home or Chōbei.
She will lie—of course. At Toémon's they are used to lies?" The
woman Matsu laughed—"No fear as to that." She looked over
the contract with care. "Ah! She is sold for life service; otherwise the twenty *ryō* would be a scandalous price. Is that her?
. . . Um! Not a likely jade. Stand a little in the light.
. . . This Matsu would never have closed the bargain without a view. But Toémon San has left no choice. In the scarcity
of women, and his good-will to Chōbei San, he would pay any sum.

At twenty *ryō* she is a gem! You can come up here. Také! Haru! A new girl. Take her in charge and show her the house and its ways. . . . Chōbei San, some tea." Chōbei put a word into this running comment and invitation. As the girls were leading off the hesitating O'Iwa he said loudly and roughly— " Remember to obey the Okamisan (wife) in everything. Whatever she commands is right and must be done: no nonsense. Ah! Something forgotten: a moment please." He drew O'Iwa aside, seeing that she was on the verge of tears. Speaking gently— " Be astonished at nothing; be ignorant of everything. The house of Toémon in Honjō is not the drawing room of Tamiya in Yotsuya. Deign to remember that Chōbei must play his part. Life is like an excursion in a pleasure boat. There are rough places to pass, some danger, and much refuse to get rid of. Condescend to have House and husband in mind. It is but for a week—or so." —" And Iémon San, the House; they will be secure? "—" That Chōbei is assured of. See: he has the twenty *ryō* in hand. It is mere matter of securing the compromising paper and the return of Iémon. Some negotiations are necessary for that. In the future his behaviour will be much improved." He clinked the coin before her. As O'Iwa passed up the stairs he returned to the *hibachi* of the wife. The tea was a short course. Chōbei was on needles while drinking it. He feared an outbreak from above in the course of O'Iwa's initiation into a vileness the depth of which she never even could suspect. " Yes: trade is good. Women are difficult to secure. The men prefer to have them in their homes, rather than to gain by their service elsewhere." In such professional talk of a few moments he quickly dispatched the refreshment, climbed into his clogs, and departed. O'Iwa had disappeared far into the depths.

Toémon and his wife were quarrelling. Said the woman— " Are you mad, to pay twenty *ryō* for such an ugly wench? No choice was given. This Matsu was to receive her. Chōbei is a

cheat." Toémon and the *bantō* drew O'Iwa under the light, much
as if she were a bag of rice—" The clever rascal! From crown
of the head to neck she is all made up. And perhaps elsewhere."
—" At all events she is a woman." The *bantō* spoke as in doubt.
" Never mind: we are great artists, too, if not so good at cheating
as this Chōbei. Twenty-six years! She's forty at least. . . .
What may be your honoured age? "—" Twenty-six years," replied
the distressed O'Iwa. The wife threw up her hands—" And she
does not lie! . . . Haru! Kōta! It is time to go out. The
bell already strikes the hour of the dog (7 P.M.). Take Iwa to
the reception room (*yoséba*). She is to learn the ways of the
place; where to entertain her guests. . . . Come! Along
with all of you! " Some ten or fifteen women had gathered in their
array for their night's campaign. Paint, powder, plaster, disguised the ravages of disease among the hardened set of this low
class house. O'Iwa accompanied O'Haru to what had been
called the *yoséba*. The girl explained to her. Here was the place
to bring and entertain any guest picked up on the street. They
were not the degraded wretches who made the darkness of an
alleyway the reception room for their lovers. It was to be remembered that the wine drunk not only profited the house, but
paid in commissions for their own cosmetics and other little
gratifications. On entering the place O'Iwa shrank back to the
wall in horror; to shrink away in turn from the filth and obscenity
to be seen on that support. She would have fled, but the entering
crowd pressed her further in. It was a long room. The entrance
formed a sort of parlour or place to sit. The rest of the apartment
was divided longitudinally into little cubicula, rooms of the space
of the one dirty mat with which each was furnished. A shelf
contained its cynically filthy and suggestive furniture.

O'Iwa's disgust and terror was too obvious. O'Haru held on
to her arm to prevent flight. The attention of the others was
drawn to them. " Does the beauty want an apartment to herself?

That is the privilege of the Oiran, the Go Tayu, the Kashiku.[1] Ah! Sister dear; it is to be learned that this place is Hell—First Block. There is no ' second block ' (nichōmé). One gets used to anything here; even to use a demon's horns for toothpicks." Thus spoke a hard-faced woman of some thirty odd, by her looks. Said the frightened O'Iwa in low tones—" Iwa has not come for this service. She is but a pledge. This redeemed, within the week she returns to her home. This place upsets one's stomach." Those present laughed loudly. " We all say that. The real reason for our coming is not to be told. Be assured that you must perform the service, or suffer. Condescend not to fall into the hands of the Okamisan. In anger she is terrible." There was a general movement of the women. Said O'Haru, drawing along O'Iwa by the hand—" Come! Make no trouble. A newcomer, you are sure to be successful and please Matsu Dono." O'Iwa resolutely held back. No matter what the suffering she would undergo it. Ah! A week in this place indeed was to be life in Hell. She called up the sight of the dismantled house, the figure of her grandfather, anything to strengthen her will to resist. O'Haru left the room. " Okamisan, the new girl refuses to serve. Haru makes report." The wife of Toémon leaped up from her cushion. Dressed in night clothes, a long pipe in hand, she rushed into the room. " What nonsense is this? Which slut is it that refuses the service of the house? . . . You! The ink on the receipt for twenty ryō paid for your ugly face and body is hardly dry. . . . Pledge? A week's service? You lie: as your uncle said you would lie. You are here for life service as a street harlot. Out with you! . . . No? No? " She was about to throw herself on O'Iwa,

---

[1] High sounding titles given to the *great hetairae*. The difference from the Greek world lay in their not being independent. They were confined to the houses of their owners. But these noted women were ransomed at times—even by great nobles. Thus Daté Tsunamune the 3rd *daimyō* of Sendai bought the famous Oiran Takao, weighing in the scales the woman against gold. In a fit of passion he killed her soon after, and had her body cast into the Edogawa.

to cast her into the street. Then her passion, to outward appearance, cooled. She was the woman of her business, malevolent and without pity. " O'Kin! O'Kin!" The others now gathered around O'Iwa. O'Haru and the girl O'Také plead with her to obey. They tried to hustle her off by force. Said O'Haru—" Report had to be made. This Haru acted for the best. Truly such obstinacy deserves punishment. But Haru is filled with pity. Deign to obey. Go forth to the service. The result of refusal is terrible." O'Iwa shook her head—" O'Haru San is free from blame. Iwa is grateful for the kind words. To go out to this service is impossible." The woman O'Kin strode into the room; a big, strapping wench, and the understudy of O'Matsu in her husband's affections. " A new recruit? " She spoke in inquiry— " Yes: and obstinate. It is a matter of punishment in the *seméba.* . . . Now! Out with you all! No dawdling!" The irate woman turned on her flock. They fled like sheep into the open.

CHAPTER XIV

THE PUNISHMENT

O'Iwa did not move. The two women approached and laid hands on her. Her yielding made no difference in the roughness of their treatment. Dragged, hustled, shoved, with amplitude of blows, she was already much bruised on reaching the place of punishment—the *seméba*, to use the technical term of these establishments " for the good of the community." During a temporary absence of the mistress, a ray of kindliness seemed to touch the woman O'Kin. She pointed to the square of some six feet, to the rings fastened in the rafters. " Don't carry self-will to extremes. Here you are to be stripped, hauled up to those rings, and beaten until the bow breaks. Look at it and take warning. Kin is no weakling." She shoved back her sleeve, showing an arm as hard and brawny as that of a stevedore. With disapproval she observed O'Iwa. The latter stood unresisting, eyes on the ground. Only the lips twitched from time to time. As the only person in the house, male or female, not to fear the Okamisan, O'Kin could only put down the courage to ignorance. She shrugged her shoulders with contempt. " A man would cause you no pain. The same cannot be said of Kin. You shall have the proof." Perhaps severity would be more merciful, by quickly breaking down this obstinacy.

The wife returned with the instrument of torture, a bow of bamboo wound with rattan to strengthen it. O'Kin took it, ostentatiously bent and displayed its stinging flexibility before the eyes of O'Iwa. The latter closed them. She would cut off all temptation to weakness. At a sign O'Kin roughly tore off the *obi*. A twist, and the torn and disordered *kimono* of O'Iwa fell to her feet with the skirt. She had no shirt. Thus she was

131

left completely naked. In modesty she sank crouching on the
ground. The cold wind of the March night made her shiver as
O'Kin roped her wrists. Again the woman whispered her counsel
in her ear—" When you get enough, say ' Un! Un!' " Detecting
no sign of consent she took a ladder, climbed up, and passed the
ropes through the rings above. She descended, and the two women
began to haul away. Gradually O'Iwa was raised from the sitting
posture to her full height of extended arms, until by effort her
toes could just reach the ground. In this painful position the
slightest twist to relieve the strain on the wrists caused agonizing
pains through the whole body. " Still obstinate—strike! " shouted
the wife. O'Kin raised the bow and delivered the blow with full
force across the buttocks. A red streak appeared. O'Iwa by a
natural contortion raised her legs. The blows descended fast,
followed at once by the raised welt of flesh, or the blood from the
lacerated tissue. Across the shoulder blades, the small of the back,
the buttocks, the belly, they descended with the full force of the
robust arms and weight of O'Kin. Every time the legs were
raised at the shock the suspended body spun round. Every time
the toes rested on the ground the bow descended with merciless
ferocity. The sight of the torture roused the fierce spirit in the
tormentors. O'Kin redoubled the violence of her blows, seeking
out the hams and the withers, the shoulders, the tenderest points
to cause pain. The wife ran from side to side, gazing into the face
and closed eyes of O'Iwa, trying to detect weakening under the
torture, or result from some more agonizing blow. O'Iwa's body
was striped and splashed with red. O'Kin's hands slipped on the
wet surface of the rod. Suddenly she uttered an exclamation.
Blood was now gushing from the nose, the eyes, the mouth of
O'Iwa. " Okamisan! Okamisan! It won't do to kill her. Deign
to give the order to cease. She must be lowered." The wife coolly
examined the victim. " She has fainted. Lower her, and throw
salt water over her. The sting will bring her to." O'Kin followed
the instructions in the most literal sense. She dashed the bucket

of water with great impetus right into O'Iwa's face. "Un!" was
the latter's exclamation as she came to consciousness. "She consents! She consents!" cried O'Kin with delight. The wife
was decidedly sceptical, but her aid plainly would go no further
at this time. Said she—"Leave her as she is. There are other
matters to attend to than the whims of an idle vicious jade. She
would cheat this Matsu out of twenty *ryo?* Well: time will show
the victor." She departed—"to drink her wine, pare her nails,
and sing obscene songs to the accompaniment of the samisen."

Tied hand and foot O'Iwa lay semi-conscious in the cold shed
of punishment. At midnight the girls returned to this "home."
They gathered around the prostate O'Iwa. From O'Kin they
had an inkling of the courage displayed. They admired her, but
none dared to touch her bonds. At last O'Haru San, unusually
successful in her night's raid, ventured to approach the half
drunk mistress of the house. "Haru makes report." She spread
her returns before the gratified Okamisan. Timidly the girl
added—"O'Iwa San repents. Deign to remit her punishment.
She looks very ill and weak."—"Shut up!" was the fierce retort.
Then as afterthought of sickness and possible loss came to mind.
"She can be untied and sent to bed."—"And food?"—"She
can earn it." The woman turned on O'Haru, who bowed humbly and slipped away. That night the girls contributed from their
store to feed O'Iwa; as they did on the succeeding days and nights.
The wife would have stopped the practice, but Toémon interfered.
He meant to keep his dilapidated stock in as good repair as possible. He fed them pretty well. "The woman is not to be
starved—at least too openly. The last case gave this Toémon
trouble enough, and on the very day this epileptic came into the
house, to bring confusion with her. Beat her if you will; but
not enough to kill her. O'Matsu followed his words to the letter.
One beating was followed by another; with interval enough between the torture to insure recuperation and avoid danger to life.
These scenes came to be regarded as a recreation of the house.
The other inmates were allowed to attend, to witness the example
and fascinate their attention. But at last the Okamisan despaired.

Amusement was one thing; but her hatred of O'Iwa was tempered by the desire to find some use for her, to get a return for the twenty *ryō* of which she had been swindled. Finally the advice of the *bantō* was followed. " The men of the house cannot be tempted to approach such an apparition. The other girls have not time to devote to making up O'Iwa as for the stage. They have not twenty *ryō* at stake, as had Chōbei. Let her wash the dishes." Thus was O'Iwa " degraded " from her high estate as street-walker. Turned into a kitchen drudge she shed tears of joy. She almost forgot the matter of the pledge in this new and pleasant life. The time and the place, perhaps the drug she took, had done their work on the mind of O'Iwa. Iémon, the house of Samonchō, the *ihai* in the Butsudan, the pleasant garden —all were of the tissue of a dream amid a toil which deposited her on the straw wrappings of the charcoal and in a shed, thoroughly worn out at the end of her long day. The O'Iwa of Samonchō at this end of the lapsing year of service was dormant. But accidents will happen.

There was excitement in the house. Mobei, the dealer in toilet articles—combs, brushes, jewel strings—was at the grating. The women were clustered before the wares he exposed in his trays. This Mobei, as dealer in toilet articles (*koma-mono*) wandered all the wards of Edo, his little trays fitting neatly into each other, and wrapped in a *furoshiki* or bundle-handkerchief. His wares formed a marvellous collection of the precious and common place, ranging from true coral and tortoise shell, antique jewelry and curious *netsuké* of great value, to their counterfeits in painted wood, horn, and coloured glass. " Mobei San, long has been the wait for you. Is there a bent comb in stock?"—" Truly this Mobei is vexing. He humbly makes apology, lady. Here is just the thing. . . . How much? Only a *bu*. . . . Too high? Nay! With women in the ordinary walks of life it is the wage of a month. To the honoured Oiran it is but a night's trifling." The other women tittered. O'Haru was a little nettled at the high

sounding title of Oiran. She would not show her irritation.
Mobei continued his attentions. He laid before her and the others
several strings of jewels, their "coral" made of cleverly tinted
paste. "Deign to look; at but one *bu* two *shū*. If real they
would cost twenty *ryō*."—"And Mobei has the real?" The
dealer laughed. As in pity, and to give them a glimpse of the
far off upper world, he raised the cover of a box in the lower tier.
They gasped in admiration before the pink of the true coral.
Hands were stretched through the grating to touch it. Mobei
quickly replaced the cover. "For some great lady," sighed O'Haru
—"Just so," replied Mobei, adjusting his boxes. He had sold two
wooden painted combs and a string of horn beads in imitation of
tortoise shell. He pocketed the hundred "cash," those copper
coins with a hole in the centre for stringing. Then briefly—"The
necklace is for no other than the Kashiku of the Yamadaya, the
loved one of Kibei Dono of Yotsuya. The comb (*kanzashi*)
in tortoise shell and gold is for the honoured lady wife of Iémon
Dono, the *go kenin*. But Mobei supplies not only the secular
world. This—for one who has left the world; for Myōzen Oshō
of Myōgyōji, the gift of Itō Dono. For the custom of Mobei the
Yotsuya stands first in order." He took a box from his sleeve
and showed them the rosary of pure crystal beads. Even in the
dull light of a lowering day the stones flashed and sparkled. The
women showed little interest. A priest to them was not a man—
ordinarily.

He shouldered his pack. "Mobei San—a comb with black
spots, in imitation of tortoise shell. Please don't fail me on the
next visit." Mobei nodded agreement. Then he halted and
turned. One of the women had called out in derision—"Here
is O'Iwa San. Surely she wants to purchase. Mobei San! Mobei
San! A customer with many customers and a full pocketbook."
These women looked on O'Iwa's assignment to the kitchen as the
fall to the lowest possible state. At sight of the newcomer Mobei
gasped. O'Iwa on leaving the door of Toémon's house, *miso*

(soup) strainers for repair in one hand, fifteen *mon* for bean paste (*tōfu*) tightly clasped in the other, came face to face with the toilet dealer. " The lady of Tamiya—here! "—" The lady of Tamiya! " echoed the astonished and curious women. Said O'Iwa quickly—" Mobei San is mistaken. This is Iwa; but lady of Tamiya . . ." Hastily she pulled her head towel over her face. In doing so the " cash " slipped from her hand. A *mon* missing meant no *tōfu;* result, a visit to the *semeba*. In recovering the lost coin Mobei was left in no doubt. " 'Tis indeed the lady of Tamiya. It cannot be denied." O'Iwa no longer attempted the impossible. She said—" It is Iwa of Tamiya. Mobei San, a word with you." The women were whispering to each other. " He called her ' *shinzō*.' " Said O'Haru—" There always was something about her to arouse suspicion; so ugly, and with such grand airs. And how she endured the punishment! Truly she must be a *samurai* woman." The minds of all reverted to their master Toémon, and how he would take this news.

O'Iwa had drawn Mobei somewhat apart from the grating. With downcast face she spoke—" Deign, Mobei San, to say nothing in the ward of this meeting with Iwa." To Mobei's earnest gesture of comprehension—" Affairs had gone badly with Tamiya. Iémon San was misled into gambling by Natsumé Kyuzō and Imaizumi Jinzaémon. He was carried away by the passion. It was no longer possible to stay in Samonchō. Worse conduct followed. In the kindness and advice of Itō Dono, of Akiyama and Kondō Sama, this Iwa found support. But she disobeyed. She would not follow the advice given. However, gratitude is felt by Iwa. One cannot leave this place, or long since she would have paid the visit of acknowledgment. A matter of importance arose. Chōbei San came to Iwa's aid, and saved the situation. This place is terrible, but the consequences of not coming would have been more so. To Chōbei gratitude is felt. It was the opportunity offered the wife to show her faith and courage." Now she looked bravely in Mobei's face. It was the toilet dealer's turn to show confusion—" Honoured lady, is nothing known? "—

"Known?" answered O'Iwa in some surprise. "What is there
to know? When this Iwa left Samonchō to be sure the house
was cracking apart everywhere. The light poured in as through
a bamboo door. . . . Ah! Have matters gone badly with
the Danna in Iwa's absence?" Mobei shook his head in dissent.
"Alas! Itō Sama, Akiyama or Kondō San, has misfortune come
to them, without a word of condolence from Iwa? Perhaps
Chobéi San, in his precarious life . . ." The poor isolated
world of the thoughts of this homely creature was limited to these
friends in need.

Mobei had sunk on his knees before her. He raised eyes in
which stood tears of pity and indignation. "The Ojōsan knows
nothing of what has occurred in Yotsuya? This Mobei will not
keep silent. With the affairs of Iémon Sama, of Itō Dono and
Akiyama San nothing has gone wrong. The absence of the lady
O'Iwa is otherwise related. She has abandoned house and husband to run away with a plebeian, the bantō at the green-grocer's
on Shinjuku road. Such is the story circulated." O'Iwa drew
away from him as from a snake—then: "Mobei, you lie! Why
tell such a tale to this Iwa? Are not the words of Itō Dono,
of Akiyama Sama, of Chōbei San still in Iwa's ears? What else
has she had to console her during these bitter months but the
thought of their kindness? This dress (a scantily wadded single
garment), these bare feet in this snow, this degraded life—are not
they evidences of Iwa's struggle for the honour of husband and
House? Mobei, slander of honourable men brings one to evil.
Mobei lies; lies!"

He seized her dress. The man now was weeping. "The
lady of Tamiya is a saint. Alas! Nothing does she know of the
wicked hearts of men. Too great has been the kindness of the
Ojōsan to this Mobei for him to attempt deceit. Deign to listen.
This day a week; was it not the day to a year of the Ojōsan's
leaving the house in Yotsuya?" O'Iwa turned to him with a
startled face. He continued—"A week ago Mobei visited Yot-

suya. He has many customers there, not too curious about prices. Hence he brings the best of his wares. Coming to the house in Samonchō a feast was in progress. There were present Itō Dono, Akiyama Sama, Natsumé and Imaizumi Sama, Kondō Dono; O'Hana San, of course. All were exceedingly merry. Iémon Dono poured out a cup of wine. 'Mobei! Mobei! Come here! Drain this cup in honour of the occasion. We celebrate the anniversary of the expulsion of the *bakémono*. The demon is driven forth from the Paradise of Yotsuya. Namu Myōhō Renge Kyō! Namu Myōhō Renge Kyō!' This Mobei was amazed—'The O'Baké. . . . What O'Baké?'—'Why: O'Iwa San. A year since, with the aid of these good friends, and one not present here, Iémon freed himself from the clutches of the vengeful apparition. Our *Kumi-gashira* granted divorce in due form. The son of Takahashi Daihachirō—Yanagibara Kazuma—Tamiya Iémon no longer catches at sleep to wake in fear. Chief, deep is the gratitude of Iémon for the favour done by Itō Dono.' The Ojōsan a *bakémono*! At these outrageous words Mobei felt faint. Receiving the cup, as in modesty returned to the *rôka* to drink, the contents were spilled on the ground. Ah! Honoured lady, it is not only that the Ojōsan has been driven out. Her goods have been cleverly stolen by false messages of gambling losses. Stored with Kondō Sama they were brought back on the success of the wicked plot. The whole is a conspiracy of Iémon Dono with Itō Dono, with Akiyama, Chōbei, Kondō, and others. They bragged of it, and told the tale in full before this Mobei, laughing the while. Why, lady! On the word of Chōbei San the order of divorce was issued by Itō Dono. Within the month O'Hana San left the shelter of the house of Kondō Sama to enter the Tamiya as bride. Deign to look. Here is a jewelled comb reserved by Iémon Sama as present for O'Hana San his wife. Here is gift of Itō Dono to Myōzen Oshō for his efforts ' in the cause.' "

O'Iwa stood as one frozen. With Mobei's words the light

was flooding into mind and soul. Step by step she now followed clearly the stages of this infamous conspiracy against her peace and honour. She had been fooled, cheated, degraded—and by Itō Kwaiba, the enemy of Matazaémon; by Iémon, son of the hereditary foe Takahashi Daihachirō. Mobei remained huddled at her feet, watching with fright the sudden and awful change in her face. The words came in a whisper. At first she brought out her speech with difficulty, then to rise to torrent force— " Cheated, gulled by the hereditary foe! And this Iwa lies bound and helpless! 'Tis understood! The end is at hand—Ah! The poison! The poison! Now it, too, rises; flowing upward to heart and head of Iwa. Accursed man! Accursed woman, who would play the rival and destroy the wife! The time is short; the crisis is at hand. Chōbei's dark words become light. Hana would poison Iwa through this treacherous leech. Iémon would kill her by the foul life of this brothel—Gods of Nippon! Buddhas of the Universe! All powerful Amida, the Protector! Kwannon, the Lady Merciful! Deign to hearken to the prayer of this Iwa. Emma Dai-ō, king of Hell, summon not the daughter of Tamiya before the dreaded throne for judgment—through the course of seven existences—until the vengeance of Iwa be sated with the miserable end of these her persecutors. May the sacred characters of the Daimoku, written on the heart of Iwa for her future salvation, be seared out as with hot iron. On Itō Kwaiba, Iémon, Akiyama Chōzaémon, Chōbei, all and every one engaged in this vile plot, rests the death curse of Iwa. Against these; against Natsumé, Imaizumi, Yoémon of Tamiya, lies the grudge of Iwa of Tamiya. Gods and Buddhas—grant this prayer!"

A violent hand was laid on the bosom of Mobei's robe. He screamed in terror at the fearful face bent over him. A broad round dead white swollen face, too sharp gleaming malignant dots darting flashes as from a sword between the puffed and swollen lids, froze him into a passive object. One of these lids drooped horribly down upon the cheek of the apparition. In the physical effort exerted, the slit of the mouth showed the broad black even teeth, which seemed about to clutch at his throat; as did the vigorous hand, the nails of which sank into his gullet. Framed in the mass of wild disordered hair Mobei was isolated as in a universe of space; left alone with this fearful vision. " Lady! Lady O'Iwa! Lady of Tamiya! This Mobei has done naught. Others have wronged O'Iwa San. Mobei is guiltless. . . . Ah! Ah! " With fright and pain he rolled over on the ground in a dead faint. Screaming and shouting the women Také and Kōta rushed around and out to his rescue. O'Iwa San was now under the full control of her disorder. Takézo staggered back, her hands to her face to hide the horrible sight, to wipe from eyes and cheeks the blood streaming from the deep tears made by O'Iwa's nails. Kōta from behind seized O'Iwa around the waist and shoulders. Sharply up came the elbow shot, catching this interloper under the chin. Neck and jaw fairly cracked under the well-delivered blow. Kōta went down in a heap as one dead. A *chūgen* coming along the North Warigesui had reached the crossing. He thought it better to stand aside, rather than attempt to stop this maddened fiend tearing through space. At the canal bank there was a moment's pause. Then came a dull splash; as of some heavy body plunged in the water. With a cry the man hastened forward. Not a sign of anything could be seen. In this rural place no help was to be had, and he was little inclined to plunge at random into the foul stream. In haste he turned back to where a crowd was gathering around the prostrate Mobei, the groaning harlots to whom punishment had been meted out.

CHAPTER XV

CHŌBEI GETS THE NEWS

THE *chūgen* stood over the toilet dealer now coming out of his half-trance condition. The eyes of the two men met and showed mutual astonishment. "Naruhodo! Mobei San! In a quarrel over his wares with the vile women of this district?"—"Kakusuké San! Ah! There is much to tell. O'Iwa San . . ." The *chūgen* of Itō Kwaiba was amazed attention. "This Mobei to his ill fortune, met with the lady of Tamiya. Her condition, her ignorance, was too pitiful. Learning all the truth from Mobei she inflicted on him this punishment. May it cease there! Namu Amida Butsu! Namu Amida Butsu! . . . Heavy the grudge against your master Itō Dono; against Iémon Sama, his wife O'Hana San, all in the plot against the Lady O'Iwa. 'To seven existences grant this Iwa opportunity to vent her anger. Every one of the perpetrators of this deed shall be seized and put to death.' She invoked all the gods and Buddhas; Nay, the king of Hell—Emma Dai-ō himself. Look to yourself, Kakusuké San. Deign to seek employment elsewhere." Kakusuké completed his task of raising the battered and scratched toilet dealer to his feet. "Mobei San, you have acted the fool; without doubt. Relate what has happened." Mobei did so in full detail. Kakusuké was thoughtful. "Much of ·this Kakusuké hears for the first time. A servant gets but snatches of the inside of such matters. Just now the mission has been from his master, Itō Dono, to the Inagaki *yashiki* near Hōonji; matter of transfer involved in the late adoption of Kibei Dono into the House of the Danna Sama. . . . So that scoundrel Chōbei sold the lady of Tamiya to Toémon for a harlot. Alas! She deserved a better fate. One way or another they would kill her; and Chōbei, his money in hand, abetted the crime. Where is this brothel?"

141

Surrounded by his women Toémon was listening to their excited statements. Takézo was crying with rage and pain, as she examined her fissured countenance before a toilet stand (*kyōdai*). Kōta, brought back to consciousness, lay groaning in a corner. They were applying cold compresses to her broken jaw. Toémon looked up suspiciously as Kakusuké entered, supporting the lamed and maimed Mobei. " Look to this man's wares, scattered in the roadway; and to the man himself." He spoke roughly, and with authority. Toémon did not dare to resent his manner. With well feigned solicitude he addressed Mobei—" Ma! Ma! A terrible punishment. Your face has the blush of the plum blossom marked upon it. . . . O'Haru, run to the house of Wakiyama Sensei. Kōta is badly hurt; his skill is needed. Stop at the drug store. Here is the ' cash ' to bring salve for this good man's wounds. Alas! That a woman of Toémon's house should so maltreat others. When caught her punishment. . . ."— " Shut up! " said Kakusuké. He had already taken his line of conduct in his master's interest. " How comes it that the Lady O'Iwa is found at the house of Toémon? "—" The Lady O'Iwa! " replied the brothel keeper in well-feigned surprise." Turning to Mobei—" It is true, then, what the women report; that Mobei San called the O'Iwa of this house ' Shinzō.' Who is this O'Iwa? " Said Kakusuké coldly—" The Lady O'Iwa is the granddaughter and heir of Tamiya Matazaémon, a higher *dōshin*. She is the wife of the *go-kenin*, Tamiya Iémon."

Toémon now was truly aghast. " Heir and wife of *go-kenin!* This Toémon had not the slightest inkling of her *status.* Chōbei has juggled this Toémon most outrageously." He turned savagely on O'Matsu. " So much for stupid brutality. One must give you head, or have no peace. Why not treat the woman kindly, learn her story? Lies or truth that of all the women in the house is known. But O'Iwa San was a mark for malice. Chōbei has lied. Between you the house is ruined. Since when were *samurai* women sold to life service? Fool! It means imprisonment, exile, to those implicated. This Toémon ends his days among the savage fishermen of Sado." He would have struck her. Kakusuké and the *bantō* interposed. The woman did not budge. Defiant, she stood with folded arms—" It was Toémon's arrangement to buy her in blind belief of Chōbei. Why blame this Matsu? Since when were women exempt from service or punishment? The rule of the house is one or the other. How long has it been since O'Seki left the house—in a box; and Toémon had to make answer at the office." Then catching herself up in the presence of strangers—"Danna Sama, this is no time for a quarrel. Those of the house will say nothing; in their own interest. As for this worthy gentleman, the Lady O'Iwa was wife and heir neither of himself nor his master. Toémon San is grossly neglectful of courtesy due to guests. Leave Mobei San to this Matsu." She whispered in his ear.

Toémon had now recovered his balance. Kakusuké was a *chūgen*. He had an object in coming to Toémon's house, instead of making report at once to his master, to the outraged Iémon Dono. Of course Toémon misintrepreted this motive; and Kakusuké was quite ready to profit by his mistake. To the now courteous brothel keeper he was equally cordial. O'Matsu and her women carried off Mobei, to salve his wounds, regale him with fish and wine and good treatment, carefully to make inventory of his goods, and repack them with substantial diminution of purchases. What more could Mobei ask. His valued rosary, the necklace, the *kanzashi,* all the treasures were uninjured. His exchequer was palpably swollen, and more pleasingly than his phiz. His beating had turned out a good day's venture; and without misgiving he can be left in the careful hands of O'Matsu and her women. Meanwhile Kakusuké and Toémon sat over their wine. From the *chūgen* and toilet dealer the latter secured a complete view of his situation. It was bad, but not irreparable. As Kakusuké with due tardiness prepared to depart, the hospitable innkeeper had ample time to prostrate himself in salutation, meanwhile pushing over a golden *ryō* wrapped up in decently thin paper which permitted the filtering through of its yellow gleam." Great has been the trouble and delay of Kakusuké San. Mark not this day in memory, good Sir." Kakusuké was equally polite in salutation—"Fear enters: thanks for the kind entertainment of Toémon San. This alone is to be kept in mind, mark of a day otherwise of but little import." These last words were a healing balm; and Toémon rejoiced.

With the departure of Kakusuké, the chief of the "nighthawks" turned at once to his aids. "Také! Haru! . . . Ah! Kōta is completely done up. You, Také, bear the marks of the day's encounter. Go to Asakusa Hanagawadō. Chōbei is to be brought here at once. The house must clear its skirts of this affair. If he refuses to come, put a rope about his neck and drag him here." The women bowed. At once they prepared for the street, a mission welcome enough under other conditions. O'Také was smarting from her wounds and not very willing to be an object lesson. O'Haru had in mind the fearful curse of O'Iwa, plainly heard by the women. Very willingly she would have had nothing to do with the affair.

Chōbei was engaged at *go* with the metal dealer of his neighbourhood. The fish and wine were in course of preparation in the kitchen close by and under the skilled hands of O'Taki. The perfume, vinous and of viands, came to the noses of the competitors, to the disturbance of their game. Chōbei had just made a profitable stroke. He had five *ryō* in hand, commission from the worthy *doguya* for the successful sale of a daughter to the Yamadaya of Nakanochō. This enterprising plebeian, having a son to succeed him in the business, had secured the necessary furnishing and adoption of a second son into the rival house of the ward, by means of the fifty *ryō* secured for the girl through the experience and clever tactics of Chōbei. Many the compliments and congratulations exchanged by these excellent men and worthy representatives of their class as they tussled over their game of *go*. Profuse were the thanks of the metal dealer for past services and future feasting. It was with some displeasure therefore that O'Taki had her offices interrupted to respond to a loud and harsh—" Request to make!" sounded at the house entrance. Said she crossly—" Who is it? . . . Ah! O'Také and O'Haru San of Toémon Sama." Then in wonder—" Oya! Oya! O'Také San. . . . Your honoured face. . . . Has O'Také San gone to bed in the dark with the cat?" Answered O'Také, in no amiable mood—" It could well have been. Your man Chōbei deals in such articles. There are the marks of O'Iwa's nails. As for Chōbei, is the precious rascal at home?" O'Taki heard her with rising rage—" O'Iwa? What has Chōbei San to do with any O'Iwa and the house of Toémon San? Why call the man of Taki a scoundrel?"—" Because he is such. Nay, Okamisan, don't get angry."—O'Haru was speaking—" has your husband a brother in Abegawachō, a brother in need of twenty *ryō* and with a daughter who would do nothing but run after the men?" O'Taki was puzzled. " Chōbei San has no brother, in Abegawachō or any other *chō*. Hence such brother has no daughter O'Iwa; nor are there children of his own, except the one born to him by this Taki, and a girl already sold. . . ." A light was breaking in on O'Taki. Months before she had come home to find that the Ojōsan had taken her departure. Explained Chōbei—" At Yotsuya everything has been adjusted. Iémon Dono is established again with his wife. The Okusama will not come back to us. Deign to rejoice at the auspicious settlement of her affairs." Which O'Taki did; all the more as Chōbei often was in funds in the successive days through Tamiya. Now she looked from one woman to the other, her fists clenched and working. Said the harsh voice of O'Také—" Chōbei lied then; just as the Danna Sama thought. Nearly a year ago he brought to the house the daughter of his brother Kanémon. He sold her into life service as a nighthawk. For this she turned out to be worthless. O'Taki San knows our Okamisan. No matter how severely

10

beaten, even until the blood came, O'Iwa would not consent to serve. Other means were tried, but the men of the house would have nothing to do with her. She was too ugly. Finally she was degraded into being the kitchen wench, to fetch and carry, and do the hardest and most nauseating tasks. At this downfall in her prospects like a very fool she rejoiced. To-day she met the toilet dealer Mobei. He recognized her as the Lady O'Iwa of Tamiya in the Yotsuya. Drawn apart they spoke together. Suddenly she was transformed into a demon. Leaping on Mobei she tore and clutched at him. Kōta and this Také ran to aid him. Kōta lies helpless and with a broken jaw. Truly it might have been the kick of a horse she received. This Také is—as can be seen. The Lady O'Iwa disappeared toward Warigesui. A *chūgen* saw her leap in. Probably she has killed herself. . . . And now, O'Taki San, is not your man Chōbei a scoundrel? "

Said O'Taki—" Rightly spoken ; more than right. Wait here." Abruptly she entered the inner room. To Chōbei—" You . . . my fine fellow . . . is this a time for *go?* Up and off with you ; to accompany O'Také and O'Haru from Toémon's in Honjō. A pretty business is in preparation there." Said the embarrassed and enraged Chōbei—" Wh-what does this rude entrance of Taki mean ? Is not the master of the metal shop present? Is such language, such abruptness, to be used in his presence ? "— " The Danna of the *doguya* is certainly present," coolly replied the woman. " It would be better if he was at home. . . . Honoured Sir, pray betake yourself there. This Chōbei has business with Toémon Sama of Honjō, the brothel keeper and chief of the nighthawks, to whom he has sold for life service as a street harlot the Lady O'Iwa, wife of the *go-kenin* Iémon Dono and heir of Tamiya Matazaémon the *dōshin*. A man can be too clever—as this Chōbei, who cheats his wife and all others. Do you be clever enough to take the hint and depart. . . . Off with you! " The *doguya* had sat in silence. His eyes were popping out of his head in frightened amaze. Chōbei bounded up in a rage—" You huzzy—shut up! Would you publish the affairs of this Chōbei to the world? Many a bridge is to be passed in the course through this world; and none too sure the footing. Money must be had to live and enjoy life. The result, not the means, is the important factor in its acquisition. Such rudeness to a guest! Vile jade, Chōbei will . . ." O'Také and O'Haru had to interfere—" Fight it out later, Chōbei San. This quarrel is no concern of ours. The sooner the master is seen, the better for Chōbei San. His rage is great, and mounting. You have the contract? With that face the master; if you can."—" Just so! Just so! As for this wench—she shall have something to remember this Chōbei by . . ." The worthy and trembling metal dealer took this remark as threat of renewed violence. " For the kind reception and entertainment: thanks. Jubei calls later." Nimbly he was on his feet. Diving under the *haori* into which Chōbei was struggling he bounced out the front, leaving Chōbei on the ground and floundering in the folds of his garments, from which issued most violent language. For the first time that day O'Také and O'Haru had something to amuse them. O'Taki refusing, they assisted Chōbei to his feet and adjusted his robe. Then one on each side of him they set out for Honjō Yoshidachō. As parting salute to O'Taki, Chōbei finished his sentence. . . . " Something to remember on Chōbei's return." Her laugh in reply was so savage that the women turned to look at her. In fright they hastened off with their prize.

At Honjō the reception of Chōbei called forth the whole house. The pimp entered the presence of Toémon with confident and jaunty air. " He has the contract? " said Toémon to the woman. O'Haru indicated a sleeve. The *bantō* and one of the *wakashū* (young men employes) grasped the arms of Chōbei. The incriminating document was deftly removed by O'Haru and passed over to Toémon. " Now the fellow can neither produce it, nor play his tricks with it." He looked it over carefully; then placed it with his own copy. Chōbei was too outraged and frightened to do more than squat and gasp as he looked around the circle of hostile faces. Without cushion he sat on the bare *tatami*, much as does a criminal at the white sand. Said Toémon severely—" For once Chōbei has drunk hot water with this Toémon. Does he think to act thus with impunity. The younger sister of his brother Kanémon, ' a noted wench for the streets,' was brought here for life service; sold to Toémon for twenty *ryō*. Toémon does not intend that the price shall be too high for him. Chōbei cannot lie out of his own contract. Toémon has it in his hands. Chōbei has the twenty *ryō*. Toémon loses his money. Well and good: Toémon clears himself from the affair. The responsibility lies wholly with Chōbei. Let him look to it." Chōbei seized the moment when lack of breath in his anger halted the speech of Toémon. He would have lied, but Toémon again broke in. " Chōbei has no brother. Chōbei has no woman to dispose of on his own signature. The one he did have, the one he possesses, Toémon knows where to find. Toémon had a woman O'Iwa in his house. You sold the wife of a *go-kenin*, Iémon Dono of Yotsuya; a woman who was the heir of Tamiya Matazaemon the *dōshin*. The Lady O'Iwa is traced to the hands of Chōbei. Settle the matter with those in office—*machibugyō, dōshin, yakunin*— when the affair comes to light . . ."—" Easily," burst in Chōbei, once more himself. " Honoured chief, matters do not call for such earnestness. All this is mere froth and fury. It is true that Chōbei has deceived the chief; but it was at the orders of those much higher. The lady of Tamiya was an obstacle. The sale was ordered by Iémon Dono himself; backed by Itō Kwaiba the head of the Yotsuya ward."—" Chōbei, you lie," said Toémon. The words and advice of Kakusuké still rang in his ears. " Iémon Dono? Itō Dono? Who else will Chōbei bring in as his bails? Such a man is not to be trusted. With this Toémon there is no more dealing. The guild is to be warned by a circular letter."

At this fearful threat all Chōbei's jauntiness left him. His livelihood, his existence, were at stake. He prostrated himself before

Toémon, dragging his body over the *tatami* to the *zen* (low table) at which was seated this autocrat of the nighthawks, this receiver of the refuse and worn-out goods of his greater brothers in the trade. Toémon harshly repulsed him with his foot. Chōbei in despair turned to O'Matsu—" Honoured lady the chief is unreasonably angry. There shall be no loss of money, no harm suffered by the affair. Deign to say a word for Chōbei."— " Since when has Matsu had aught to do with the affairs of the house? The women are her concern. She goes not outside her province." The pimp sought the feet of O'Také—" Condescend to plead for Chōbei. His fault is venial. When no injury results, pardon follows. This is to cut off the breath of Chōbei, of wife and child. Deign to intercede." The street harlot laughed. Her cracked voice was rough—" The commission of Chōbei San has no attractions. This Také has had enough to do with the matter. Truly Chōbei is a wicked fellow. Také would fare badly in such intercourse. Besides his company is too high flown. Officials! Samurai! Chōbei San seeks and will find promotion in the world. Lodgings are preparing for Chōbei Sama in public office—on the Ryōgokubashi; of such he is assured." She drew away from him, harshly cackling. Thus he crawled from one to the other. It was " Chōbei Sama," " Chōbei Dono," in derision they would call him prince—" Chōbei Kō." All stuck out their tongues at him. The young fellows of the house, several of them, stood round the entrance, ostensibly occupied, but with one eye on the scene. As Chōbei sought the *banto's* aid, the man raised a long lean leg and gave him a violent kick in the breast. Strong hands seized him as he rolled over and over to the edge of the platform, to land in the arms of the enthusiastic *wakashū*. The next moment, and Chōbei was picking himself up out of the mud and snow of the street. The lattice of the house entrance closed noisily.

In his confusion of mind by force of habit Chōbei turned round and bowed with ceremony toward the place of his uncere-

monious exit—"The time is inopportune. Chōbei intrudes. He
will call again." The opening of the wicket gate, the peering,
scowling face of the *bantō* recalled the past scene to mind. With
all the haste his tottering gait allowed Chōbei sprang off north-
ward to the Adzumabashi and home. As he sped, swaying along,
his active mind was making calculations. " Ryōgokubashi, the
last home of the outcast beggar—other than the river which flows
beneath it!" He shuddered at the prophecy. "Bah! One rascal loses; another gains. Toémon loses twenty *ryō*. From
Iémon San ten *ryō* was the commission. Itō Dono gave five *ryō*
and asked no questions. The total to Chōbei sums up thirty-five
ryō. For a year the affair of O'Iwa has fattened Chōbei; with
something still left." His foot struck a stone in the roadway.
He looked up and around to find himself before the Genkwōji.
About to enter on the maze of temple grounds and *yashiki* separat-
ing him from the bridge his gaze fell on the stagnant squalid
waters of the canal. It was in the dirty foulness of this North
Warigesui that O'Iwa had disappeared. Chōbei pulled up short.
A dead cur, copper hued, with swollen germinating sides and grinning teeth, bobbed at him from the green slime. Chōbei slewed
round—"A vile ending; but after all an ending. Iémon profits;
Chōbei gets the scoldings. Ah! If it was not that Itō Kwaiba is engaged in this affair; Tamiya should pay dearly. There is a double
ration to share with Chōbei—and not to be touched! Itō Dono
is no man to trifle with. There was that affair with Isuké; and
now, as he says, Iémon is a very son to him." A memory seemed
to touch Chōbei. His pace became a crawl. "Why hasten?
Chōbei rushes to the fiend—that demon Taki. Chōbei would
rather face O'Iwa than Taki in a rage." He laughed—"The
attenuated hands of a ghost and the thick fist of Taki, the choice
is not uncertain. From the lady mild and merciful there is nothing to fear. Evidently she has settled matters once and for all
in the Warigesui. But at the tenement—there it is another affair.
This Chōbei will fortify himself against the shock. A drink; then

another, and still more. The scoldings will fall on a blunted mind wandering in some dreamland. Time will soothe her rage. To-morrow Chōbei wakes, to find the storm has passed and Taki his obedient serving wench." Near the Adzumabashi, following his prescription against domestic enlivenment, he entered a grog shop; to turn his good coin into wine.

The quarter at Hanagawadō in Asakusa was in an uproar. What had occurred was this—There was an old woman—" Baba " in the native parlance for Dame Gossip—a seller of the dried seaweed called *nori* (sloke or laver), still called Asakusa *nori*, though even at that time gathered at Shinagawa, Omori, and more distant places. This old trot had returned, to make her last sales to the excellent metal dealer who lived opposite her own home in the *nagaya*, in which she lived next door to the Chōbei, husband and wife. The tongue of the *doguya* was still in full swing of the recital, not only of his own experiences, but of the revelations of O'Taki. He was only too willing for this twenty-first time to repeat the tale to the *nori* seller, his good neighbour. The good wife and wives listened again with open mouths. The Baba was the most interested of them all. This choice morsel of gossip was to be gathered at the primal source, from the lips of O'Taki herself. She was all sympathy in her curiosity—ranging in the two cases of Chōbei and wife on the one part, and the metal dealer and his insulted household on the other part. Away she stepped quickly from the assembly of ward gossips. At the door of Chōbei's quarters she stopped—" Okamisan! Okamisan! . . . Strange: is she not at home? Is she so angered that no answer is given? However, this Baba fears no one. . . . Nesan! Nesan!" She passed the room entrance and went into the area. Glancing into the kitchen—"Oya! Oya! The meal is burnt to a crisp. It has become a soppy, disgusting mass. Nesan! Nesan! The rain falls, the roof window (*hikimado*) is open." She put down her empty tubs in order to play the good neighbour. The first thing was to close the window against the descending rain.

Quickly and deftly she proceeded to wipe the moisture off the shining vessels, to put everything in order in O'Taki's usually immaculate kitchen. Women of this class are finicky house-keepers in their own homes. As the old wife became less engaged she began to hear strange sounds above. Some one was in con-versation—and yet it was a one-sided queer kind of talk. The voice was threatening and wheedling. Then she heard a child cry. Surely O'Taki was in the upper room; and thus neglectful of her lord and household.

The old Baba went to the foot of the ladder and listened. " Nesan! Nesan!" No answer came, beyond the curious dron-ing monotone above, varied by an occasional wailing cry of the child. It seemed to be in pain. Resolute, the sturdy old Baba began to climb the steps. At the top she halted, to get breath and look into the room. The sight she witnessed froze the old woman in horror to where she stood. A woman was in the room. She knelt over the body of the child, which now and again writhed in the hard and cruel grasp. The queer monotonous voice went on—" Ah! To think you might grow up like your father. The wicked, unprincipled man! To sell the Ojōsan for a street whore, for her to spend her life in such vile servitude; she by whose kindness this household has lived. Many the visits in the past two years paid these humble rooms by the lady of Tamiya. To all her neighbours O'Taki has pointed out and bragged of the favour of the Ojōsan. The very clothing now on your wretched puny body came from her hands. While Chōbei spent his gains in drink and paid women, Taki was nourished by the rice from Tamiya. When Taki lay in of this tiny body it was the Ojōsan who furnished aid, and saw that child and mother could live. Alas! That you should grow up to be like this vil-lainous man is not to be endured. . . . Ah! An idea! To crunch your throat, to secure revenge and peace, security against the future." She bent down low over the child. Suddenly it gave a fearful scream, as does a child fallen into the fire. The Baba, helpless, could only feebly murmur—"Nesan! Nesan! O'Taki San! What are you about? Control yourself." She gave a frightened yowl as the creature began to spread far apart the child's limbs, and with quick rips of the sharp kitchen knife beside her dissevered and tore the little limbs from the quivering body. At the cry the woman turned half around and looked toward her. Jaws dripping red with blood, a broad white flat face with bulging brow, two tiny piercing dots flashing from amid the thick swollen eyelids, it was the face of O'Iwa glowering at her. "Kiya!" The scream resounded far and wide. Incontinently the old woman tumbled backward down the steep steps, to land below on head and buttocks.

Some neighbours, people passing, came rushing in. A crowd began to gather. "Baba! Baba San! What is wrong?" She could not speak; only point upward and shudder as does one with heavy chills. As they moved toward the stair a roar went up from the crowd in the street. O'Taki had appeared at the window, her face smeared with blood and almost unrecognizable. She waved a limb of the dismembered infant. The crowd were frozen with horror. · As some shouted to those within to hasten the woman brandished the bloody knife. Thrusting it deep into her throat she ripped and tore at the handle, spattering the incautious below with the blood spurting from the wound. Then she fell backward into the room. When the foremost to interfere rushed in they drew back in fear at what they saw. The child's head was half knawed from the body; its limbs lay scattered to this place and that. The body of O'Taki lay where she had fallen. It was as if the head had been gnawed from the trunk, but the head itself was missing. Search as they would, it was not to be found. Meanwhile the news of these happenings spread rapidly. In the next block it was shouted that the wife of the pimp Chōbei had gone mad and killed and eaten five children. A block further the number had risen to twenty-five. At the guardhouse of the Adzumabashi she had killed and gnawed a hundred adults.

These rumours were mingled with the strange tale of the old woman as to O'Iwa San. In time there were many who had witnessed the suicide of O'Taki, who were ready to swear they had seen the fearful lady of Tamiya. Chōbei first learned of the affair by being dragged from the grog shop to the guardhouse of the Adzumabashi. Here he was put under arrest. Distressed and discomforted he stood before the ruin in his home, under the eyes of his neighbours. These stood loyally by him. As happens in ward affairs in Nippon the aspect of the affair not immediately on the surface was slow to reach official ears. Thus it was as to the Tamiya phase involved. Chōbei had suffered much, and was in to suffer more. His fellow wardsmen were silent as to all but the actual facts needed for interpretation. The marvellous only filters out slowly. But they had their own way of dealing with him. The *kenshi* (coroner) made his report. Examinations, fines, bribes, the funeral costs, reduced Chōbei to his worst garment. With this after some weeks he was permitted to go free. The house owner had turned him out. The wardsmen had expelled him. Enough of Kazaguruma Chōbei—for the present.

CHAPTER XVI

NEWS REACHES KWAIBA

KWAIBA was hard at it, practising his favourite arts. His *saké* cup stood before him, and from time to time he raised the bottle from the hot water, testing its temperature with skilled hand. He accompanied the action with a continual drone of a *gidayu*. Kwaiba by no means confined the art of *gidayu* recitation to the heroic tales usually therewith associated. His present effort was one of the suggestive and obscene *ukarebushi*, quite as frequent and as well received in the *gidayu* theme containing them. Kibei listened and applauded, with cynical amusement at the depravity of the impotent old man. Kwaiba had found an excellent bottle companion, and renewed his own former days in the " Quarter," with the fresher experiences retailed by Kibei. Said Kwaiba—" All has gone well. For half the year Kibei has been the son of Kwaiba. He has brought luck into the house." Kibei bowed respectfully. Continued the old man— " Iémon with his whore is fast destroying Tamiya by riot and drinking. Chōzaémon is a fish in the net. The debt of ten *ryō* has doubled into twenty *ryō*, which at any cost he must repay. Kwaiba will make him cut belly if he don't. And Tamiya! Old Tamiya; Matazaémon! O'Iwa is paying her debt to Kwaiba by becoming an outcast, perhaps a beggar somewhere on the highway. If she shows her face in the ward, seeking ' cash ' to keep life in a wretched carcass, this Kwaiba will send her to the jail, to rot as vagrant. But what did become of her? Iémon has never spoken." Kibei shrugged his shoulders. " A close mouthed fellow ; too wise to talk of himself. He would but say that Chōbei took the affair in hand." Kwaiba threw up his hands in horror and merriment. Said he—" 'Tis rumoured the fellow is a pimp.

But surely he could not dispose of O'Iwa in his line. The very demons of the Hell of lust would refuse all intercourse with her." Just then Kakusuké presented himself. " Report to make to the Go-Inkyō Sama. Inagaki Dono sends his compliments to Itō Sama. The papers of transfer are these; by the hand of Kakusuké." As he took the documents, said Kwaiba in answer to Kibei's inquiring look—" Your honoured parent has favoured this Kwaiba. The transfer is of farms in Kazusa for others in Shimosa. Thus all can be brought under one hand. A single *nanushi* (bailiff) can manage the whole property in the two villages."—" But the office . . .," objected Kibei. He had the *samurai* instinct against the slightest taint of failure in obligation. " Let Kibei San deign to follow in.the footsteps of Kwaiba. The successor to the *nanushi* recently deceased is a child. Kwaiba is in no haste to provide a substitute pending majority. The right will lapse, and at majority the boy can be found occupation elsewhere, to no small gain in the revenue. Out of sight, out of mind. Kwaiba's present manager is unsurpassed; so is the income he manages to gather." He looked around in some surprise, seeing that Kakusuké still maintained his position, although dismissed. Then noting him closely—" What has happened, Kakusuké? Your colour is bad. Too cordial entertainment by the *chugen* of Inagaki Dono? Or has Kakusuké seen a ghost? "

" Kakusuké has seen O'Iwa San; of Tamiya. Rather would he have seen a ghost; if indeed it was not a demon he saw." Kwaiba started—" O'Iwa! Where? "—" It was at the brothel of Toémon, chief of the night-hawks, at Yoshidachō in Honjō. Mobei the toilet dealer had suffered direfully at her hands. Meeting her unexpectedly, the fool let out all he knew of the happenings in the ward. In a rage she flew on him. ' To seven lives a curse on Iémon Dono, on Akiyama Sama, on Kondō Sama.' "— He hesitated; then added—" on the Go Inkyō Sama. Then in a straight line she flew off toward the canal. Did she drown herself? This Kakusuké c̄ould not ascertain. Going to the aid

of Mobei, mauled and prostrate on the ground, the whole story
was learned. Chōbei had sold her for life to Toémon, to serve
as a night-hawk."
Itō Kwaiba sat straight up. His idle braggart words of a few
moments before came home to him. In Kibei he found no encouragement. After all Kibei was a *samurai;* harsh, but with
the courage of his caste and profession. He spoke openly—" It
was an outrageous deed. To sell a *samurai* woman to such a life!
It stinks. This comes of bringing in a low dog (*yarō*) such
as this Chōbei. Did Iémon know of his intention?" He looked
Kwaiba in the eye, but the latter met him squarely—" What
Iémon knew or did not know, this Kwaiba knows not. But of this
event he must know—and at once. Kakusuké, go in all haste to
the house of Tamiya Sama. Kwaiba would consult with him."
Kibei fidgetted and fumed. He walked up and down the room.
Then abruptly—" Condescend to pardon the presence of Kibei.
The honoured father having matters to discuss with the diviner—
he finds no amusement in the counsellor." As he was withdrawing
Iémon entered. Their greeting was cold to the extreme. Iémon
knew that Kibei hated and despised him; as much as he, Iémon,
hated and feared Kibei. Kwaiba called sharply to his genial
son—" Pray be within call, if needed." He was glad to see the
surly fellow's exit. In some things Kwaiba felt fear. The stiff
courage of Kibei made him ashamed openly to air his weakness.
He broke the news at once to Iémon. " Kakusuké has seen
O'Iwa." Iémon looked at him curiously. Was Kwaiba frightened? Said the one-time priest—" What of that? She lives in
Edo. A meeting with her is quite likely; at least for a man
of the grade of Kakusuké." He smiled grimly—" But . . .,"
said Kwaiba. He plunged into the story of the *chūgen* in its full
details. Iémon listened carefully. " Ah! She is likely to come
here."—" Come here!" bellowed Kwaiba. " Just so," answered
Iémon. " If she seeks vengeance on this Iémon, on Kwaiba, or
the others, where else would she come than Yotsuya. We cannot

run away." Kwaiba gasped at his coolness—" And Iémon Dono, does he open Tamiya to the presence of its ex-lady and mistress?"
—" A beggar, an outcast, importuning Tamiya; the severed body will lie in the ditch, for the gatherers of offal to cast as food to the dogs on the moor. Fear enters, but—honoured chief, condescend to follow the example of Iémon."

The round eyes in the round face of Kwaiba stood out. He leaned over and touched Iémon's sleeve. In astonishment Iémon noted the fright depicted in his face. The blustering old man at bottom was an arrant coward. Two knaves should understand each other—as did he and Chōbei. He felt that he had been gulled during the whole of his intercourse with this old fool. He should have bluffed; and not been bluffed. Said Kwaiba in lowered voice—" Kakusuké could see nothing of her. She disappeared into the waters of Warigesui. Suppose O'Iwa appears as a ghost, to take vengeance on Kwaiba   . . ." He straightened up in astonishment and some anger at the derisive smile playing over the face of Iémon. Indeed Iémon was more than amused. Not at the circumstances, but at finding at last this weak spot in the man who had dominated him. Conditions, however, controlled him. It was fact that the physical O'Iwa might appear—to the distress and discomfiture of all concerned. They must stand together. He spoke with severity—" Rich and afraid of ghosts! Has not Itō Dono two spearmen when he goes abroad? When he has an interview with his lord does he tremble with fear? When the enemy in life, with all physical powers, is not feared; why fear a disembodied spirit deprived of all means of venting its wrath and spite? It is but the imagination which works havoc. None are more helpless than the dead. With them time and occasion has reached an end. If O'Iwa returns to Yotsuya, it will be in her own person. With O'Iwa, the beggar and night-hawk, our *kumi-gashira* knows how to deal."—" Then Iémon knew the lot dealt out to O'Iwa."—" At first hand; from Chōbei himself. The lean knave has prospered by the affair.

Iémon had no such desire to see him, as to secure his costly presence at the dinner so unfortunately witnessed by Mobei. . . . But deign to call for wine; drive out these vapours with wine. Honoured chief, condescend to play the host to Iémon." Iémon's manner was not wholly natural, as Kwaiba could have detected if more himself. He felt immensely relieved. A priest—surely he was one to know all about the nature of ghosts; was one to speak with authority. Iémon was hardly to be regarded as in ecclesiastical good odour. But Kwaiba was easily satisfied. He, too, roared —"Wine! Wine! Bring wine!" As by magic Kibei appeared at the welcome sound. He disliked Iémon, but he liked wine. The servants bustled around. The wine was heated—again and again. A feast of fish—with more wine—followed. It was late when Iémon left the house, the only sober member of the party. Of his hosts; one was maudlin, the other asleep. The ample resources of Tamiya, if not of benefit to his person, in these past two years had given him the chance to harden his head; and he had grasped it.

Iémon by no means had all the confidence he displayed before Kwaiba. He was a priest, but environment influences everybody. There was a possibility—discountenanced by experience, but existing. As he walked slowly along Teramachi his thoughts strayed back into the past. "It was an ill bond between this Iémon and O'Iwa San. Without question she has drowned herself in the Warigesui. The body must be found and buried. Memorial services are to be recited, for one dying without relatives or friends (*segaki*)." The virtuous resolution was the outcome of his meditation and glances into the many graveyards passed in his progress through the temple-lined street. It was a beautiful street, with its overhanging trees, its open spaces populated by the many dead, its temples gorgeous in red and gilding amid the dark green of pine and cedar. Iémon on this night had to hasten his steps. Rain threatened. Gusts of wind came sharply from this side and that, driving the first drops of the coming storm. He reached home just as it broke with all its fury.

To O'Hana he would say nothing of Kwaiba's mission. On her remarking on the lateness of the hour, he made answer that the old man was out of sorts. Kibei was too robust a bottle companion for a man reaching toward his seventieth year. No matter how vigorous, Kwaiba's wine was showing on him. The two prepared for bed. O'Hana listened as the rain dashed in streams against the *amado,* as if trying to break its way in. She gave a little chuckle—" Who would have thought it! "—" What? " asked Iémon, perhaps a little tartly. He was nervous. O'Hana laughed—" That Iémon and this Hana should be where they now are. Their parting was on a night like this. Ah! At seeing a man weep Hana could have retired into a cave—forever. Only the fortunate accident of a drunken *yakunin* (constable) as guest enabled her to give warning. . . . And now! Once more united Iémon and this Hana live in luxury. Every wish is gratified. Thanks for the past which contained this meeting in its womb; thanks for the present in which happiness is secured:

> ' Losing one's way, again roads meet!
> The hill of flowers.' "[1]

A terrific gust struck the rain-doors. They bent and cracked before the force of the gale. The vivid white of lightning showed that one door had been forced from its groove. Iémon rose and replaced it. As he turned away suddenly the room was plunged in darkness. Said the voice of O'Hana—" The light of the *andon* has gone out. Oya! Oya! The lights in the Butsudan (altar) are lit. And yet this Hana extinguished them." Grumbled Iémon —" The wind has blown out the light in the *andon.* Doubtless a spark was left in the wick of the altar light. Fire is to be dreaded; great care should be taken in extinguishing the light." As he relit the light in the night lamp, O'Hana went up to the

---

[1] " *Hagurete mo mata afu michi ya hana no yama*."

Butsudan to extinguish the lights there. She put her hand out to take one. A sharp scream, and she fell back in confusion and fright. " An *aodaishō* in the Butsudan! Help! Aid this Hana!" As she fled the snake with a thud fell on the *tatami*. Unrolling its six feet of length, it started in pursuit. Iémon stepped behind it and caught it by the tail. A sharp rap behind the head stunned it. It hung limp in his hand. " Hana, please open the *amado*."— " No, no: this Hana cannot; move she will not."—"Coward!" said Iémon. " Time comes when Hana, for generations in the future existence, will wander hill and dale in such form."— " Ara!" The woman was properly shocked at this speech, wicked and brutal as an imprecation. " Has the life of Hana been so foul as to deserve such punishment in a future life? Surely 'tis not the priest of Reigan who speaks; nor Iémon." She could only see his lips move as he stood at the *amado*. " Evil was the connection between O'Iwa and this Iémon. Wander not as one unburied, but becoming a Buddha at once enter Nirvana. Namu Myōhō Renge Kyō! Namu Myōhō Renge Kyō! Wonderful the Law, wondrous the Scripture of the Lotus!" With the invocation he cast the stunned reptile far out into the garden. Returning, he said—" The aodaishō is the most harmless of snakes. The farmers keep it to destroy the rats which infest house and store rooms. How can Hana be afraid of snakes, living in this *yashiki* overgrown by weeds and grass, from roof to garden?" O'Hana did not reply in direct terms—" It is evil fortune to take a snake in the hand."—" Never mind such talk. It is the priest who speaks. This Iémon knows all about snakes. Go to sleep." She obeyed, knowing nothing about O'Iwa and the events of the day; yet her slumber was broken and restless. By morning she was in a high fever.[2]

---

[2] The *aodaishō* is something of the nature of a black snake. Says Brinkley's Dict. " *elaphis virgatus*."

CHAPTER XVII

NEWS FROM KWAIBA

KWAIBA was reported as ill; very ill. His friends and dependents who had to pay visits of condolence, spoke of this illness with awe and terror. To understand what follows something must be said of the past of this man. The actor, drawing on the presumed knowledge of his audience as to the story in the gross, can pass this over with a speech or two; a horror-struck gesture and allusion. Not so the *kōdan* writer, who perforce must lay before his reader all the *minutiæ* of the case.

Itō Kwaiba did not brag when he spoke of his beauty as a boy, his handsome figure as a young man. These had brought him wealth and position; gained, it was whispered, in vilest service to his lord. In these days he had in his employ a *chūgen* named Isuké, or as some say Kohei. Engaged before the mirror Kwaiba was applying the paint and powder which of late had become necessary adjuncts to fit him to appear before his lord. A gesture of pain and discomfiture, and then Kwaiba turned irritably toward his satellite. " Isuké, you are a clever fellow. Kwaiba has needed no aids to his looks—up to recent days. Now paint and powder, all the armoury of a woman, or paraphernalia of an actor, hardly avail to conceal the blotches which disfigure Kwaiba's face and body. The voice broken and husky, the lightning pains in limbs and joints, these violet patches—in such state it soon will be impossible to act as attendant on his lordship's household service, as *kami-yakunin*. What disorder eats into the life and happiness of Kwaiba? "

For a time Isuké made no answer, beyond a bow at his master's acknowledgment of his cleverness, and in which he heartily concurred. He seemed engaged in a close contemplation of the end

162

of his nose. "Hei! Hei!" It was all that Kwaiba could get out of him for the moment. Then noting the growing anger Isuké began with—"Condescend beforehand to pardon this Isuké. Though the anger of the Wakadono (young lord) is hard to bear, yet a faithful servitor should speak. Deign to step this way." He conducted Kwaiba to one of those small retired rooms, opening on an inner garden and common to every properly built house of any size in Nippon. He closed the few rain-doors, shutting out the light. Then fetching a piece of camphor, he set fire to it. When the thick yellow light flared strongly he took up a hand-mirror and passed it to Kwaiba. Kwaiba was frightened at what he saw. His face was dark as that of a peasant of Satsuma. Said Isuké—"The darkness is shown up by the light of the burning camphor. The colour is due to the poison circulating between the body and the outer skin. The white sunlight does not show up this symptom. But there is another test." Lighting a candle, he took a long steel *kanzashi* needle and heated it to redness. Holding the cold end by his head towel he grasped the arm of Kwaiba, The latter drew back, afraid. "Nay, it will give no pain," said Isuké. He thrust the hot length of the needle several inches under the skin. As far as Kwaiba was concerned he might as well have thrust it into the straw matting (*tatami*) at his feet. Isuké withdrew the needle and carefully pressed the arm. A brownish liquor oozed out; not blood. "The Danna has a nose—as yet." Kwaiba hastily applied his arm to that member. He turned his face to one side in disgust and horror—"Is this Kwaiba already dead and rotten? In such condition all is lost. Duty no longer can be performed. Service and income cease together. Isuké, there remains naught but to get out the mats. Kwaiba will cut belly."

Isuké examined him carefully and quizzically. Satisfied with his inspection, he said—"Deign to have confidence in Isuké. In former days he was not Isuké the *chūgen*. Son of a doctor of the Dutch practice at Nagasaki; gambling, wine, women have reduced Isuké to the state of a servant. Family and friends long since have discarded and cast him out. The severance of relations between parent and child was formal. Isuké owes naught of service or duty to any but his master Kwaiba. Here is his refuge. Deign to give Isuké three silver *ryō*. The disease is curable. Trust the matter to Isuké. *Soppin* (mercury) duly applied will remove the poison, and with it all the disastrous symptoms. The two hundred and thirty *tawara* of income are enjoyed by the Wakadono. Service can be performed; and Isuké preserves such a good master." Flattered and frightened Kwaiba at once handed over the money. Isuké disappeared to secure the drug necessary to the " Dutch practice." Baths and potions, potions and baths, followed in due course. The promises of Isuké were fulfilled. The fearful symptoms gradually were alleviated. In the course of six months Kwaiba was himself again; his position was assured to him. He heaved double sighs— of relief from the nightmare which had pursued him; of anxiety at the nightmare substituted for it.

Kwaiba was a rake and a gambler. So was Isuké. The two hundred and thirty *tawara* of income was saved to Kwaiba—and Isuké. Not long after the cure was thus assured Isuké disappeared. Kwaiba sighed gently, with relief at the departure of one who knew too much of his affairs, and with a scared feeling on losing the only " doctor " in whom he had confidence. " These fellows come and go, like leaves on a tree. Isuké has grown tired, and deserted. Some day he may return. This Kwaiba is a good master." Isuké did return—in the form of a note from the Yoshiwara. Twenty *ryō* were needed to pay his debts to pleasure and gambling. Severely reprimanded, Isuké opened his eyes in astonishment. " Respectfully heard and understood: has the income been reduced? But that does not affect the share of Isuké. He keeps well within his limit." This was the first intimation Kwaiba had of Isuké's views as to his rôle of physician. In those days the doctor usually had the pleasure of performance, not of payment. Moreover with the great—like Kwaiba—per-

formance was carried out at a distance; the pulse felt by the vibra-
tion of a string attached to the wrist, or at best by passing the
hand under the coverlet. For a time Kwaiba's strange medical
attendant devoted himself to his more prosaic duties of *chūgen*.
Within ten days his master ransomed him from a resort in
Shinagawa; price, ten *ryō*. A few weeks later he was heard from
at a gambler's resort in Shinjuku. The note was peremptory—
and for fifty *ryō*. Kwaiba lost all patience. Moreover, just then
he held office very favourable for bringing this matter to an issue.
But he must have Isuké; and have him in Yotsuya. As usual
payment secured the presence of a repentant Isuké, full of promises of amendment. Kwaiba smiled, used soft words; and shortly
after Isuké was confined to the jail on a trumped up charge of
theft from another *chūgen*. Kwaiba, then acting as magistrate
for the district, had full power. On notification he assured Isuké
of a speedy release. This the unhappy man secured through a
poisoned meal, following a long fast. He died raving, and cursing
his master. No one heard him but his two jailers, who considered
him crazy—this man of bad record.

Years had passed, but Isuké merely lay dormant in the mind
of Kwaiba. Then came up the affair of Tamiya—the threatening
curse of O'Iwa San. Iémon's counsel lasted but over night.
With soberness and morning Kwaiba straightway showed the
results of wrecked nerves and distorted imagination. Sleepless
nights he now visited on his friends by an increasing irritability.
The first few days of this state of Kwaiba were laughable. He
spoke of O'Iwa San; not freely, rather with reticence. He made
his references as of jesting expectation of her advent. Then he
passed to boisterous tricks; springing out on the maids from dark
corners or the turns in the corridors. Alarmed by these manifes-
tations of the old man—not entirely strange, for he was a terror
to the female element in his household—they soon noted that there
was an unnatural wildness in his amusement at their discomfiture.
Now he would talk of nothing but O'Iwa. From this hysterical

mirth he passed to an hysterical fear. Afraid of visions of the Lady of Tamiya he stayed awake at night. To be alone appalled him. He would have others keep awake with him. He was now at the gibbering stage. " Night in the house of Kwaiba is to be turned into day. The day shall be the time for sleep. Lights! Lights! More lights!" He sat surrounded by his household, until the white light of dawn filtered through the spaces above the rain-doors. One of his women, her hair down for washing, met him unexpectedly in the corridor. With a howl of terror he started to flee. Then recognizing her, he flew on her and beat her almost to a jelly in his insane rage. People began to talk of the eccentricities of Itō Kwaiba—the honoured ward head.

Barely three weeks after Iémon's visit a violent scene occurred in the mansion of the *kumi-gashira*. Shouts and screams, the smashing of screens and sounds of a terrific struggle were heard in Kwaiba's room. Kibei, who with the men preferred night for sleep, rushed in. He found the old man standing, stark naked and alone. His attendants had fled—to a woman. His pillow sword drawn, Kwaiba was dancing to this side and that. " Isuké! O'Iwa! Pardon! This Kwaiba is a wicked fellow! Isuké was poisoned by Kwaiba. O'Iwa San? Kwaiba sold her for a street whore. For seven lives they pursue him. Ah! A merry chase! But Kwaiba deals not with night-hawks. His game is higher. Away with the huzzy!" He had grasped in both hands the flower vase standing in the alcove (*tokonoma*). Kibei dodged, and catching him by a wrestler's hold, threw him to the ground. Kakusuké, just entering, was knocked flat by the heavy missile. Groaning, he rose, and with other servants came to the aid of the Wakadono. Kwaiba was overpowered and guarded during the remainder of the night.

With daylight he knew nothing of what had occurred; at least he made no reference to it, no response to the talk of others. His fear was now full on him. He babbled of nothing but Isuké and O'Iwa San. Now he was incapacitated, downright ill. There was no more turning of day into night, and *vice versa*. He was in the hands of his nurses. But to humour him Kibei marshalled the women. Their beds were made encircling that of Kwaiba in the midst. Kibei and Kakusuké were present. Thus they lay in this room brilliant with its scores of lanterns, its wax lights blazing on the lamp-stands. At the sides and in each corner were placed the scrolls of the holy *sutra*. Kwaiba in despair sought a sleep which would not favour him. " Some one walks in the corridor. . . . Namu Amida Butsu! Namu Amida Butsu! . . . Kibei! Kibei!" The appeal to the man would bring quicker response than that to the Buddha. Indeed there was a sound, as of hair rubbing across the paper screens, of some one or something trying to peer through the opaque material. There was a rattle and dash of rain. A gust swept through the corridor, the *shōji* slightly parted. Kwaiba gave a shriek— "O'Iwa! O'Iwa San! Ah! The bloated face, the drooping eyelid, the corpse taint in the air. It catches Kwaiba's throat. O'Iwa the O'Baké would force away Kwaiba the living. Ha! Ha!" A stronger gust, and the *shōji* dislodged from its groove whirled round and fell noisily into the room. Terror gave strength to the sick man. Kwaiba sprang madly forward. It was horrible to see the ghastly renovation of this tottering, flabby, emaciated man, who yet inspired the fear of a maniac's reckless strength. The frightened women huddled and crouched in the now darkened room, lit but by a single *andon* near the alcove. Was Kwaiba mad? As the men fought over the ruins of the *shōji*, in the darkness of the corridor, at first faint as a mist, then distinctly seen, the women were assured of the presence of O'Iwa. In long black robe, face wide and bloated, of a livid greenish tint, hair in wild disorder, bulging forehead, swollen eyeless lids, she stood over the struggling men. Suddenly she thrust the severed head she carried into the face of Kwaiba, leering horribly at him the while. With a yell he fell flat on his back. The braver entered with lights. All gathered round the unconscious Kwaiba.

This scene was the crisis of his disorder. The disease, once dormant, now fell on him suddenly and with full force. Perhaps these mental symptoms were its first indication. More annoying to his comfort, ulcers broke out all over his body. The itching drove the man nearly frantic. His mad scratching spread the sores. The boils developed. They ran with pus. So terrible was the stench that few would stay by him. The women fled the room in terror, driven away by the running stream of physical corruption, the continual babble of lewdness from the corrupt mind. He soon noted their absence. Kibei, attended by the sturdy and faithful Kakusuké, remained to nurse him. Suddenly said Kwaiba —" O'Hana, the harlot of Reigan; this Kwaiba would have talk and dalliance with her. Summon her hither. Let wine and the *samisen* be brought, a feast prepared. O'Hana! O'Hana!" He raved so for the woman that Kibei thought her presence would quiet him. A request was sent to the house of Iémon. Wishing her to know nothing of the affair of O'Iwa, Iémon had kept silence. He would have refused the mission—on the pretext of a quarrel with Kwaiba and Kibei. O'Hana showed herself unexpectedly obstinate—" It is to the favour of Kwaiba Sama that Iémon' owes this Hana. She has a duty to the past, as well as to the present." With a snarl she turned on him, glowering. Iémon shrank back. He passed his hand across the eyes into which O'Iwa had just looked. He no longer opposed her going.

O'Hana was still weak from repeated attacks of the fever which had visited her ever since the night Iémon had cast forth the *aodaishō*. She said that the snake had bitten her. It was the poison, not fever, working in her. Iémon had laughed at her proposal to try the exorcisms of the priest. Behind the irritation aroused by his scepticism was that peculiar clinging of a woman to an old lover, to a man with whom she had been intimate. In the heart of O'Hana there still remained a strong leaning to the man who had removed her from the rapid and nauseating life of the Fukagawa brothel, which cast her into the arms of anyone who paid the price and raised his finger. With time and the old conditions probably she would have been as unfaithful to Iémon as she had been to Kwaiba. The latter showing his desire, she would have answered his call. Even before this disease-eaten swollen mass of dropsy, she showed but temporary repugnance. Leaning over him, almost overcome by the stench, with endearing terms she strove to rouse him to consciousness and recognition of her. It seemed fearful to have him die without the word of parting. Kibei aided her by raising the old man. The result was a horrible frightened stare in eyes made large by fever and delirium. Long he gazed at her. Said the woman—" 'Tis Hana; Hana once the intimate of Kwaiba. Deign to take courage. This is but a passing affliction. With Hana as nurse recovery to health is assured." She laid her hands on his shoulders. In so doing her hair, come loose, fell down around her wan face. Kwaiba was as galvanized. With a howl the old man pushed her violently away. " Scrawny wench! What impudence to show your face here! Ah! To the last moment, waking and in dreams, she pursues this Kwaiba. I sold you. 'Tis true—I sold you for a night-hawk—to Toémon of Honjō. Does Kwaiba consort with wenches of such ilk? Raising his fist he dealt her blow after blow, all the time shouting—" O'Iwa! O'Iwa! The O'Baké solicits Kwaiba. Broken loose from Hell and the waters of Warigesui she would force away Kwaiba. Help! Help! Aid for Kwaiba! Away with the O'Baké!" The old man again had broken into his mad fit. The shouts of Kibei brought Kakusuké. Kwaiba's hands were detached from the masses of O'Hana's hair. The wounds on her face were not so deep as those inflicted on her mind. At last the secret was out. In bare feet she fled along the muddy street toward the Samonchō house.

It was true that the vileness of the disease, the vileness of Kwaiba's tongue, had driven the women from attendance in the sick room to the remotest quarters of the house. But there was a deterrent even to their now limited service. All said the place where Kwaiba lay was haunted. Under press of necessity a maid had brought needed medicaments to the sick man's room. Putting down the light she carried on the *rōka,* she pushed open the *shōji* to enter the outer chamber. Her robe caught as she did so. Turning to release it she gave a fearful shriek. Standing in the corridor, at the open screen behind her, were two tall figures robed in black. With dishevelled hair, broad white flat faces, bulging brows, eyelids swollen and sightless, yet they gazed through and through the onlooker and into the farther room. One creature, even more hideous with drooping lid and baldness extending far back, half moved, half fell toward the frightened maid. The woman's screams now were mingled with wild laughter. Kibei came rushing out, sword drawn, to find her in a fit of mad hysterics. Catching the drift of her broken phrases he went out on the *rōka.* There was no one there. *Haori* and *kimono,* hung up there to dry, rustled and moved a little in the draft. Had these frightened the woman? Kakusuké carried her back to her companions. Henceforth no one would enter that part of the building occupied by the sick man. Kibei as son, Kakusuké the old and faithful attendant, were isolated in their nursing.

Kibei noted the sick man's face. " Father, why the forehead so wrinkled? Is pain condescended?" Said Kwaiba—" 'Tis the rats; they gnaw and worry at Kwaiba."—" Rats?" replied Kibei in some astonishment. He looked around. The *shōji* were tight closed. Kwaiba noted the inspection. He shook his head, and pointed to the *rama-shōji,* the ornamental open work near the ceiling. This could not be obviated. " Auntie (Obasan) is old and deaf. She sleeps; while rats, attracted by the foul sores of the scrofulous child, enter and attack the infant in its cradle. The child gets thinner and weaker every day; then dies. A terrible creature is the rat." So much for the opinion of Nippon. Kibei had brought a mosquito net. Its edges were weighted down with heavy stones. Thus the watchers could not be taken by surprise. Under its protection the sick man was saved from annoyance. Said Kibei—" This illness is most tedious. Could not Kibei go to the Yoshiwara for a space? The letters of the Kashiku (*oiran*) accumulate. Kibei has nothing to give, and has given no explanation for not giving. What thinks Kakusuké?" Kakusuké was brave. Moreover he knew the Wakadono was brave. The prospect, however, of facing his old master in a crazy fit— and perhaps O'Iwa—had no attraction. He gave his advice— " The Go Inkyō Sama is in a very precarious state. He is now very weak. The worst may happen at any moment. For the Wakadono to be taking his pleasure at the Yoshiwara would arouse criticism in the ward; nay, even more than criticism. It would be held unfilial. Deign to reconsider the purpose." Kibei looked sourly at the swollen corruption which represented Kwaiba—" How does he hold on! His strength must be great." Kakusuké shrugged his shoulders—" The Go Inkyō Sama will not die easily. He has much to go through yet."—" In the name of all the *kami* and Buddhas, how has he come to such an end? He is a sight to inspire fear—in those who can feel such." Replied Kakusuké with sly look—" The Go Inkyō Sama has lived high, and loved beyond measure. The Wakadono does well to reconsider his purpose."

The night was passing. The two men, worn out by the continued watching and nursing, after vain struggle to keep awake had gone to sleep. Kakusuké was in the room with Kwaiba. In his slumber Kibei was back in the fencing room. The clash of the wooden swords (*bokken*), the cries of the contestants, rang clear in his ears. He woke to find rain and storm shaking and tearing at the *amado*. But it was the shouts of Kakusuké, standing at the *shōji*, which had aroused him—" Danna Sama! Danna Sama! Wakadono! At once! At once! Deign to hasten!" Kibei rushed into the next room. In fright Kakusuké pointed to the mosquito net. A figure stood upright within it, swaying, gesticulating, struggling. It was a figure all black and horrible. "Un! Un!" grunted Kwaiba. He was answered by a mincing, gnawing sound. "Father! Have courage! Kibei is here." He rushed at the heavy stones, to toss them to one side and enter the net. The swaying figure within suddenly toppled over in a heap. With his sword Kibei tore and severed the cording of the net. The black mass of rats scattered to the eight directions of space. On approaching Kwaiba a terrible sight met the eye. Eyes, ears, nose, chin, toes and fingers had been torn and eaten off. The lips were gnawed away and exposed to view the grinning teeth. A feeble groan—and Kwaiba had met his end. Neither Kibei nor Kakusuké dared to touch the foul body. In their panic the two men looked in each other's faces. "Namu Amida Butsu! Holy the Lord Buddha, Amida!" prayed Kibei, on his knees before the corpse. "Namu Amida Butsu!" answered Kakusuké.[1]

---

[1] The term "Inkyō," already several times used, applies to a man who has retired from active life, leaving the management of the affairs of the House to the duly appointed heir and successor. A specified portion of the income is usually assigned for his maintenance, and forms a first lien, so to speak, on such return. The modernized law of Nippon does not permit assumption of this state before the age of fifty years, unless there be incapacitation such as necessitates retirement. In ancient days (pre-Meiji) there was no such limitation. Men often retired very early in life—from caprice, family intrigue, or for the freer management of their affairs. In the latter case they had more power and less responsibility; the latter falling on the heir and successor, perhaps still a mere child. *Go* is merely honorofic.

CHAPTER XVIII

IN THE SHADOW OF THE GO-INKYŌ

SAID a neighbour next day, on meeting his fellow-gossip—
" Ah! Is it Goémon San? It is said the Go Inkyō is to be
congratulated." Kamimura Goémon sniffed. He was a long man;
with long face, long nose, long thin arms, long thin legs; a mali-
cious man, who longed to give advice to his fellows which they
much disliked to hear, and liked to see them writhe under the
infliction. In fact this epitome of length rarely spoke in good faith
or temper—" The Go Inkyō is to be congratulated? Escaping
the troubles of this world, perhaps he has fallen into worse
troubles in the next." At this unorthodox reply Mizoguchi
Hambei showed surprise. Continued Goémon—" The Go Inkyō
died a leper, eaten by the rats. Such an end hardly calls for congratulations." Mizoguchi gasped, with round eyes and round
face. " Extraordinary! "—" Not at all," replied Kamikura, com-
placently tapping the palm of one hand with the elongated fingers
of the other. " The Go Inkyō drove out O'Iwa San from Tamiya.
He gave O'Hana in her stead to Iémon as wife. Hana the harlot!
Cursed by O'Iwa in dying, he has met this frightful end. Akiyama, Natsumé, Imaizumi will surely follow. As will all those
involved in the affair."—" But is O'Iwa San really the cause of the
death? The Go Inkyō in life was not the most careful of men
in conserving health." This was timidly interjected by a third
party. Kamimura suppressed him with a scowl—" Of course
it is O'Iwa San. Has she not been seen? The women of the
house answer for it. Only Kibei the sceptic, and Kakusuké who
would face the devil in person, attempt to deny it." He threw
up a hand. With unction—" Ah! It inspires fear. Small is the
profit of wickedness and malice. He is a fool who indulges in
either. . . . How cold it is for the time of year!"

Said the interloper—" But the congratulations have to be rendered all the same. It will be necessary to attend the all-night watch. How vexatious! Perhaps O'Iwa San will not appear. There is no getting out of it? "—" Certainly not," answered Kamimura. " The Go Inkyō was the head of the ward association. Twelve neighbours have been invited to the watch. At dawn the body is to be prepared. A pleasant undertaking, if all that is said be true! The viands will be of the best, the wine no worse and plentiful. None must fail to attend." He smacked his lips. The others likewise, but much less heartily.

It was an unwilling band which crawled in laggard procession through rain and mud and the length of the Teramachi to Kwaiba's house. A *dōshin*, the ward chief, a rich man, the mansion displayed all its splendour. The atmosphere, however, was oppressive. Kibei greeted the guests with heartiness, and accepted their condolence and gifts with lavish thanks and the cheerful face of him that profiteth by the funeral. Kakusuké was his main aid in connection with the Go Inkyō's last appearance. Occasionally a timid white-faced woman was seen, but she would flit away from the scene of these festivities, to seek the companionship of her panic-stricken fellows. Entering the funereal chamber the body was found, laid out and decently swathed so as to cover, as far as possible, the horrible nature of the death. On a white wood stand was the *ihai* in white wood, a virtuous lie as to the qualities of the deceased. It ran—Tentoku Gishin Jishō Daishi. Which can be interpreted—" A man of brilliant virtues, virtuous heart, and benevolent temperament." Screens, upside down, were placed at the head:

" Alas! The screen: the carp descends the fall." [1] Akiyama, Natsumé, Imaizumi, were the last to appear. The former had been composing a violent quarrel between his two friends—the long and the fat. Much recrimination had passed, and the usually

---

[1] " Awarase ya: Byōbu wa koi no taki sagari." The living carp strives to ascend the fall.

peaceful Imaizumi was in a most violent and trucculent humour. He glared with hate on Natsumé, who now aided Akiyama in efforts to soothe his anger. On entering the assembly the looks of all were composed. "A retribution for deeds in the past world. Old; but so vigorous! The offering is a mere trifle. This Kyuzō would burn a stick of incense." Kibei extended his thanks and suppressèd his smile as much as possible. He was breathing with full lungs for the first time in weeks. The storm was over; happiness was ahead; the clouded sky was all serene. "Thanks are felt. This Kibei is most fortunate: nay, grateful. Such kindness is not to be forgotten during life."—"The Inkyō an *hotoke;* Iémon Dono and O'Hana are the husband and wife not present?" The question came from some one in the room. "O'Hana San is very ill. Her state is serious. Iémon does not leave her." Akiyama answered for the truant pair. Kibei's joy was complete.

Akiyama, Natsumé, Imaizumi were standing by Kwaiba's body. Kamimura slowly approached. The long man's face was longer than ever; longer, much longer than that of Natsumé; and Kibei was not in the running. Goémon meditatively fondled his nose; on the pretence of concentrating thought, and for the purpose of relieving that member from the savour arising from Kwaiba's bier. This was no bed of roses—"Yes, the Inkyō is indeed dead." He sniffed. "Soon it will be the turn of all of you— to be like this;" another sniff—"of Iémon and O'Hana, of Natsumé and Imaizumi, of this Akiyama San." The latter gave a violent start. With hand to his nose also, he turned on the intruder. Continued Goémon—"A plot was concocted against O'Iwa San. Beggared and driven from the ward, deceived and sold as a street harlot, this death of the Inkyō is but the first in the roll of her vengeance. Kamimura speaks with pure heart and without malice. You men are not long for this world. Is Akiyama San reconciled? And . . ." He pointed a skinny finger at Kyuzō, then at Jinzaémon. "You show it. Your eyes are hollow; your nostrils are fallen in. The colour of the face is livid. You seem already to be *hotoké*, prepared to lie with the Go Inkyō." Akiyama found his tongue. He burst out in a rage—"The jest is unseemly. Kamimura San goes too far. It is true this Chōzaémon gave counsel to Itō Kwaiba. Kyuzō and Jinzaémon took some part in what followed. But we acted on the orders of Itō Dono, of Iémon San. On the first will be visited any grudge." Goémon laughed harshly. He pointed to the corpse. "Here he lies. How did he die? Goémon does not jest, and the argument of Akiyama San is rotten. The master bids the servants to beat the snow from the bushes. The snow falls on them; not on him. How now Akiyama San?" Chōzaémon turned away discomfited. All three felt very bad—in mind and body.

The bell of Sainenji struck the eighth hour (I A.M.). Just opposite, its clangour filled the whole mansion with a ghostly sound. In the depths of night this inert mass of metal seemed a thing of life, casting its influence into the lives of those present, rousing them to face grave issues. Noting the absence of Natsumé, the round-faced, round-eyed, round-bodied Imaizumi followed after. Kibei came forth from the supper room, to find his guests all flown. "Where have they gone to, Kakusuké?" He looked around in amazement—"They were taken with pains in the belly. With this excuse they departed. Yotsuya is afflicted with a flux." The *chūgen* answered in the dry and certain tone of one unconvinced. Kibei shrugged his shoulders. "There is naught wrong with wine or viands?"—"Nor with the guests," replied Kakusuké. "They are cowards, who have caught some inkling as to the not over-nice death of the Go Inkyō."—"The latter day *bushi* are not what the *bushi* were of old; at least this brand of them. Ah! These wretched little bureaucrats; *bushi* of the pen. Two men to eat a supper prepared for twelve sturdy trenchers. Well: two are enough to wash the corpse. Lend a hand Kakusuké."—"Respectfully heard and obeyed," replied the *chūgen*.

The white dress for the last cover to the body was laid ready. Secured by Kwaiba many years before in a pilgrimage to the holy

Kōyasan, the sacred characters were woven into its tissue. Kaku-suké dragged a large tub into the bathroom.. Kwaiba's body was unswathed and placed in it. Kakusuké eyed his late master with critical and unfavourable eye. " Naruhodo! The Go Inkyō is a strange object. No eyes: nose, ears, lips gone; his expression is not a pleasant one. . . . Nay! The Wakadono is awkward. Throw the water from head to feet. . . . Take care! Don't throw it over Kakusuké. He at least is yet alive. The Wakadono is wasteful. More is needed. Deign to wait a moment. Kaku-suké draws it from the well." He opened the side door and went outside. Kibei drew a little apart from the body. It stank. A noise at the sliding window (*hikimado*) in the roof made him look up. Oya! Oya! The face of O'Iwa filled the aperture— round, white, flat; with puffed eyelids and a sightless glare. With a cry of horror and surprise Kibei sprang to the door. As he did so slender attenuated hands groped downward. "Kakusuké! Kakusuké!"—"What is it, Wakadono?"—"O'Iwa: she looks down through the *hikimado*! She seeks the Inkyō!" Kakusuké gave a look upward—" Bah! It's the cat. Is the Wakadono, too, getting nerves? They are a poor investment."—"The cat!" Kibei sighed with relief. Nevertheless he kept his hand on his sword.

He turned round—to give a shout of surprise—" Kakusuké! Kakusuké! The body of the Go Inkyō is no longer here." As the astonished *chūgen* came running to look into the empty tub, both men nearly fell over in their wonder. The body of the Inkyō was whirling around the neighbouring room in execution of a mad dance. Followed by Kakusuké, his worthy son and heir sprang in pursuit. Invisible hands led Kwaiba and the pursuers into the darkness of the garden, into the rain and storm. Kibei heard the steps just in front of him. He pursued madly after them. "To lose his parent's body—this was against all rules of Bushidō." Thus comments the scribe of Nippon. Kibei could commit all the moral and physical atrocities except—failure in filial conduct

12

to parent and lord; the unpardonable sins of the Scripture of Bushidō. Kakusuké soon lost his master in the darkness. Disconcerted and anxious he returned to secure a lantern. The wind promptly blew it out; then another, and a third. He stood on the *rōka* in the darkness to wait the return of the Wakadono. For the first time Kakusuké had noted failing purpose in his young master. He was more solicitous over this than over the strange disappearance of the Inkyō's body. Was the Wakadono losing his nerve; as had the O'Dono?

In time Kibei reappeared. To Kakusuké's inquiring glance— "Kibei pursued to Myōgyōji; then up the hill. Here sight was lost of the Inkyō. The darkness prevented further search. A lantern is next to worthless in this gale. Kakusuké, go to the houses of Natsumé and Imaizumi close by. They are young and will aid Kibei in the search." Kakusuké did not demur. Pulling his cape over his head, off he posted. He asked but to come across the Inkyō's body, in O'Iwa's company or not made no difference to this iron-hearted servitor. His mission was fruitless. The two men had expressed the intention of spending the night at the Kwaiba wake. Neither had as yet returned. Grumbled Kibei— "The filthy fellows! With this excuse to their wives they seek new pastures at Nakachō (Shinjuku), to spend the night in dissipation. 'Tis Natsumé who is the lecher. Gladly would he wean Imaizumi from his barely wed wife."—"Or wean the wife from Imaizumi Sama! Wakadono, nothing can be done now. The dawn should be awaited." With these sage comments the *chūgen* squatted at respectful distance from his master. From time to time one or other arose, to look sceptically into the empty tub in which once had reposed the Inkyō's body. Finally both nodded off into sleep. At dawn—don, don, don, don, came a loud knocking on the outer gate. Kakusuké went out, to return with astonished face and portentous news. The dead bodies of Natsumé Kyuzō and Imaizumi Jinzaémon had been found at the foot of the *baké-ichō*, a huge tree close by the guard-house. Finger tip to finger tip three men could not girdle this tree. With the bodies of the men lay that of a woman. Two corpses, man and woman, were stark naked. Kibei's presence, as the successor to Kwaiba's office, was required. He prepared at once to start for the Okidō. The tale was in time learned from the prolix Kamimura Goémon, who had witnessed part at least of the scene. As he was knocking at his door on the Shinjuku road, having just returned late from the watch at Kwaiba's house, rapid steps were heard in the street. A man, recognized as Kyuzō, passed, running at top speed. He dragged along by the hand a woman, the wife of Imaizumi. The two were nearly naked. Close in the rear pursued Imaizumi Jinzaémon, his drawn sword in his hand. They sped up the wide road. Goémon stepped out, to follow at a distance this flight and pursuit. At the *ichō* tree the fugitives were overtaken. The woman was the first to be cut down. Kyuzō turned to grapple with the assailant. Unarmed his fate soon overtook him. He fell severed from shoulder to pap. Having finished his victims Imaizumi seated himself at the foot of the tree, and cut open his belly. "Long had such outcome been expected," intoned the long-nosed man. The case needed no explanation. Others echoed the opinion of Goémon, who was merely many fathoms deeper in the scandal of the neighbourhood than most of them. It was agreed to hush the matter up. Reporting his own experience, to the astonishment of his hearers, Kibei, accompanied by Kakusuké, started down Teramachi toward Samégabashi. As they passed the Gwanshōji attention was drawn by a pack of dogs, fighting and quarrelling in the temple cemetery. A white object lay in the midst. With a shout the men sprang in. Tearing up a grave stick Kibei rushed into the pack, driving off the animals. There lay the body of Itō Kwaiba, brought hither by the hands of O'Iwa to be torn and mangled by the teeth of the brutes. Thus was it that the funerals of Itō Kwaiba, Natsumé Kyuzō, and Imaizumi Jinzaémon took place in one cortége on the same day and at the same time. The postponement in the first instance— was it providential?

CHAPTER XIX

TAMIYA YOÉMON: WITH NEWS OF KONDŌ ROKU-RŌBEI AND MYŌZEN THE PRIEST

TAMIYA YOÉMON was stumbling home in all haste from the funeral of Itō Kwaiba. He was full of news for the wife, O'Kamé. The neighbours could talk of nothing but the strange happenings in the ward, and details lost nothing in the telling; perhaps gained somewhat by the process. Most edifying was the reported conduct of the wife of the late Natsumé Kyuzō, the observed of all observers at the funeral, the object of that solicitous congratulation which embodies the secret sigh of relief of friends, neighbours, and relatives at the removal of a prospective burden. Natsumé had left behind him a wife, an old mother, an infant child, and huge liabilities. To administer this legacy—and perhaps to get rid of her mother-in-law—the wife had promptly and tearfully sacrificed her status, and sold herself for a term of years to the master of the Sagamiya, a pleasure house at Shinagawa post town. The sum paid—one hundred *ryō*—relieved the immediate future. The neighbours derided the ignorance of the Sagamiya in accepting the uncertain bail of Akiyama Chōzaémon. If the lady behaved badly, small satisfaction was to be obtained of her security. "Ignorance is bliss." Let the Sagamiya bask in both and the beauty of the prize. Meanwhile their concern and admiration were for the lady destined to this post town of the crowded Tōkaidō, the stopping place of high and low, noble and riff-raff, entering Edo town. Of the inmates of the pleasure quarters, the harlots of Shinagawa, Shinjuku, Itabashi, were held in lowest esteem.

Arrived at his door Yoémon stopped short in surprise and alarm. To his loud call of "Wife! Wife!" answer there was none. Looking within he could barely distinguish objects through the thick smoke which filled the house. The last thing the Nipponese would do under such conditions, would be to throw open doors and panels. This would convert the place at once to a blazing conflagration. Where was the fire getting its start? Choking and spluttering Yoémon groped his way through the rooms into the rear. Wherever the fire was, it was not in the living rooms. The smoke was accentuated on reaching the kitchen. Here was a smell of burning rice, of Yoémon's dinner gradually carbonizing under the influence of an element other than the juices of his round stomach. Looking into the room, through the thickened haze he saw the flame of the fire brightening. O'Kamé the wife could be made out, on her knees before the portable furnace. She was blowing a mass of slivers and brushwood into flame by the aid of a bamboo pipe. It was this stuff, green and partly wet, which gave out the choking acrid smoke. Yoémon was angered beyond measure at the sight of his ruined meal and expectations. "Kamé! Kamé! What are you doing? Have you gone mad? Ma! Ma! The dinner is being ruined. You are ill. Kamé's head whirls with head-ache. Yoémon will act as cook. Go to bed —at once." At his peremptory speech the wife looked up into the face of the husband standing over her. She scowled at him in a way to cause fear. "Not a *shō* of rice; not a *mon*. Yoémon would give freely to a beggar, rather than confer a 'cash' on Iwa. Yoémon sells me as a street harlot." He started back in fright before the snarling distorted visage. The wife sprang to her feet. Pash! On his devoted head descended the hot iron pan with its content of stew. "Ah! Kamé is mad—clean daft." With a wild laugh she seized the pot full of boiling rice and began to pour it into the drain. When he tried to stop her, he received the mess full in his bosom—"Mad? Not at all. This Kamé never felt in better spirits. When grass grows in Samonchō we enter Nirvana. Ha! Ha! Ha! To hasten the happy time!" With a kick she knocked over the furnace. In an instant the *tatami* was in a blaze. Yelling like mad, shouting for help, Yoémon leaped from the house. O'Kamé seized the burning brands in her bare hands, hurling them into this room and into that. Outstripping the old Yoémon, the younger men of the neighbours rushed in. The mad woman was soon overcome and carried from the burning building. Nothing else was saved. They took her to the house of Akiyama Chōzaémon. Here she was tied hand and foot, and put in a closet. The old man Yoémon stood by in despair, watching the progress of events. Before the conflagration was extinguished his own and four other houses were destroyed. He was a ruined man; responsible for all.

Myōzen the priest had just set foot on the slope leading up from Samégabashi to Yotsuya. A somewhat long retreat at Myōhonji, attendance at the ceremonies held on the Saint's (Nichiren) birthday, had kept him in ignorance of recent events in Yotsuya. In the dawn of the beautiful day of earliest 3rd month (our April 13th) he had set out from Kamakura. Sturdy as were the priest's limbs, yet he was a little tired. He rested at the foot of the hill. Then his eyes grew big with astonishment. In the waning afternoon a funeral came wending its way downwards. But such a funeral! Two spearmen led the way. Then came a long train of attendants. Three catafalques followed, the first a most imposing bier. Then came the relatives. Kibei on horseback headed these. The women rode in *kago*. That it was a ward funeral Myōzen had no doubt, both from its source and make up. He noted a parishioner in the cortége. "Kamimura Uji!" The long-limbed, long-faced, long-tongued man left the ranks and obsequiously greeted his spiritual father. At Myōzen's question he expressed gratified surprise, and unlimbered his lingual member at once—"Whose honoured funeral this? Nay! It is a triple funeral; that of Natsumé Kyuzō, Imaizumi Jinzaémon, the Go-Inkyō, our ward-head. It is owing to this latter that there is such an outpouring of the ward, with attendance of barrier guards and firemen. Although the ending of Natsumé and Jinzaémon was not edifying, that of our honoured once head gratified still more the public curiosity. Gnawed and eaten by the rats he died most horribly." He told of the eventful night. " Hence delay in the burial. The deaths of Natsumé and Imaizumi were almost coincident. The body of the adulterous woman, rejected by both families, was cast out on the moor." He noted with satis-faction the great impression his tale made on the priest, as also the clerical garb and rosary held in hand. " Pray join the band. A little re-adjustment . . ." He bent down. With the baton he held in hand as leader of his section he carefully dusted the robes. Adjusting the folds he pronounced the results as most presentable. " The honoured Oshō is ready to bury or be buried." Myōzen took this remark in very ill form. He prepared to answer tartly, but curiosity overcame his weariness and ill temper. The procession was moving fast. He fell at once into line, with hardly an acknowledgment of Kamimura's courtesy, as this latter hastened forward to his place.

His neighbour in the procession explained. The nature of the deaths of the three men had aroused the feeling in the ward. Their connection with a conspiracy against O'Iwa San was now gener-ally known. Without doubt it was owing to her vengeance that they had died as they did. Let them lie outside the quarter. The protest to Kibei was respectful but emphatic. A newcomer, he had made no great resistance. It was determined to bury them at the Denzu-In, close by the mound of the nameless dead of Edo's great fire of more than half a century before. Hence the direction of the cortége. As the cemetery of the great temple was approached the curiosity of Myōzen, morbidly growing the while, became overpowering. The priest slipped from rank to rank. At the grave he stood in the very front. As long-time friend he besought a last glance at the dead. Those given to Natsumé and Imaizumi called forth a careless prayer for each. The men hesitated before raising the cover concealing the body of Kwaiba. At Myōzen's peremptory gesture they complied. He bent over and looked in. Frozen with horror, he was fascinated

by those great holes for eyes, large as teacups, which seemed to
fix him. Dead of leprosy, gnawed and torn by beasts, the face
presented a sight unforgettable. The holes torn in the flesh
twisted the features into a lifelike, though ghastly, sardonic grin,
full of the pains of the hell in which Kwaiba had suffered and now
suffered. A stench arose from the box which made the hardened
bearers hold their noses and draw away. Yet the priest bent down
all the closer. In his corruption the lips of the old man seemed to
move. Did Kwaiba speak? Closer and closer: Myōzen seemed
never satisfied with this inspection. The poise and brain gave
way. Priest and corpse met in the horrible salutation. With
exclamation the attendants sprang forward. Myōzen in a dead
faint was carried apart and laid on the ground. Some priests of
the hall busied themselves over him. Somewhat revived he was
taken off to the residence quarters of the temple, and soon was able
to return to his home. "Curious fool." Kibei was greatly
angered. He was easily irritated in these days. The delay in the
rites almost maddened him. Would old Kwaiba—his father Itó
Inkyō—never be got out of men's sight? Out of Kibei's sight?

That night Myōzen sat alone in his quarters. Somewhat
shaken, he was ashamed and regretful at thought of his unseemly
curiosity of the afternoon. The priests of Denzuin had regarded
him with covert amusement and repulsion. He had noted one
passing the sleeve of his robe over his lips. Myōzen explained
the incident by more than usual weariness. They condoled with
him, and made horrified gestures of ill-disguised glee when they
thought his attention was elsewhere. In his present privacy the
scene at the grave came back to mind again and again. "Ah!
Ah! If this Myōzen had not looked. The Inkyō's face was terrible. Myōzen cannot put it from mind." He glanced at the
pages of the sutra lying before him. He turned them over. He
knew they spoke of the horribleness of death; but what was the
cold script to the actuality? It was no use, the attempt to read.
Kwaiba's face interposed. "Oh! That salute! The very idea

of that terrible salute, the contact with corruption!" He was as
if plunged in an icy bath. He started nervously. It was but rain
dashing against the *amado*, rattling and twisting in the gale.
He could not sleep. That night he would watch. The fire was
hot in the *hibachi* (brazier). He went to the closet to get some
tea. On opening it he sprang back with a shout of alarm, to
lean trembling and quivering in every limb huddled against the
wall. "Namu Myōhō Renge Kyō! Namu Myōhō Renge
Kyō!" One character of the wondrous formula secured pardon
and safety to the believer in that paradise of Amida which Myōzen
was in no great haste to visit. Shivering as with a chill intently
he watched the animal as it glided along the edge of the room, to
disappear into the shadows. He shrugged his shoulders wearily.
A rat had frightened him almost out of his wits! His heart beat
tumultuously, almost to suffocation; then it seemed to cease altogether; to resume its wild career.

Hardly was he again seated, his hand on the kettle—don—
don, don—don, don, don, don. Some one was violently knocking
on the door. Myōzen sprang up. Approaching the *amado* with
silent step he eyed the bolts: "All secure." Snatching up a stake
close by he jammed it in between floor and crosspiece. Leaning
heavily on the panel he listened. "Myōzen Sama! Oshō Sama!
Condescend to open; deign to give entrance! The storm nearly
throws one to the ground. News! News for the Oshō! A
request to make!" Myōzen held his ground against this outer
temptation. "Who are you, out at this hour of the night and in
such weather? To-night Myōzen does not open. Go away; return in daylight."—"But the honoured Oshō Sama is needed.
His presence is requested. Deign to open; at least to hear the
message. The priest aids the afflicted." There was something
in the voice he recognized, despite its terror. Regaining some
courage he parleyed. The priest was for the consolation of the
unfortunate. O'Iwa had been, was unfortunate. He could not
open. "Who are you? Unless the name be given this Myōzen

holds no further talk. To-night he is unwell, positively ill. Come
at dawn and Myōzen will receive you."—"Who? Does not
the voice answer for the person? This is Tomobei, from the
house of Kondō Rokurōbei. Deign to open. The master needs
and calls for the aid of the Oshō Sama.

Voice and speech, the importance of Kondō in the life of
Myōzen, broke down his hesitation. Slowly he removed the bars.
Tomobei entered, dripping with wet. He cast down his straw coat
at the entrance. The man's eyes and manner were wild. He kept
casting frightened looks into the wild welter of storm outside.
When the priest would withdraw into the room he held him
by the skirt. " What has happened? " commanded Myōzen briefly.
Replied Tomobei—" A terrible thing! To-day the master was
ready to attend the funeral of Itō Inkyō. The wife was engaged
in putting the house *kimono* in the closet. O'Tama was playing
on the upper *rōka*. She is but seven years old. Leaning far over
to see her father leave, she lost her balance. Down she fell, to
be impaled on the knife-like points of the *shinobi-gaeshi*. The
sharp-pointed bamboo, protection against thieves, have robbed the
Danna of his greatest treasure (*tama*). Deep into throat and chest
ran the cruel spikes, to appear through the back. The sight inspired fear, so horrible was it. He could but call out—' Tomobei!
Tomobei!' All effort to detach the child, to saw off the points,
did but make matters worse. It was necessary to fetch a ladder.
When taken down she was dead. Alas! Alas! The Okusama is
nearly crazed. The Danna Sama in his cruel distress does but
rage through the house. ' Myōzen Ōshō, he loved the child. Let
Myōzen Ōshō be summoned to say a prayer of direction, while
yet the child spirit hovers hereabouts.' Such is the cry of the
Okusama. Hence the presence of this Tomobei. Otherwise he
would rather be scourged at the white sand than face the darkness
in which O'Iwa San wanders abroad." Man and priest were
weeping. The former in his fright and over the confusion and

distress fallen on the household; the priest over the sudden and
dreadful end of this child to whom the homeless one, the man
devoted to the solitary life, had taken an unbounded affection
as of a father. Great as was his terror, he forgot his own ills in
the greater misfortune of the life-long friend. He remained
bowed in prayer. "Namu Myōhō Renge Kyō! Namu Myōhō
Renge Kyō! Oh! The wondrous law, the *sutra* of the Lotus!"
He rose—"Myōzen comes."

As they 'struggled through the storm, Tomobei kept up a non-
sensical, running talk, full of the superstitious fear of the man of
the lower classes. "Iya! The affair has been terrible, but misfortune is in the air. . . . What's that! Ah! Something
passes by . . . above. O'Iwa! O'Iwa!" He seized the
priest's arm and clung to him in terror. Myōzen's fears had all
returned. He would have run away, but was too tightly held.
"Where! Where!" He shrieked and whirled around toward
Samegebashi. Tomobei held on tenaciously to his skirts. An
object was bearing down on them in the dark. Close upon priest
and man they jumped to one side. A cold hand was laid on the
neck of the cleric, who squawked with fear. A howl answered
the howls and mad cries and blows of the two men, who now
threw themselves flat on the ground to shut out sight of the
apparition. The beast sped down the hill. Discomfited, Myōzen
disentangled himself from the embraces of a broken water spout,
which descending from the roof under which he had taken shelter,
was sending its cold stream down his neck. Tomobei rose from
the mud puddle in which he lay face downward. They gazed
at each other. "A dog! A wandering cur!" Myōzen eyed his
once immaculate garments with disgust. How present himself in
such a state! Tomobei read his thoughts and determined to
keep a companion so hardly won. "There are present but the
master and the Okusama, Tomobei, and Kiku; other company
there is none. . . . Yes; the Ojōsan."—"The corpse needs
no company," said Myōzen testily. In his disgrace and unkempt

condition Myōzen was unduly irritated at his child friend. The
business was to be gone through. They were opposite the cemetery of Sainenji, on its western side. Said Tomobei—" A paling
is loose. There is no need to descend the hill. This is no cheerful spot at this hour. Deign to sprint it, Oshō Sama. In the time
one can count ten the entrance at the rear is reached. Deign a
spurt, honoured priest; deign to sprint." Myōzen felt he was in
for everything this night. With Tomobei he tucked up his robes to
his hams, as if entering a race. Crawling through the bamboo
palings into the haunt of the dead, at it they went—a mad spurt
across to Kondō's house. Tomobei was the more active. He
turned to watch the priest tripping over hillocks in the grass,
knocking into gravestones hidden by the darkness. So near home,
courage was returning. He burst into laughter at sight of Myōzen
madly hammering a battered old stone lantern of the *yukimidōro*
style. The broad-brimmed hat-like object he belaboured as something naturally or unnaturally possessed of life, all the while
giving utterance to anything but priestly language. Tomobei
ventured back to his rescue. Myōzen was quite battered and
bleeding as the two rushed into Kondō's house.

The master was expecting them; but he threw up his hands
as they appeared in the room. " Oshō Sama! Tomobei! What
are you about! Why rush into the room, clogs still on the feet?
Deign to withdraw. The *tatami* are stained and streaked with
mud. . . . Water for the feet of the Oshō Sama! Tomobei,
are you mad? Out with you: bring water to clean up this mess."
In confusion the priest withdrew. His apologies were profuse as
he reappeared—" Alas! ·Terrible the loss, and in such dreadful
manner. Kondō Dono, Okusama, part at least of this grief
Myōzen would take on himself. Great is the sorrow at this end
of one just beginning life." The wife received the condolence
of the priest with a burst of weeping. Then she turned fiercely
on the husband—" It is all the fault of Rokurōbei. He was *nakōdo*
for O'Iwa San in the marriage with Iémon. Turning against her,

he took O'Hana into the house. Did she not spend her time in idling, and teaching the child the ways of her questionable life—'how to please men,' forsooth? . . . Ah! Tama did have pretty ways. Though but of seven years, she danced, and sang, and postured as would a girl double her age. Now thus cruelly she has perished." Her mind, reverted to the child, again took a turn. "The plot against O'Iwa—with Itō Kwaiba, Iémon, Chōzaémon—here is found the source of this calamity. O'Iwa in dying has cursed all involved. Now 'tis the turn of Kondō and his unfortunate wife." She ended in another outburst of tears, her head on the mats at the feet of the priest. Rokurōbei was tearing up and down the room, gesticulating and almost shouting—"Yes! 'Tis she! 'Tis she! The hateful O'Iwa strikes the father through the child. Ah! It was a cowardly act to visit such a frightful ending on one budding into life. O'Iwa seeks revenge. O'Iwa is abroad; and yet this Kondō cannot meet with her." Myōzen was almost deafened with his cries and noisy earnestness. Truly to bring peace into this household, with division reigning between husband and wife smitten with fear of the supernatural, would be no easy matter. His priestly experience taught him the safest way to bring about his object.

"'Tis true; 'tis true. But loud cries avail nothing. The aid of the Buddha for the deceased is to be sought." Apologetically he showed something of his condition to the wife. At once she rose. Outergarments were removed. Muddied undergarments were renewed. Myōzen went into the mortuary chamber. The little "Jewel" was laid out as in sleep. The wounded chest, the torn throat, were concealed by garments and a scarf-like bandage adjusted by a mother's sad and tender care. The incense sticks lay in clay saucers near the couch. "Oh, the wonderful Law! The *sutra* of the Lotus! Namu Myōhō Renge Kyō! Namu Myōhō Renge Kyō!" He looked long at the little silent figure. His eyes were full of tears as he turned and took the hands of the weeping mother who had followed him into the

room. Then for long he spoke in consoling tones. She was somewhat quieted when they returned.

Kondō Rokurōbei was still moving restlessly about the room.
Now he was here, now there; from the death room he returned
to the company; from them he passed to the kitchen. The wife
thought of the friend and priest. " Tomobei, go to the store-room
and bring wine." Myōzen was a curious mixture. His weak
spot was touched—" Deign it, honoured lady, for all. Let the
occasion be made seemly, but more cheerful. Cause not sorrow to
the dead by an unmeasured grief. This does but pain the Spirit
in its forced communion with the living. Death perchance is not
the misfortune of subsequent existence in this world, but a passage to the paradise of Amida." He spoke unctuously; as one full
informed and longing for its trial. His homily had no effect in
moving Tomobei, who was flatly unwilling to perform the service
ordered. " The wine . . . .," broke in Kondō harshly.—" The
go-down is at the end of the lot. The hour is very late, and the
storm . . . and other things . . . it rages fiercely. This
Tomobei . . ."—" Shut up! " roared his master, with easily
roused anger. The maid O'Kiku timidly interposed—" There is a
supply in the kitchen. This Kiku early brought it there, anticipating the need. Indeed the storm is terrible. One gets wet to
the bone in traversing the yard." The wife caught the last words
—" Aye! Wet and chilled the lost child spirit wanders, ringing
its bell and vainly seeking aid and shelter; no aid at hand but that
of the heartless hag in the River of Souls." [1] At the thought
of the little O'Tama in cold and storm she broke down. Crying
bitterly, she crept from the room and laid down beside the bier.
    The wine was served. Myōzen drank. Then he drank again.
His potations gave him confidence—for more drink—and recalled

---

[1] The old hag who lurks in the River of Souls, waylaying little
children, robbing them of their clothes, and compelling them to con-
struct huge piles of stones. Her counterfeit presentment (by Unkei)
can be well seen at the Ennōji of Kamakura.

him to his functions. "Let us all pray. Namu Myōhō Renge Kyō! Namu Myōhō Renge Kyō! Wonderful the Law! Wonderful the *sutra* of the Lotus, explanatory of the Law by which mankind are saved, to enter the paradise of Amida. Be sure the wanderings of O'Tama will be short. Scanty is the power of the Shozuka no Baba. Soon shall the child sit upon a lotus. Early shall be her entrance into Nirvana. Namu Myōhō Renge Kyō! Namu Myōhō Renge Kyō! . . . Honoured master, let all join in. Command the servants to join in the recital of the Daimoku." Kondō waved a hand at Tomobei and O'Kiku, in assent and command. Vigorous were the tones of all in the responses. Myōzen drank again. He pressed the wine on the others; drinking in turn as they agreed. The night was passing. It was the eighth hour (1-3 A.M.). Said he—"Don't get drowsy. By every means avoid it. Now! A vigorous prayer." He raised his hand—"Namu Myōhō Renge Kyō! Namu Myōhō Renge Kyō!" But the responses were flagging. Said Myōzen—"This will never do; at this hour of the night." He drank again—to find that the supply had come to an end. Kondō was nodding. Tomobei, if awake, was deaf to words. Myōzen rose himself to fetch a new supply.

Kondō pricked up his ears. The temple bells were booming the hour watch in solemn unison. The rain splashed and pattered on the *amado*. A rustling, swishing sound was heard, close by, in the next room. Now it was as if a hand was passing along the screen. He sprang up, drawn sword in hand. His eyes were riveted on the *shōji*, anticipating an appearance. Then he laid a violent hand on the interposing obstacle and threw it back. A tall figure robed in black, with broad flat face and bulging brow, puffed eyelids in which were sunken little dots in place of eyes, hair in wild disorder framing the dead white face, stood before him. "O'Iwa! O'Iwa!" The lamp was knocked over, but not before he dealt the one fierce upward blow. Madly he sprang on the apparition and slashed away in the dark. "Kiya!" The

cry rang loud. Kondō danced with joy, calling loudly for lights.
"O'Iwa! O'Iwa! Kondō has slain the O'Baké, the enemy of his
child! Rejoice with Kondō! The vendetta is accomplished!" In
the darkness and confusion a groan was heard; then another, still
fainter; then there was silence. Tomobei appeared with a light.
He leaned over the long black robed body; to raise an alarmed face
to his joyful master. "At what does the Danna Sama rejoice?
What has he done? 'Tis Myōzen Sama, the Oshō Sama, who lies
cut down. Dreadful has been the mistake of the Danna Sama.
This is like to cost the House dear."—" Namu Myōhō Renge Kyō!
Namu Myōhō Renge Kyō!" The sword had slipped from
Kondō's hand, and in genuine grief he knelt beside the body of
the unfortunate priest, seeking for some sign of life. Alas!
Myōzen had almost been cut in two by the upward sweep of the
sword. From liver to pap was one gaping wound. He lay in the
pool of almost all the blood in his body. Gathered around the
corpse the four people eyed each other with terror.

Don—don—don, don, don, don. They sprang up in a huddled mass. The sound was at their very shoulders. "Some one
knocks at the back door," said Tomobei. "Go open it," commanded Kondō. Tomobei flatly refused, and without respect,
nay with insolence. Kondō picked up and weighed in his hand the
bloody sword. Why mingle vile blood with good? Instead of
cutting the man down he went himself and opened the half door
at the top. A woman, dripping with water, her hair in wild
disorder, her face white as chalk, stood outside in the storm.
Kondō gave an exclamation of surprise—" O'Kamé of Tamiya!
How comes O'Kamé here? It was said that Yoémon San had
shut her up, as one gone mad." The woman smirked with satisfied
air—" Kondō Rokurōbei is seer as well as murderer. This Kamé
was bound and imprisoned; nay, almost divorced. Myōzen, just
dead at Kondō's hands, to-morrow was to pronounce the divorce.
For so much, thanks to Kondō Dono. But O'Tama has died.
Kamé would condole with Kondō San; burn a stick of incense for

O'Tama. Condescend to grant entrance." Said Rokurōbei abruptly—"How knows O'Kamé of the death of Myōzen; who told her of the fate of O'Tama?" She laughed wildly—"Who? O'Iwa; O'Iwa is the friend of Kamé. It was she who loosed the bonds. 'O'Tama of Kondō's house is dead. O'Kamé should condole with the wife, the friend of this Iwa. Get you hence, for Kondō has murdered the priest.' . . . So here we are; O'Iwa accompanies Kamé. Here she is." She waved a hand into the storm and darkness. "Deign to give passage to the chamber where lies O'Tama. O'Iwa and Kamé would burn incense to the darling's memory, to the little Jewel." With a roar Kondō seized the breast of her robe—"Vile old trot, off with you!" He gave her a violent push which sent her on her buttocks. The woman remained seated in the mud, laughing noisily. She held out two skinny arms to him. With a slam he shut the door.

He knelt by the priest's body, truly grieved—"Ah! O'Iwa is abroad. How has this mad woman knowledge of this deed? What was the offence of Myōzen thus to deserve the hatred of Tamiya O'Iwa?" O'Kamé had seen the priest enter, had stood in the wet listening to the wild talk of Kondō, had seen the bloody sword in his hand. Her mad brain had put riot and death together. The talk as to O'Tama she had overheard from her closet. Kondō thought of neither explanation. He was at odds with Akiyima, and had sent no message to his house. As he speculated and thought how best to compound matters with the temple, now grieved at the rash blow fallen on a friend, now aghast at the certain and heavy indemnification which would be exacted by the enraged clerics, an uproar arose outside. There were wild cries and a scream of pain. Then came a loud triumphant shout— "Heads out! Heads out! O'Iwa is slain! This Akiyama has killed the O'Baké. The incubus of the ward is lifted. Help!" Kondō sprang up and out of the house. Were the words true? Had another succeeded where he had failed? His lantern, the lanterns of many others, threw light on the place where Akiyama

13

Chōzaémon bravely stood ward over the prostrate body of the apparition. Returning late from Shitamachi he had entered the ward with shrinking terror. As he skulked along, with eyes on every dark corner, the figure of a woman was seen close by the eaves of the house of Kondō Rokurōbei. As he approached she came forward laughing wildly the while. The light of his lantern fell on the ghastly white face, the disordered hair. In a spasm of fright he dropped the lantern and delivered his blow in drawing the sword. The cut was almost identical with the one delivered to Myōzen the priest. The men there gathered looked into each other's faces, then at the body of O'Kamé lying in their midst. The crowd parted, and Tamiya Yoémon appeared. Kondō Rokurōbei and Akiyama Chōzaémon stood by with bloody swords, their own skins without a scratch. They were self-accused.

The upshot of the affair was ruin for all. Matters in Yotsuya were coming to the official ears. Yoémon was forced to make charges against Akiyama; the more willingly as therein lay a chance to recoup his own losses through the wife he intended to divorce on the morrow. Kondō easily cleared his skirts of this offence, but was involved with the irate temple priests. All were entangled in the heavy costs of the law of those days. Of these three men something is to be said later.

CHAPTER XX

KIBEI DONO

KIBEI was in great straits, financial and domestic. The death of Kwaiba had brought him anything but freedom. In Nippon the headship of a House is much more than the simple heirship of our western law. Relieved of his obligation in office the old man's hands were wide open to shower benefice or caprice on the most worthless. Endorsement for cash and goods to Natsumé, Imaizumi, and Kamimura; donations to the temples of Teremachi and the Yotsuyazaka; favours in every direction except that of Akiyama Chōzaémon, in the pursuit of whom Kwaiba found much amusement; all these items added to the very free living in his household had pledged deeply the ample revenue of two hundred and thirty *tawara,* and would have upheld the *samurai* trait of not knowing the value of money—if Kwaiba had been of that kind. Between Kwaiba and Kibei, the wild debauchery of the last year had brought the House to the verge of ruin. Kibei was aghast. Long since he had become deeply involved with the Kashiku Tamagiku of the Yamadaya in Edomachi Itchōme of the Yoshiwara. The ugly fellow was madly in love with the beauty. On her he had poured out the treasures of the Itō House during the six months which preceded the illness of Kwaiba. During his prolonged absence from her the letters of the Kashiku had inundated the writing table of Kibei. Had he deserted her? Was all affection gone? Where now were the promises of ransom, the blood-sealed vow to become husband and wife, to assume the relation which endures for two worlds? Kibei sullenly read these lines; cursing Kwaiba and cursing himself. Ransom! With strict living for the next five years *he* might set matters straight and free the Tayu; and any day *she* might be bought by some

195

rich country *samurai* or *gōshi* (gentleman farmer), or be carried off to ornament the *bessō* of some *hatamoto*. Kibei wiped the bitter saliva from his lips.[1]

The domestic difficulties were accompaniment to these more important matters. In the large mansion Kibei was now alone. The tenth day had witnessed the flight of the last of the servants. The women had departed with the funeral, through fear, sacrificing wages and even such clothing as could not surreptitiously be removed. What woman—or man—could remain in a house which was the nightly scene of such fearful sounds of combat. Shrieks, wails, groans, came from the quarters once occupied by the dead Kwaiba. As to this there was no difference of opinion. The more venturesome had been favoured with actual sight of the scenes enacted. They had seen the old man as he was in death, pursued from room to room by two frightful hags, as gaunt, blear, sightless as himself. Dreadful were the cries of the dead man as the harpies fastened upon him, descending from above like two huge bats. These scenes took place usually at the eighth hour (1 A.M.), not to cease until dawn. As for the men servants, they took their leave in the days following, asking formal dismissal (*itoma*) with recommendation to another House. They scented the approaching ruin of their present employer.

One day Kakusuké presented himself. Kibei looked up. He understood at once that the man had come in his turn to take leave. Kakusuké alone had remained with him. He was *chūgen*, stable boy, cook, maid; and did the work of all four without complaint. The change in his master was too marked. Kibei, in his turn, had become irritable, timorous as a girl, subject to outbreaks of almost insane rage. To Kakusuké the young man seemed to have lost all nerve. Kakusuké wanted to serve a man. As long as the Wakadono gave promise of redemption, of rising above his difficulties and emerging into a splendid career in which

---

[1] An ordinary disposition of these women; who often preferred their Edo lover to such lot.

Kakusuké could take pride, the *chūgen* was ready to take the
bitter with the sweet. To be maid servant and keeper of a man
half mad had no attraction for this blunt-nerved fellow. He spoke
plainly—" The Wakadono should deign to throw up the whole
connection. Under the present conditions the ruin of the House
is unavoidable. Condescend to return to the original House in
Honjō Yokogawa. This course will be best. At least the Wakadono secures his own salvation. This is the advice of Kakusuké,
grown old in experience of service in a *samurai* household. In
naught else is there hope. As to himself, would the Wakadono
condescend to grant dismissal." Long had been the intimacy between Itō Kwaiba and Inagaki Shōgen. Kakusuké, the messenger
between the two Houses, had watched this Fukutarō (Kibei)
grow to manhood, had noted his prowess. It was with delight
he had carried the documents which were to bring this new and
vigorous blood into the home of his decadent master. This was
the result. " A pest on these witches—and their craft! "
Kibei heard him out with growing anger. As the man's words
gathered vigour and plain spokenness his hand wandered to his
sword. He had a mind to cut him down then and there for his
freedom of speech. More than half induced to recognize the truth
of the indictment his better feeling halted him. With harsh
and sardonic tone he gave unbelieving thanks for the implied
reproof of the *chūgen*. The service of Kakusuké had been faithful beyond measure. It should have its proper reward. If others
had chosen to depart as do those who run away, they had shown
ignorance of this Kibei. From a drawer of the desk he took out
a letter already prepared, a roll containing wages. He pushed
the *zen* toward Kakusuké. This readiness, as if foreseen, hit the
man hard. Respectfully he pressed the letter to his forehead,
bowing with extended hands on the *tatami;* the money he did not
touch. Finally he raised a timid questioning glance to his one-
time master. Said Kibei jeeringly—" Kakusuké has given his
advice. Is it part of his long experience that a servant should

question the wages placed under his nose? Off with you! This Kibei would be alone; most willingly so." At the peremptory threatening gesture Kakusuké no longer hesitated. He had no inclination to be a victim of one of the mad outbreaks of the young man. Taking the roll humbly he backed out of the room. His steps were heard a few minutes later passing the entrance. Then the outer gate shut to with a clang.

For a long watch Kibei sat in meditation. He was as one who sleeps. Then he rose with decision. " 'Tis the last chance. Kakusuké is right. The matter is to be brought to an end." Dressing for the street he left the house. He opened the big gate; then went to the stable, and saddled and bridled his horse. He led it outside, closed the gate, and mounting he rode forth, to go to Honjō Yokogawa and the *yashiki* of his father, Inagaki Shōgen. Coming unaccompanied he was received with surprise and some discomfiture, as he was quick to note. He was very quick to note things in these days. Prostrating himself before his mother—"Kibei presents himself. Honoured mother, deign to pardon the intrusion. Fukotarō would solicit her pity and influence." The lady looked at him with amazement. "Fukutarō! What then of Kibei? Is some jest deigned at the mother's expense? It is in very bad taste. . . . But the face of Kibei implies no jest. Pray put the matter plainly. Why does her son come in petition to the mother?" Began Kibei—"The matter is most serious . . ." He went into the full details; from the time of his entrance into the Itō House, through the course of dissipation and illness of Kwaiba, down to the present ruined state of affairs. "All this is due to the curse of O'Iwa San, to this plot in which Kibei foolishly engaged." Of this he now fully felt the force. The events of the past weeks had wrecked him in mind and body. One disaster after another, in house and ward, had been visited on Kibei. The bitterness and dislike of the people toward Kwaiba was visited on his representative, who was held responsible. In his great mansion he lived alone. No servant would enter it to attend to his wants. Was he to cook and be valet for himself— and pose as the Kumi-gashira, the great chief of the ward! The position was an impossible one. Deign to use a mother's influence with Inagaki Dono. " Condescend to secure permission for the return of this Kibei to his original House, for the cancellation of the adoption."

The wife of Shōgen sat frightened; at the tale, and at this radical way of finding an exit from the situation. The mother's heart was full of pity for the distracted son, whose haggard looks showed the strain of the past weeks. Besides she was a woman, and as such fully believed in and feared the curse of this dead O'Iwa, one who had died without funeral rites or prayer. " Fortunately the honoured father now is on the night watch at the castle. He is at home, drinking his wine. His humour is excellent. Wait but a moment." Leaving Kibei she went to the room of Shōgen's light indulgence. The severe and conscientious nobleman was bending under the genial influence of the saké. " Kibei? He comes in good season. The heir of Kwaiba Inkyō has not favoured his real father of late. Ah! The boy was well placed. Kwaiba soon made way for him; and none too willingly, one can believe." He chuckled. Then noting his wife's troubled looks. " But there is something to tell."—" So indeed; none too pleasant." She went into the story Kibei had told her. " His fear of O'Iwa San is deadly. The House is ruined, with no profit in the connection. Deign to permit the cancellation of the adoption, his return to the House of his true parent." She stopped before the stern astonished look of the husband. Said he harshly —" Let him come up. Shōgen answers Kibei Dono in person. . . . Heigh! Up here with you! For Itō Dono there is wine . . ." Kibei entered joyfully at his father's call. Success was in his hands. Once more he was to marshal his father's retainers and accompany him to the castle; once more be the habitué of the fencing rooms. " Honoured father, fear enters: for long this Kibei has not ventured into your presence."—" And need not for long again," thundered the old man. " What stuff is this for the ears of Shōgen? Kibei would sever his connection with the Itō House. Kibei is afraid of a ghost! He fears a girl! A *samurai* wearing two swords shrinks from an encounter with a woman! Has Shōgen no obligation toward his old friend Kwaiba? In more serious matters and in life Shōgen would share Kwaiba's lot. Back with you to the house in Yotsuya! If this matter become known, both Kibei and Shōgen will be the laughing stocks of Edo. At least keep such fears to yourself. Off with you! Shōgen had wine for Itō Dono. For the fellow who would call himself—Fukutarō, he has none." With a kick he sent rolling the *zen* (table) with its burden of bottles and heating apparatus. In a rage he left the room.

Kibei's face was white as he raised it from the *tatami.* " Father has no experience of ghosts; he speaks at random and in anger. Terrible is the actuality." Said the mother, slowly and painfully—" He is the father; he is to be obeyed." Kibei was sitting upright. He nodded grave assent. Then suddenly he prostrated himself ceremoniously before the *shōji* through which Shōgen had disappeared. He repeated the salutation before his mother. Then he rose—" Itō Kibei takes leave. May good health and fortune visit those of this House." At his exit the mother rejoiced. Severe had been the father's words, but they had brought the boy to reason. She wept and trembled at the reproof. Men had best knowledge of such affairs. She would pray at Reiganji, and have memorial service held for the peace of this O'Iwa in the next world. Then the curse would not rest upon her son.

On his appearance at the house entrance an *ashigaru* (foot soldier) led up the horse. Kibei waved him away—" For the present keep the animal in charge. With matters to attend to close at hand Kibei will use other conveyance." The man took the animal away. Leaving the gate of the *yashiki* Kibei walked the short distance to the Hōonji bridge. Here was a *kago* (litter) stand. "To Yamadaya in Yoshiwara." As the *kago* men went off at a trot—"Kibei has played and lost. How does the account yonder stand? Seventy *ryō* owed at the Matsuminato-ya. For the rest, this Kibei can claim a night's attendance from the *kashiku*. If affection would not grant it, the huge sums bestowed in the past have a claim upon her. Then to end matters and die like a *samurai*. To-morrow Kibei cuts belly." It was the debt which sent him direct to the Yamadaya, and not first to the tea house. Sitting over the wine all effort of the Kashiku to enliven him failed. Noting her discomfiture he smiled gloomily. Then in explanation—"The thoughts of Kibei go astray. The House is ruined. Ransom is impossible. This is the last meeting. To-morrow Kibei cuts belly, and dies like a *samurai.*" At first the girl thought he was joking. Then noting the wild look of despair in his eyes, she was frightened. Partly in disbelief; partly seeking to postpone this desperate resolve, to turn his thoughts and gain time for reflection; partly in that sentimental mood which at times affects this class of women—"Is Kibei truly ruined? Lamentable the fate of Tamagiku. Why not join him in death? But the idea is too new. Deign to postpone the execution for a space. To-night shall be a night of pleasure with the Kashiku Tamagiku. With the morrow's darkness she dies with Kibei. Hand in hand they will wander the paths of Amida's paradise." She came close to him in service of the wine; put her arms about him, and drew him to her bosom; in every way cajoled and sought to comfort him, and corrupt his purpose. Consent was easy. The night was passed in love and wine. In the morning he left her.

Kibei was making his final preparations; writing directions which would benefit as far as possible the House in Honjō at the expense of that in Yotsuya. In the Yoshiwara a very different scene was taking place. With his departure the Kashiku sprang up. Hastily throwing a robe around her person she sought the room of the *yarité*—the bawd of the house. "The Kashiku! At this hour—what has happened?"—"Something of importance. This night Tama dies with Kibei Dono. The compact is closed, hard and firm." The astonished bawd had been rubbing the sleep out of her eyes. The last words brought her full awake—"Is the Kashiku drunk with wine? Is she mad? Truly it would seem so. And the bail? What is to become of the unfortunate? True it is Toémon of Honjō; and he has trouble enough already. He will never leave his prison." Tamagiku made a gesture of impatience—"This Tama has acted but to gain time. Can she have affection for such an ugly fellow? Was she to be the victim of some crazy outburst? Perhaps the day will bring better counsel; but the night's conversation does not augur it. His plans are most complete. The master must be seen. Deign to mediate; prevent the admittance of Kibei Dono as guest." O'Kayo the bawd nodded intelligence and assent. At once she sought the master of the house. "A dangerous guest," was his comment. "Send to the Matsuminatoya. They must be warned. We can look after ourselves." As an attendant of the tea house presented himself— "And the master, Teisuké San!"—"Is absent; this Tōsuké represents him. He has gone to Edo. Perhaps the house will deign to look at a new inmate. A true Tayu! The daughter of Akiyama San of Yotsuya sacrifices her caste. But sixteen years, she is a jewel. Less than a hundred ryō will buy her. He is in great difficulties." Tōsuké spoke with enthusiasm. The master of the Yamadaya answered promptly and with emphasis—"Accepted: let her be on hand in the course of the day. But Tōsuké, there is another matter. Kibei Dono no longer can be accepted as a guest." He went into details. Tōsuké drew a long breath. "A dangerous fellow! The Danna Sama never liked his presence. But he owes the house much money; seventy ryō."—"That is your affair," coldly replied the master of the Yamadaya. "This house answers not for the accounts of the tea-house. Previous notice has been given. Kibei Dono cannot be received as guest." —"That is not to be denied. He is most undesirable. But the seventy *ryō!* And the week's settlement to make with this house?" The Yamadaya had an idea—"It rarely passes a hundred *ryō.* . . . Five years is accepted? Then take thirty *ryō* and deliver this girl to the Yamadaya. . . . A true Tayu? If so the debt of Kibei finds payment." Tōsuké agreed with joy. At night the *kago* man set Kibei down before the Matsuminatoya. Teisuké, the *teishū* (host), regarded his arrival with mixed feelings. His coming meant something. Giving up his two swords, and once seated, Kibei's first act was to give thanks for past services. Calling for his account he produced the seventy *ryō* in its settlement. Prompt and profound were the humble thanks of the house for this unexpected liquidation. Kibei had secured the money by the transfer of obligations of Akiyama Chōzaémon to the usurer Suzuki Sanjurō. Three hundred and fifty *ryō* immediately due against seventy *ryō* in cash satisfied even this shark. Teisuké was impressed. How deny such a guest? He would get rid of him, and profit both ways. Yamadaya now would promptly pay the additional seventy *ryō* due on the girl with whom they were so delighted. He had paid fifty *ryō* for her. At Kibei's call his order was prompt. "Tōsuké, accompany Kibei Dono to the Yamadaya." Kibei's calm and collected manner reassured him. This man did not contemplate suicide.

With the appearance of Tōsuké and Kibei at the Yamadaya there was a flutter. The Bantō Matsuzo respectfully came forward. As Kibei came up to the *rōka* and shook off his *geta* he interposed. "Deign to wait, Kibei Dono. Matters have changed since morning. The Kashiku is very ill. She can see no one. Condescend to come another time. For one ill in body pleasure is no pastime. Pray consider; grant excuse for this one occasion." Kibei was surprised. He had left her perfectly well in the morning. Something in the *banto's* face, in the massed position of the men standing by, apprised him of the truth. He was enraged at the lie and the insult. "Ill? That is very strange, when so well at morning. But it is immaterial. Kibei goes to the room."—

" Impossible," was the firm reply of the *bantō*. " The Kashiku lies isolated from all. It is the order of the physician. Even those in the rooms around her have been ordered out. Pray forbear." But Kibei was obstinate—" Then a glass of wine at her bedside; Kibei has matters to impart." The *bantō* stuck to his post—" Wine! Amid the smell of drugs, the unseemly vessels of the sick room! Such could not be permitted." Kibei stretched out an arm. The *bantō* went flying a dozen feet. Kibei made a leap toward the stairway. But the bawd O'Kayo interposed her vinegary presence. She was brave; having the support of great numbers, of the whole household. " What rudeness! How inconsiderate your way of acting! You behave in very bad taste; with the roughness of an *ashigaru* (foot soldier). The Yamadaya does not entertain such miserable scamps. The Tayu is ill. This Kayo says it. Get you hence—to some coolie house. Return the day before yesterday." [2] Kibei gave a yell—" Yai! You old bitch! The whole affair is plain to Kibei. Out of money, his presence is no longer desired. Ah! Kibei will have vengeance." Without arms, before the sullen determination of these plebeians, he felt his helplessness. An unseemly brawl, in which he would be worsted, must not be entered on. He must leave. In a towering rage he strode back to the tea-house. Tōsuké tried to keep pace with him.

Said Teisuké in feigned astonishment—" Kibei Dono! What has happened? " Kobei did but stutter and fume. The *teishū* turned to Tōsuké. This latter made answer for his charge—" At the Yamadaya they were very rude. Admittance was refused to Kibei Dono. The bawd O'Kayo told him to come back day before yesterday! "—" Very rude indeed! Were such things said? It is unpardonable. An explanation must be had with the house.

---

[2] *Ototoi oidé:* It is the salutation of the good Buddhist to the captured insect, thrown without and requested to return " the day before yesterday " = the Greek Kalends. As used above it is a gross insult to the person addressed.

Danna Sama, for to-night deign to leave this matter to Teisuké. Ample satisfaction shall be had for the outrage." Teisuké threw up his hands as with uncontrollable anger. Kibei paid no attention, but demanded his swords. Outwardly he had regained his self-control. The maid O'Moto looked with diffidence at her mistress. The woman was accustomed to such scenes. At her sign the girl brought the weapons, carefully wrapped up. She placed them before Kibei. Unrolling the cover he put them on. With scanty salutation he strode off. Teisuké watched him—" It would be wise for the Yamadaya to close early to-night, to take in their lanterns; nay, even to board up the front and take refuge in the store-house." Tōsuké was in no hurry to face Matsuzo, the *bantō* of Yamadaya. Continued the easy old fellow—" Well, 'tis their affair. They are as good judges as Teisuké; and they could have been more civil in refusal. At all events the house has seventy *ryō*, and Kibei Dono is sober. He will cut belly before dawn; and perhaps nothing will happen hereabouts." The old pimp went off to his inner room; to sit down before his wine about the same time that Kibei did the same in a cook shop opposite the great gate of Yoshiwara. Here he idled, barely touched his drink, and passed the time in bantering the maid servant. He was in a riotous humour. He would take her to wife—and sell her the next morning. " As they do yonder." But O'Kiyo was not of that kind. " There is a lover? "—" Of course! " In admitting it she blushed, somewhat offended at hint of suspicion that such was lacking. Jibed Kibei—" He will do the same. Better to be the wife of a *samurai;* even for an hour." In the end he frightened the girl a good deal, so boisterous was he. She had gone out to buy him a deep hat. With relief she saw him put it on and set forth into the darkness and the rain.

The eighth hour (1 A.M.) was nearly ready to strike. The pleasure quarter was silent. Passersby were few. The occasional shuffling sound of *zōri* (sandals) could be heard behind the closed *amado*. Kibei smiled cynically as he recognized this mark of revolting passage from one room to another. In doubt he stood before the gate of the Yamadaya. How break in and kill them all? If Kibei had his way the Kashiku would keep her word. Just then a noise of voices was heard within, the falling of the bar. Several belated guests came forth. They were in the charge of O'Moto, the maid of the Matsuminatoya. Affectionate were the leave-takings with the quondam wives. " Condescend an early visit. This Haya lives but in the thought of Mosuké."—" Bunzaémon San,. be faithful to this Hana. In his absence she is always ill. She receives no one." At this there was a roar of laughter from the others of the company. Bunzaémon answered with re-proaches. Kibei followed behind. This fellow was somewhat lamed. He lagged behind. Kibei pulled his sleeve. Bunzaémon, the cit, turned in surprise and fear at sight of the *samurai* in his deep hat. Said Kibei—" Don't be afraid. Bunzaémon San has forgotten pipe, or purse, or something. He must go back to the Yamadaya." At the fellow's groping in his garments and failure to understand he grew impatient. " A friend lies at the Yamadaya. It is late, and they will not open at an unknown voice. Entrance somehow must be had. Deign to lend your aid." At last the fellow comprehended—" O'Moto San! A mo-ment: my pipe . . ."—" Oya! The Danna Sama has forgotten his pipe? " The girl went back the short distance to the gate. She knocked and called. With sleepy tones the voice of Matsuzo the *bantō* was heard. The bar fell. The girl turned to look down the street toward her guests. She looked right into the face of Kibei. Dropping her lantern, with a smothered scream she fled.

Matsu, the *bantō*, looked with horror at the man before him. As Kibei threw off his hat he turned to flee. Tripping, he fell. Kibei drew him back by the leg. A blow cut him through the shoulder. As he rose staggering a second vicious side swing sent the severed head to the ground. The gateman took the chance. Fleeing to the recesses of the kitchen, he swarmed up a post and hid himself among the rafters of the roof, amid the darkness of their shadows. Kibei turned back and carefully barred the gate. With the key at the girdle of Matsuzo he locked the bar chain. All was now ready for his visitation and search.

On the floor above they had a drunken guest in hand, trying to get him to depart. A *bantō* and several women formed the committee of expulsion. "Ah! Money gone, one's welcome is quickly worn out in this hell. But Jusuké does not budge. He fears not the whole pack of foxes. . . . Thanks: deep the obligation of this Jusuké, extending to the next life." A woman had picked up and restored his purse. "The bill is paid? An early start Tōkaidō way? Ah, true! Jusuké had forgotten." He was now all compliments and thanks. Then in a rage—"Oh! The huzzy! What is Jusuké's purse worth with nothing in it? Who has robbed the purse of Jusuké?" He was madly fumbling his tobacco pouch. A woman put his hand on the missing object in the folds of his girdle. He was mollified. As they moved to the head of the stairs—"Take care! Jusuké San, don't fall! Bantō San, deign to aid the guest." Refusing all help the man lurched half way down the flight. Then he stopped, staring and looking before him. At the foot stood Kibei, bloody sword in hand. "Down with this Jusuké? But Jusuké cannot down. A fool blocks the way. . . . Fool, you block the way of Jusuké."— "Out of the road, drunkard!" The words of Kibei came between his teeth, half growl, half snarl. The man obstinately held his own. When Kibei would push past him—"Beast!" He struck the *samurai*. Kibei whirled the sword. The head rolled to the bottom of the steps. The blood bathed Kibei from head to foot.

His appearance was horrible. The women fled in all directions. The *bantō* covered their retreat. "Kibei Dono! Pray be reasonable. Control yourself!" Kibei made a step toward the women's rooms. The *bantō* was dreadfully frightened, yet bravely he interposed to save them. He shouted for aid; below and to the neighbours. Kibei reached him. A blow and he fell severed. Kibei gave a howl of joy. O'Kayo the bawd came out to ascertain the cause of the brawl. She turned livid with fear on recognizing Kibei. They were standing together in the sort of entresol or room at the head of the stairway. Only a large brazier separated Kibei from his vengeance. Its massiveness of three or four feet breadth baffled him. The woman was fleeing for life. As he strove to get within striking distance fear gave her wings. From one side to another she leaped and dodged. Kibei was hampered. He had to cut her off from stair and *rōka*. As he hesitated she discharged the iron kettle at his head. One implement followed another. In hurling the iron tripod ashes entered her eyes. At once Kibei leaped to close quarters. The first sword blow she dodged. As Kibei recovered she sprang by him and over the *hibachi*, seeking the safety of the stairs now open to her. Her night-dress caught on the handle of the brazier and brought her to the ground. Next moment she was severed from shoulder to midriff.

Methodically Kibei began his examination of the rooms. To most of the inmates this uproar was a mere quarrel in the house, the cause of which they neither knew nor cared to know. The first search was at the room of the Kashiku, close to that of O'Kayo the bawd. Her reception room was dark. Here the Kashiku's bed usually was prepared. The inner room, her dressing room, showed the dim light of an *andon*. Noting her absence from the usual place a hasty stride brought him to the *shōji*. As he violently shoved them apart a man rose from the bed in the room. A mere glance showed that this was no lover. As Kibei with drawn sword stood over him, he squatted on his hams, crouching and begging for life. To Kibei's astonishment he called him by name—" Deign, honoured Sir, to spare this Chōbei. Be assured the Kashiku is not in this place. She lies to-night with the Danna of the house. Deign to seek her in his company." He pointed vaguely as he spoke, to give direction. Kibei laughed ferociously. From this source these directions were atrocious. He lowered the weapon—" Chōbei! At this place and time! Well met, good

Sir. Kibei is doubly grateful for what he has learned. Chōbei and Kibei are fellows in fortune. Willingly Kibei leaves him to O'Iwa San and her mercies." His attentive gaze never wandered from the face of the one-time pimp. With a gesture of horror he rushed from the room. In fright Chōbei rolled his head up in the coverlet, to keep out the vision evoked.

He continued his search—"Is it my little black fellow?" Such the greeting of one woman aroused from sleep. Trembling she rose at sight of Kibei. Harshly told to lie down, she gladly obeyed. Her quivering limbs already were nearly yielding as he spoke. In but one place did he encounter opposition. Pushing open the *shōji* of the merest closet of a room he came upon a girl whose face somehow was familiar. She was a mere slip of a creature to be called a woman. The undeveloped hips, the yet immature bosom, aroused his astonishment at finding her in such a place as inmate; that is, until the pure oval and beauty of the face caught his glance. As he entered she sprang up in alarm. Just roused from sleep she hardly knew where she was—"Father! Father! A man! A man is in the room! Help!" Kibei pushed her back on the bed. With his bloody sword he rolled over the bed-clothes. Then he made a move to get at the closet behind. Perhaps mistaking his action the girl sprang upon him. Kibei was startled at her mad energy. When he thrust her down she seized his hand in her teeth, sinking them deep into it. Pain and impatience—after all he was pressed for time—overcame him. Unable otherwise to shake her off he thrust the point of the sword into her throat and gave a vigorous downward push. Coughing up great clouts of blood, the girl sank back, dying on the *futon*. As he left the room remembrance came to Kibei's mind. He had seen her in Yotsuya. More than once O'Tsuru had served him tea in the house of her father, Chōzaémon. How came she in this vile den? He took a step back to aid her if he could. She was stone dead.

14

The Tayu Nishikiyama [3] now knew the cause of the disturbance. To the frightened page (*kamuro*) who came running to her—"Be quiet child. This is no time to lose self-control. Aid me in preparation. She dressed herself with the greatest care; "all in white, as befitted a lady in attendance on a nobleman." Then she took down her *koto* and struck the opening bars of an old and famous song— the "Jinmujō" (Inexhaustible Happiness)—said to have been sung by the famous Shizuka Gōzen when she danced the Hōraku, or sacred dance, before the Shōgun Yoritomo at Kamakura Hachimangū. As Kibei turned into the corridor the voice of the Oiran caught his ear as she sang in accompaniment to the instrument. She was bending over the *koto* as the *shōji* were flung apart. Kibei, his hair hanging in disorder and framing a face ghastly white in contrast to the red streaks splashed over it and his garments, stood transfixed at the entrance. The Tayu looked up. With calm pose and courteous salute—"Kibei Dono, what manner of acting is this! Is not Kibei Dono the *bushi?* Truly madness has seized you, honoured Sir. This is Nishikiyama. . . . Deign to be seated. 'Tis Nishikiyama who serves Kibei Dono. What has been done cannot be undone. The last cup of wine in life is to be drained. Deign to accept it from these humble hands." Kibei continued gazing on her. The unhappy man, his mind was opened to a flood of light. The hurricane of passion was passing. Slowly he advanced into the room. "Truly the Go Tayu is right. Kibei has gone mad; mad indeed!" He sank down on the cushion before her. At a sign the page placed the stand containing the bottle of cold *saké* before the lady. Skilfully the slender hands held it, gracefully poured it for the man doomed to death, taking this final cup served by her. Kibei raised it, drained it to the last drop. "The Kashiku: she is on this lower floor. Where lies she?" Nashikiyama noted the wild light returning to his

---

[3] Damask hill: the names taken by these great *hetairai* were most fanciful.

eyes. She bowed her head before him—"The life of Nishikiyama is at the command of Kibei Dono. Her lips are sealed.
Honoured Sir, how answer Kibei Dono's question?" For the
moment he looked down. Then he rose—"Whose daughter can
the Oiran be! Truly no lady in the land could show a higher
courage, a finer courtesy. The final salute of this Kibei in life is
to the Go Tayu." In grave ceremony it was performed. As he
left the room the woman buried her face in her hands, weeping
bitterly. In wonder and gratitude the frightened page extended
her hands, her face hidden in the white robes of the Go Tayu.

Kibei trod this lower corridor with sombre tread. He would
cut belly at the garden pond. With some surprise he noted an
amado open at the end of the *rōka*. Voices were heard. Standing
at the opening he saw lanterns. Some frenzied women had raised
a ladder to the garden wall. They would thus escape, but the
knife-like bamboo stakes prevented. Said a voice outside, and
close to him—"The key to the gate: here it is." The Kashiku
at a run passed by him. Kibei gave a shout. The frightened
woman turned, recognized him, then sped on. In a few steps
he was on her. The raised sword descended as she fell on her
knees before him, in attempt to swerve its course. Through
wrist and collar-bone, from neck to navel, the keen blade passed.
Kibei threw the weapon aside. He leaned over her, his dagger
drawn. Then he rose, holding by its tresses the head. For a
moment he gazed on it. Slowly he walked to the pond in the centre
of the garden. Carefully he washed the bloody trophy and placed
it on the curbing. Confronting it he made reverential salutation.
"Kibei keeps his promise to the Kashiku. With Tamagiku he
treads the gloomy paths of Shideyama. Honoured lady—a moment and Kibei follows." Seated before the head reposing on
the curb he opened his clothes. Thrusting the bloody dagger deep
into his left side he slowly drew it across the belly; then made the
upward cut. The body fell forward. Kibei indeed had kept
his word.

CHAPTER XXI

MATTERS ECCLESIASTICAL

INAGAKI SHŌGEN received the news at dawn, just as he was leaving the castle on completion of his night watch. The old knight smiled gravely, thanked the bearer of the message, and rewarded him with lavish hand. The *kago* bearers jolted on. The news had reached the train, and *chūgen* and spearman exchanged whispers. On arrival at the Inagaki *yashiki* his lordship made no motion to descend. The chamberlain raising the curtain gave a cry of horror. The old man lay stretched at the bottom of the little chamber. The dagger and the pool of blood told the tale. Shōgen had followed the example of his son. He, too, now trod the paths of Shideyama.

With laggard tottering step Akiyama Chōzaémon entered his house. Regardless of wife and the cushion she offered, of the hardly repressed tear in her salutation, he cast himself full length on the mats. He buried his face in his arms. The groans which issued from the prostrate body frightened the woman. " The honoured return; has other misfortune fallen on the House?" A shrug of the shoulders, a shiver; then the man half rose and faced her. She was startled at his expression. He was facing the most dreadful, not mere thought of ruin to him and his—" Suzuki San is liar and thief. Fifty *ryŏ* in hand the promise was for abstention. Now he demands twenty *ryŏ* more—the interest on the debt in full." His voice rose to a harsh scream. He laughed despairingly. " Seventy-five *ryŏ* interest, for the loan of a month; and that loan forced on this Chōzaémon by Ito Kwaiba! Kibei has squandered everything. The loan comes back on the bail. If Suzuki holds the interest in hand, he allows the principal, three hundred and fifty *ryŏ*, to stand for the month. Unless he has the

212

lacking twenty-five *ryō* by the fourth hour (9 A.M.) to-morrow, complaint is laid at the office. As usual the interest is written into the face of the bond. The end is certain. This Chōzaémon must cut belly or suffer degradation (*kaieki*)." He looked her over critically. The light of hope died out of his eyes—" Ah! If this Tsuyu could but be sold, the money would be in hand. But she is old and ugly. Pfaugh! . . . " How he hated her at this moment. Some half a dozen years older than Chōzaémon the marriage had been arranged by the parents on truly financial principles. Mizoguchi Hampei was rich, and reputed stingy and saving. Just recently he had fallen into the Edogawa as he returned home late one night. Drunk and surfeited with the foul waters of the stream they had fished him out stone dead. Then it was learned that the old fellow of sixty odd years had several concubines, of the kind to eat into house and fortune. The reversion of the pension, of course, went to the House. In all these years Chōzaémon had never received the dower of O'Tsuyu ; nor dared to press the rich man for it, too generous to his daughter to quarrel with. The funds eagerly looked for by Chōzaémon were found to be *non est inventus*. Probably, if alive, Mizoguchi would have argued that the dower had been paid in instalments. In his grave difficulties Akiyama could find no aid in his wife. She mourned her uselessness—" Willingly would Tsuyu come to the aid of House and husband, join her daughter in the bitter service. But past forty years. . . . 'Tis useless to think of it. Perhaps some expedient will come to mind." She brought out the arm rest and placed it near his side. Then she sat apart watching him. From time to time was heard the tap of her pipe as she knocked out the ashes. At last, overcome by sleep and seeing no sign of movement on the husband's part, she went off to bed, expecting that he would soon follow.

She woke with a start—" Father! Father!" The voice of O'Tsuru rang sharply in her ears. Dazed she half rose and looked around her. Tho daylight streamed through the closed *amado*.

She had been dreaming. With surprise she noted her husband's absence. Had he gone forth? The cries of a bean curd seller were heard without—" *Tōfu! Tōfu!* The best of *tōfu!* " The palatable, cheap, and nutritious food was a standard meal in this house as in many others of Nippon. Akiyama was most generous in indulgence of his passions for gambling, wine, and the women of Shinjuku; and his household with equal generosity were indulged in an economical regimen of *tōfu*. The wife rose to answer the call of the street huckster. Her surprise increased as she found every means of exit bolted and barred, as during the night. The open sliding window in the kitchen roof caught her eye. Surely he had not departed that way! As she opened the back door a murmur of voices, as in the roadway or close by, struck her ear. The *tōfu* seller had his head turned away looking upward. At her call he turned quickly with apology—" Good day, honoured lady. A strange event! Ah! The honoured household still sleeps. All is silent. . . . Strange indeed! A man has hung himself on the big oak tree in the temple ground. Deign to look." He pointed to the big tree close by in the grounds of the Myōgyōji."[1] Sure enough : forty feet from the ground dangled the body of a man. It swayed gently to and fro in harmony with the movement of the branches. A hand seemed to grasp the heart of Tsuyu. The branches of the tree reached far over their roof. The open *hiki- mado!* With feeble voice she said—" My husband; he is strangely absent. Deign, somebody, to climb up and find out whether this man is—of the ward." The startled *tōfu* seller hastened to get aid. Several men entered the garden, quickly mounted to the roof, and thus reached the tree. Said the topmost fellow—" Ma! Ma! It is no pretty sight. He makes a hideous spectacle. The face is black as a rice boiler. The eyes stand out as if ready to burst. The tongue hangs out like a true guard (*hyōtan*). The grin on

---

[1] Next to the Ten-ō Jinja; not that of Samégabashi. To-day retired, neat and clean; without the dirty publicity of larger temples. It is a bit of country in crowded Yotsuya.

the distended mouth is not nice to see. Ah! The rascal has used the merest cord to cut himself off. And he has nearly done so. The head is almost severed." He gave a shout—"Naruhodo! Why, its . . ." One close by silenced him. The men above looked down. They made signs to those below. The women gathered around O'Tsuyu as if to keep her from the sight. She broke away from them as the body was gently lowered to the ground. Her shrieks rang loud. They strove to detach her from the dead body of Chōzaémon. The House ruined, daughter and husband taken out of her life in a single day; the blow was too crushing for a brain harassed by a life with this debauched worthless man. Her warders struggled with one gone clean daft. Years after men grown up from childhood in the ward looked with pity at the feeble ragged old mad beggar woman who crouched by the beautiful bronze dragon which ornaments the water basin of the Ten-ō Jinja. They would drop in her hand a copper "cash," and drive off with rebuke the children who taunted and annoyed her— as they had done years before. Thus were mother and daughter— the innocent—involved in the father's crime against the dread Lady of Tamiya.

All these events created a tremendous stir in Yotsuya. Men disliked to go abroad at night. Women, to their great inconvenience were confined to the house. Two figures approaching each other in the darkness would be seen to hesitate and stop. "What's that—standing, slinking yonder by the wall? Alas! This Kinsaburō, this Genzaémon has evil fortune led him into the clutches of the O'Baké? O'Iwa! O'Iwa!" With that and mad cries they would fall on each other; at times only to exercise restraint after some injury had been done. Hence quarrels arose; feuds, started in all innocence, came into being. Women, as suspects, were chief sufferers. The local atmosphere was overcharged, nerve racked. And so from Honjō to Nakachō (Shinjuku), from Nakanochō (Yoshiwara) to Shinagawa, even in the nearer post towns of Kawasaki, Tsurumi, and Kanagawa the talk was spreading of the strange happenings in Yotsuya of Edo town. Katada Tatéwaki, descendant of that Katada Sámon who, as vassal of Gongen Samon (Iyeyasu) had had this Aoyama-Yotsuya district in fief, now first began his inquiries into the affair. The Katada had wide possessions elsewhere at the time of the grant. Samon had gifted much of his new fief as temple land, and on the old maps of the day this part of Edo is a blood red splash, indication of these many establishments. But the Katada influence still prevailed through the ward, indeed through the more than good will of the beneficiaries. Tatéwaki's *yashiki* was at the top of Ushigomézaka. His modest pension of a thousand *koku* by no means represented the extent of his power. Iémon became frightened at the storm gathering against him. He was open to all suggestions of remedy for the cataleptic state into which O'Hana had fallen. The neighbour gossips suggested calling in the Daihō-in of Shiomachi. A service kept part at least of the money in the ward. They had their share in provision and consumption; the fifty *ryō* necessary were much to them—and to Iémon in his present circumstances.

The neighbours were assembled at Tamiya. Iémon went forth to greet the Daihō-in. With his attendant *kannushi* and train he presented himself at the entrance. Iémon was prostrate in salutation before the great man.—"Reverential thanks for the condescension. Deign to enter this unfortunate house." The Shintō priest was brusque, as is the way of the kind. Himself he was the *samurai*, with all the tone of official manner. "Ha! Ha! Salutation to all." He gave a comprehensive glance through the assembly and lost none of them in the process. He approached the couch of O'Hana. He opened the closed eyes, which stared fixedly into space as of one dead. He raised an arm upright from the body. Stepping aside, he squatted. Some moments passed. The arm remained rigidly upright. Satisfied, the Daihō-in signed to his attendants. Raising O'Hana they placed her in a sitting posture on a mat. Her hair was arranged in *ichōmage*.[2] A *gohei* was placed between her hands. Then the Daihō-in began the recitation of the prayers and charms. The other priests gave voice at times in response. All present were awe-struck. The women hardly breathed, leaning eagerly forward. Their eyes took on a vacant stare, as if themselves mesmerized. The *gohei* began to tremble; then to shake violently. The woman's hair fell down in disorder around her face. All turned away their faces. Some women gave smothered cries. It was O'Iwa San who glared at them out of those eyes. The Daihō-in eagerly leaned close over O'Hana—" O'Iwa: where are you? What has become of your body? Be sure to speak the truth. Don't attempt to lie to the priest. . . . You don't know? Ah! you would be obstinate in your grudge. The charm shakes and quivers; it possesses O'Iwa. . . . You would rest in Samonchō ground? That is much to ask; particularly when the body is not in hand. . . . A substitute will do? Ah! Prayers? . . . For a year, at morn and night of each day? That is terrific. Consider the cost. . . . You care not for the cost! Only then will you cease to afflict the ward? . . . Very well: humbly this Daihō-in transmits the will of the dead."

Thus did the priestly mediator interpret to his gaping auditors the mumbling and cries given forth by O'Hana. The wild look faded from her eyes. She rolled over as in a faint. The priests raised her up. The Daihō-in turned to Iémon and the assembly— " The words of O'Iwa have been heard through this woman. O'Hana has been possessed by O'Iwa. Hence her trance. . . . Heigh! Water!" He began making passes over his patient— " The stage has passed. O'Hana no longer is possessed by O'Iwa. The wronged lady leaves O'Hana to peace. O'Hana is completely herself again. O'Iwa is all delusion. O'Hana believes this. She

[2] A young girl's method of fixing the hair; but Ryuō uses the term. Gohei are the paper strips used as offering. Usually attached to a short stick.

believes firmly. The Daihō-in tells her to believe. O'Iwa does not haunt O'Hana. O'Iwa has no ill will against O'Hana." He looked fixedly and with command into the eyes of O'Hana. His voice rang clear and authoritative. Then he began gently to stroke the back of her head, her neck and spine. "All is well?" "Hai! Hai! This Hana is completely restored. All is well." With a little sigh she sank back, to be laid on the cushions in a sleep which all wondered to see was most natural. Those present were in transports of delight. They buzzed approval as the Daihō-in addressed Iémon. "The Daihō-in has done his part. All have heard the words of O'Iwa San. The rest lies with the temple. Deign to receive these words. The Daihō-in returns." With his pack voicing loudly at his tail he left the entrance gate. The assembly streamed after. Iémon was left alone, biting his thumbs in helpless rage. He was aghast. "The old fox! What is to be done, pressed as Iémon is for funds? How is this Iémon to act? Refusal means the open hostility of the whole ward. It will turn against him. Ah! What a miserable old scamp. He did it all himself; he and his confederates. The gods descend from above; the Daihō-in shakes the *gohei* from below— and those fools believe, to the ruin of Iémon!"

Hence he would have postponed the costly appeal to the temple. Within the week a committee of the ward waited upon him. As if expecting them, Iémon gave ready compliance. With four or five other gentlemen he waited upon Shūden Ōshō, the famous priest of the temple of the Gyōran Kwannon. The Lady Merciful, Kwannon Sama, seemed the fitting deity to whom appeal should be made. A word is to be said as to this famous manifestation of the goddess. Told by Ryuō at length, of necessity here the account is much abridged. Gyōran Kwannon—Kwannon of the fish-basket—has several other names. She is called the Namagusai Kwannon, from the odour of fresh blood attached to the pursuit; the Byaku Kwannon, or the white robed; the Baryufu Kwannon, as wife of Baryu the fisherman. The image of the Byaku Kwannon exists.[3] It is carved in white wood, stained black, with a scroll in the right hand, and holding a fish basket (*gyōran*) in the left hand. The story of Baryu, and of his connection with Kwannon, is of more moment.

In Morokoshi (China) there is a place called Kinshaden. Across the bay from Edo-Tōkyō is Kazusa with its ninety-nine villages, one of which has the same name—Kinshaden. The fishing population of Nippon is a rough lot. From babyhood there is little but quarrelling and fighting between the bands which control the different wards of the villages. The relations between the people are very primitive. One of the important occupations is the *iwashi*, or pilchard, fishing. To pull in the nets loaded with the fish requires the united effort of the whole village population, men, women, even children. Among their toilers the people of Kinshaden noted a young girl of some sixteen or seventeen years; easily noted by the great beauty and attraction of face and figure, the willing readiness and wonderful strength she showed in her struggles with the weighted net. As she appeared several times at last some men went up to her—"Girl, you are a stranger here. For your aid thanks are offered. Who may you be; and whence from? Strangers, even in kindness, in Nippon must not conceal their names." The girl smiled—"I come from Fudarakusan in the South Ocean. . . . Where is Fudarakusan? It is in India. . . . And India? It is in the South Ocean, the Nankai." To the wonder expressed at her coming such a distance of thousands of *ri.*—" I come, I serve, for my husband."—" Your husband? Pray who may he be, in these parts?"—" Not yet is he chosen," answered the girl. " Come! The nets are drawn, the fishing ended for the day. I will ascend that rock; read the sutra of the Lady Kwannon. He who can first memorize it shall be my husband." Ready was the assent to such an attractive proposal— a beautiful helpmate in prospect, one endowed with surprising strength for her frail form, and who seemed to bring luck to the

---

[3] At the Gyōranji of Matsuzakachō in the Mita district of Tōkyō.

efforts of the village in the struggle for a livelihood. Even the
Nipponese prejudice against strangers paled before such practical
qualification.

The maid ascended to the rostrum. For three days she read
and expounded the holy sutra of the Lady Kwannon. On the
fourth day the fisherman Baryu—young, handsome, strong—felt
sure that he could answer to the test. "Woman, descend! To-
day this Baryu will repeat the sutra, expound its meaning." With
seeming surprise and merriment the girl obeyed. Baryu took her
place. Without slip or fault he repeated the sutra, expounded
the intricacies of its meaning. The girl bowed low in submission.
"Condescend to admit my humble person to the hut of Baryu the
fisherman. To-night she pollutes with her presence a corner of
his bed-chamber." Rejoicing Baryu at once took her to his home,
where he would act the husband. At first gently she rebuked him.
"These rough people of Kinshaden have regard to nothing! There
is such a rite as marriage. Nine times are the saké cups to be
drained between husband and wife. Thus is established this important relation. In the connection between man and woman
there is such a thing as etiquette. This observed, the woman
passes to the possession of the man. For the woman, second marriage there is none."

Thus were the decencies of the marriage bed taught to the
rough fisherman. Near dawn Baryu awoke with surprise. His
bed-fellow was in the last extremities. Dripping with sweat, she
seemed to be melting away. Already she was unconscious. Then
vomiting forth water she died. Baryu was tremendously put out.
To lose a wife, who barely had been a wife; one so beautiful, so
strong; this was extremely vexatious. "This won't do at all!
Why has such a misfortune befallen this Baryu? O'Kabe (Miss
Plaster) and O'Nabé (Miss Stewpan) endured without mishap
the passage of their marriage night. . . . Hai! Hai!" in reply
to a friend knocking at the door. "Baryu cannot go to the fishing
to-day. . . . The woman? She has died. Baryu's wife is

dead." Opening the door he retailed his experience to the wondering friend. As they talked, along came a priest most strangely dressed for this land. Approaching them he said—" Is this the house of Baryu? " At the fisherman's acknowledgement—" Has a girl come here? . . . Dead! Deign to let this foolish cleric hang eyes upon her." Baryu thought he would take his turn at questions. " And you; whence from?" " From Fudarakusan in the Nankai." " Get you hence, frantic interloper," broke in Baryu with grief and anger. " Enough has this Baryu heard of Fudarakusan. Baryu must needs observe his state as widower. The month must pass before he seeks a wife. And more than half its days remain! But look." Mollified by the humble attitude of the priest he went and raised the coverlet from the woman's body. He uttered a cry of surprise. " Oya! Oya! She has disappeared. There is naught here but a wooden image. Ma! Ma! what a curious figure—with scroll and fish basket, just as the wife appeared at the beach. This is what one reads of in books." He turned to the priest in wonder and as seeking explanation. Said the latter with earnest and noble emphasis—" Favoured has been this Baryu. The Kwannon of Fudarakusan of Nankai has shown herself before his very eyes. For the reform of this wicked people, to teach them the holy writing, she has condescended to submit to the embraces of the fisherman. Let not Baryu think of other marriage. For him has come the call to leave this world. Fail not to obey." Baryu rushed to the door, to catch but a glimpse of the departing form. All sign of the priest quickly faded. Baryu returned to the wooden figure lying where once had reposed the body of the beautiful girl. It was a most unsatisfactory substitute for the flesh and blood original. But Baryu made the most of it. He took his vow. He shaved his head, becoming a priest to recite and preach the sutra of the Lady Kwannon. Hence this Kwannon is known as the Baryufu Kwannon—wife of Baryu the fisherman. Hence she is called the Kwannon of the fish basket, in honour of the aid she brought the people of this village and land.

CHAPTER XXII

THE RITES FOR O'IWA SAN

Iémōn fared as badly at the hands of the Buddha as at those of the Kami. Shūden Ōshō, as guardian of the sacred image of the Gyōran Kwannon, was a very great man indeed. After some delay the deputation from Samonchō was ushered into his presence. Iémon made profound obeisance and explained the cause of their presence. The visitations of O'Iwa to the district were causing the greatest public commotion. Not as a matter of private interest, but of public utility his interference was sought. If Iémon thought to abstract a copper "cash" from the priestly treasury he made a gross mistake. Besides, the individual who disturbs the public peace suffers severely from official mediation, no matter what form this takes. Shūden inquired minutely as to the visit of the Daihō-in, of which he seemed to have heard. What information Iémon might have withheld, or minimised, or given a different complexion, was cheerfully volunteered by others, who also corrected and amplified any undue curtailing or ambiguity of their spokesman. Shūden listened to Iémon with a gravity and an expression hovering between calculation and jeering comment. He turned from him to the committee, giving great attention to those scholiasts on the text of the orator. He gravely wagged his head in agreement with the rival prelate, whose acumen he highly extolled. Memorial services were to be provided for a year. It was, after all, merely a form of restitution to the wronged lady. But also the wandering spirit of O'Iwa was to be suitably confined. Here lay the difficulty. Recitation of the sutra for seven continuous days; proper inhumation of the substitute beyond possibility of disturbance, would surely lay a spell on the enraged lady, and put an end to the curse of one dying an unworshipped

222

spirit. For the burial a bamboo was to be provided—of length one *shaku* eight *bu* (one foot nine inches) between the joints.

With this notice Iémon and his companions withdrew. He was resigned to the payment of the fifty *ryō* necessary for the memorial services extending over the year. The inclusion in the bamboo was another affair. The finding of such was about as easy as the fishing for black pearls. He soon found that securing the substitute and securing the body of O'Iwa San for proper inhumation were kindred problems. After looking over all the bamboo which had drifted to Edo and was in the hands of the world secular—and most of it at surprisingly cheap rates—the committee was driven back on the religious world. They soon found that the article in question was kept in stock only at the Gyōran Kwannondō. Resorting to the priestly offices, Iémon felt convinced that the grave salutation of the incumbent official—they directed him to the treasury—concealed a derisive grin at his expense. He was sure of it when he learned that this rare object could be had—for another fifty *ryō*. The temple gave no credit; but Suzuki, the usurer who was one of the party, after some demur agreed to hand over the amount, which he had just received from Akiyama Shōzaémon, the service bounty of the daughter O'Tsuru. With some reluctance the long nosed, long faced, long limbed Kamimura went security for the repayment on their return to the ward. With cheerful recklessness Iémon pledged the last chance of any income from the pension and resources of Tamiya for the next three years; so heavily was he in debt. Shūden on his part lost no time. With at least one member of the committee in attendance, to see that he played fair, for seven days vigorously was the sutra intoned by the loudest and most brazen of his subordinates, backed by the whole body of priests. Day and night a priest would slip to the side altar, to invoke the pity of the Buddha on the wandering spirit of the deceased lady in few pithy but hasty words, and to spend the rest of his vigil in a decent slumberous immobility.

The seven days accomplished, the procession formed. Six men in new uniforms—provided by Iémon—made pretence of great difficulty in carrying the long box (*nagamochi*). Four men carried the *sambo,* or sacred tray of white wood, on which rested the section of bamboo wrapped by the hands of Shūden himself in the sacred roll of the sutra of Kwannon. Officialdom of the ward was present. The citizens turned out *en masse.* For long Yotsuya had not witnessed such a scene. Within its precincts the *yashiki* of the great nobles were conspicuously absent; their long processions of spearman, *chūgen, samurai* and officials were only to be witnessed at times on the highway which leaves Shinjuku for the Kōshūkaidō and the alternate and then little used Ashigaratōge road. Arrived at Samonchō the ground selected was inspected by Shūden. The bishop's eyebrows puckered in questioning mien. "Here there are too many people. Is there no other place?" They led him to another site. The wrinkle deepened to a frown—"Here there are too many children. Their frolics and necessities are unseemly. These would outrage the tender spirit. Is there no other place?" The committee was nonplussed. Iémon was in terrible fear lest all his effort and expenditure would go for naught but to swell Shūden's cash roll. A thought came into his mind. "There is no other open land, but the garden of Tamiya is wide and secluded. The wall prevents public access." People looked at him aghast. He was either mad with courage, or obstinate in disbelief in the power of O'Iwa San so plainly manifested. Shūden paid no attention to that surprised whispering. "Deign to show the way thither." Thus the procession took its course back to Teramachi and through the gate of Tamiya. A spot was selected, just before the garden gate. It was open to the salutation and vows of passers-by, yet could be shut off from direct access toward house and public. At Shūden's order a hole was dug, just four *shaku* (feet) in depth. The Oshō began the recitation of the sutra. The priests stood by in vigilant attention. As the last word reverberated on the bishop's

lips they seized the sutra wrapped bamboo, slipped it in the long
box—bum! the lock snapped. The congregation was tremendously
impressed. For a decent time Shūden remained in prayer and
meditation. " The charm is complete. O'Iwa no longer wanders,
to her own penance and the disaster of men. Henceforth he who
says she does so lies. Hearken to the words of Shūden. Admit
none such to your company. Let not children make this place a
playground. Shūden has given warning. Pollution surely follows. Their habits are unseemly, an insult to the dead. Even
as to parents, those with infants on their backs are specifically to
be excluded." He tied a paper covered with Sanscrit characters
to a bamboo stick. This was placed on a white wood stake. On
the stake he wrote kindred words, converting it into the counterfeit of a *sotoba*. Neither he nor any present knew what the words
meant, or had care as to their ignorance of this essential of re-
ligion. Then he and his train gathered up their gowns and gal-
loped out the gate, after practice and receipt of grave courtesy,
so much did temple differ from shrine in its contact with secular
life. The assembled multitude departed ; much edified by the day's
proceedings, and with low comment to each other on the dilapida-
tion of Tamiya, its fall from the one time spruce and flourishing
state. Introduce a spendthrift in the door, and the wealth leaks
from every crevice. The spirit of Tamiya Matazaémon must
grieve at this sight. But why did he bring in as *muko* a stranger?"
    Iémon could flatter himself on the efficacy of the divine
interposition. The public mind was quieted. Nothing more was
heard of O'Iwa San. Only the daily summons, on one pretext or
another, to the ward office troubled him. The *yakunin* also made
a practice of taking in Tamiya en route to performance of their
various missions. This he knew was a practice as to men under
observation. He went over his career as known to Yotsuya.
There was nothing in it to call for question. Official censure does
not rest its case on a ghost story. The famous investigation of
Echizen no Kami (Ōoka) into the Yaeume case of Yamada was

15

matter of later days. Moreover, all his troubles were lightened
by the state of O'Hana, the devoted object of unwavering affection. Ever since the Daihō-in had mesmerized her, impressed his
will on her, the daily improvement could be marked. Now again
she was her normal self; sadly thin and worn in spirit, a woman
tired out, but yet the figure of O'Hana and in her right mind. To
him she was the beautiful tradition of the past and just as beautiful as ever in actuality. Two weeks had passed since Shūden's
experiment. One night, as the hour of the pig (9 P.M.) was
striking, there came a knocking at the door. O'Hana rose from
her sewing. "Danna, Kamimura San would say a word." Iémon
made a gesture of annoyance. The long man had shadowed him,
ever since entering on the engagement of bail. He went to the
door and looked at his caller with amazement. Kamimura, his
hair in confusion, was stark naked except for his wife's under
cloth—and she was almost a dwarf. He stretched out a hand to
Iémon, half in threat, half in begging. "Iémon Uji, a word:
condescend to grant this Goémon ten *ryō* in silver, not in words.
Suzuki the usurer has come on Goémon as bail of Iémon, in the
matter of the exorcism. To-day he stripped the house of everything. Wife and children, hungry and almost naked, lie on bare
boards. When Goémon begged mercy, that he go to Tamiya, the
wretched fellow jeered. 'Tamiya? Tamiya has but *hibachi* and
three mats; the clothes worn by himself and wife. The house
and land of Tamiya is but a reversion. Suzuki gets nothing at
Tamiya but a lawsuit which would not pay the office fees.
Kamimura is rich; his house is well supplied. One petition; and
not only expenses, but the debt finds payment. Hence Suzuki
troubles not Tamiya.' With this off he went deriding me. Deign
the loan, Iémon San. Condescend at least the shelter of clothes
and food."

To the wretched fellow Iémon could make no reply. Ten *ryō*!
Kamimura might as well have asked for ten thousand *ryō*. In
house and land Iémon was secure. These belonged to the heirship

of Tamiya as long as the House maintained its status. The pension was long mortgaged. The farms had disappeared. The trouble of Goémon pained him. He could only refuse; palliating the refusal with vague promises as to the near future. He would effect a loan. The debt of Suzuki repaid, all his goods would be restored to Kamimura San. Goémon took this talk at its real value. Shaking his fist he berated Iémon with violent words. "Ah! Shame is brought to the House of Kamimura, wretchedness to his family—and by this vile stranger. It is Iémon with his heartless wicked treatment of O'Iwa San, who has wrought distress and ruin to the ward. For Goémon there is neither food nor clothing? Wait! Time shall bring his vengeance on Iémon and his House." Iémon would have detained him; sought in some way to mollify him, at least get a hint as to how he purposed injury. Goémon shook him off as one would a reptile. With a wild laugh he went out naked as he was into the darkness.

He had no definite purpose in mind. However, as he passed the garden gate of Tamiya his eye caught the factitious *sotoba* standing white in the fitful moonlight. He stood stock still; then clapped his hands in mad joy and decision. Hastening to his home he sought out an old battered mattock and a rusty spade. Soon he was back at the garden gate. A blow and the bar fell. Goémon passed within. "She lies but four *shaku* deep. The task is quickly performed. None pass here at this hour." The dirt flew under his nervous arms. Soon he had the box out on the ground beside him. A peel of thunder; he must hasten, or stand a ducking from the coming storm. He laughed. What had a naked man to fear from getting wet? The clothes he wore would not spoil. Why did not man dress in a towel, as after the bath; its use, to wipe the moisture from the body. Now his eyes were fixed in curiosity on the bamboo staff before him. The first few drops of the rainstorm fell on his bare shoulders, but he disregarded them. "Naruhodo! How heavy it is! O'Iwa in life hardly weighed more. Lady of Tamiya—show pity on this

Goémon. Iémon and O'Hana—those wicked voluptuaries—prosper and flourish, while Goémon is brought to beggary and starvation. Deign to visit the wrath of O'Iwa San on these vile wretches. Seize and kill them. Goémon sets O'Iwa free." He seized the mattock. Raising it overhead he brought the edge sharply down on the bamboo stake. At the moment there was a violent peal of thunder rolling off into a crash and rattle. The landscape was lit up by the vivid lightning. People uneasily turned over on their beds.

Shortly after dawn Iémon woke with a start. Don-don-don, don-don-don. There was a tremendous rapping at his door. O'Hana could hear but a whispered consultation going on without the *amado*. Iémon returned to the room. His face was white; his step tottered. Hastily he donned an outer robe. To her question he made scant reply, so agitated was he. His one idea was to keep from her what he had just heard. In the garden he found his wardsmen assembled. All were dumbfounded and aghast. They looked at each other and then at the broken bamboo tube. Close by lay the body of the man who had done the deed. Brains and blood had oozed from the hole in the skull in which yet stuck the pointed end of the mattock sunk deep within. Evidently the instrument had rebounded from the resilient surface of the bamboo. A by-stander pointed to the tiny fracture near the hard knot of the staff. It was a small thing, but enough to destroy all the past labours. Iémon went up to look at the body. " Why! 'Tis Goémon." To their questioning he told how Kamimura had called on the previous night, his rage at the inability of Iémon to aid him in distress. With hanging heads, eyes on the ground, and wagging tongues, all departed to their homes. Later the body of Goémon was borne to his house by neighbours. Iémon picked up the bamboo staff. Carrying it within he placed it in a closet. It was as costly an object as the house had ever held. He was in despair.

It was on that very day, at the seventh hour (3 P.M.), that

O'Hana heard a call at the door. " A request to make! A request to make!" She recoiled from the sight presented. A beggar stood at the entrance of Tamiya. A dirty mat wrapped around his body, feet and arms emerging from bandages, making him like to some hideous insect with its carapace, his face wrapped in a towel, the effects of leprosy were hideously patent."—" What do you here? There is naught to be had. Pray depart at once." The answer was in tones the very harshness of which seemed to cause pain to the utterer—" The request is to Iémon Dono Condescend to notify him." With fearful glance O'Hana shrank within. Iémon noted her nervous quivering. Promptly he was on his feet —" A beggar has frightened Hana? Such are to be severely dealt with." He went to the entrance. " A beggar, and such a fellow? How comes it entrance has been had to the ward? There is nothing for you here. If you would escape the dogs and bastinado, get you hence at once." The man did not stir from the spot on which he stood. Slowly he opened the mat held round his body (*komokaburi*), one of the coarse kind used to wrap round *saké* barrels. He was clothed in rags glued together by the foul discharges of his sores. He removed the towel from his face. The ghastly white and red blotches, the livid scars of the leper, the head with patches of scurfy hair ready to fall at a touch, startled even Iémon the priest. He would not have touched this man, expelled him by force, for all the past wealth of Tamiya. The intruder noted the effect produced.

" To such has the wrath of O'Iwa San brought this Chōbei. Does not Iémon, the one-time neighbour Kazuma, recognize Chōbei? And yet all comes through Iémon. Child, wife, means of life, all these have failed Chōbei. In the jail robbed of everything, degenerate in mind and body, Chōbei has found refuge at nights in the booths of street vendors; on cold wet nights, even in the mouths of the filthy drains. Fortunate is he when fine weather sends him to rest on the river banks. To seek rest; not to find it. O'Iwa stands beside him. When eyelids drowse

Chōbei is aroused, to find her face close glaring into his. Beg and implore, yet pardon there is none. ' Chōbei has a debt to pay to Iwa. In life Chōbei must repay by suffering; yet not what Iwa suffered. Think not to rest.' Some support was found in a daughter, sold in times past to the Yamadaya of Yoshiwara. There the child grew up to become the great profit of the house. The influence of the Kashiku was all powerful to secure entrance. For a night Chōbei was to find food and a bed. But that night came Kibei San. He killed the Kashiku—crushed her out, as one would crush an insect. This Chōbei nearly died; but Kibei left him to the mercy of O'Iwa. Her mercy!" He would have thrown out his arms in weary gesture of despair. The pain and effort were too great. He moaned. "Last night Chōbei sought relief. Of late years the river has been spanned, for passers-by and solace of the human refuse. Standing on Ryōgokubashi the dark waters of the river called to Chōbei as they swept strongly by to the sea. A moment, and all would be ended. About to leap hands were laid on Chōbei's shoulders. He was dragged back. Turning—lo! 'twas O'Iwa San. Another creature, still fouler than she, with sloping eyelid, bald head, and savage look, stood by. Said O'Iwa San—' And Chōbei would end all—with luxury before his eyes! Chōbei dies not but with the consent of Iwa. Get you to Yotsuya; to Iémon and Hana, living in luxury and Tamiya. Aid will not be refused you.' And so she brought me here. Deign to hear the prayer of Chōbei. Allow him to die in Yotsuya, upon the *tatami;* not on the bare earth, to be thrown on the moor for dogs to gnaw. Grant him burial in temple ground."

He changed his theme; the feeble quivering hands clasped his belly. "Ah! This pinching hunger. Double Chōbei's suffering; of mind and body. Apply for alms or food, and the leper is repulsed. See! Two fingers remain on this hand. Count of the rest fills out the tale for but one member. O'Hana San, condescend a rice ball for this Chōbei. You, at least, know not the pinch of hunger. . . . Ah! She still possesses some of that beauty and charm for which Iémon has brought ruin upon all." Before the horrible lascivious leer of this object O'Hana fled. Left alone Iémon spoke. He had been thinking—" Chōbei has spoken well. From Iémon he is entitled to relief. Chōbei shall die on his mat. But in such shape nothing can be done. Get you hence. Buy clothing fit to appear before men's eyes. In the bath wash that pus-laden body. Then come to Iémon. Relief shall be granted Chōbei." Wrapping a *ryō* in paper he passed it to the leper. It was the last coin he possessed. O'Hana now returned with five or six rice balls savoured with salt. Fascinated, the two watched the horrible diseased stumps awkwardly shoving the food into the toothless mouth, cramming it in, and breaking it up so as not to lose the savour of a grain. "Until to-morrow," said Chōbei. He picked up his stick. In silence the man and woman watched him. "Leaning on his bamboo staff he crawled away like some insect." O'Hana looked inquiringly at Iémon. He turned away his head.

Through the dusk Chōbei crawled across the Ryōgokubashi. The words of the woman O'Také had come true. He had a sense of being followed. He turned at the sound of footsteps. At sight of a *samurai* in deep hat, mechanically he stretched out hands and self in the roadway, begging an alms. The man drew apart, passing him in disgust and haste. Chōbei went on. He had no aim. It was with surprise that he found himself, as often of late, on the embankment of the North Warigesui. He looked down on the foul place of O'Iwa's disappearance. "A foul ending; but after all an end. One night! One night's sleep! Deign, lady of Tamiya, to grant pardon and respite to Chōbei. Just one hour of sleep." Carefully he adjusted his mat. Painfully he stretched himself out on it. "To die on the mat. Such was the word of Iémon." He felt his rags. "It was well he agreed. Chōbei had other means to force compliance. Well, 'tis for later use." A continued rustling aroused him. Some one was cautiously picking a way through the dry grass of the past winter, was creeping toward him. He half rose. Seeing that concealment was no longer possible, the man rushed on him. Chōbei struggled to his feet, as one to fight for life. "Life is dear. Why kill Chōbei the leper? Is he a test for some new sword? Deign to pardon. The flesh of the leper is too rotten. It defiles the weapon. Chōbei has been the *samurai;* he knows. . . . Ah! Respite there is none. 'Tis Iémon! Iémon of Tamiya would kill Chōbei!" He shouted and coupled the names in his despair. Fearful of discovery, of being overheard, Iémon did not delay. The gleaming weapon descended. Standing over the body Iémon showed uncertainty. He had some thought of search; even bent down over it. But he could not touch those foul rags. His nicety of feeling, almost womanlike—recoiled. Besides, what more had Iémon to do with the leper Chōbei. Their account was closed. Should he leave the body where it was? Recognition might convey some danger, at least inconvenience. He looked around for means to sink it in these waters, and yet not handle its repulsiveness. A *shōyu* tub, old but fairly intact, lay upon the bank. It caught his eye. He rolled it up to the corpse. Gingerly he girdled the body of the dead man with his *tasuki* (shoulder cord). Now tight fast it clasped the roundness of the barrel. This he filled with stones, drove in the head, and with a shove sent it and its burden into the Warigesui. "That will hold him down. The rotten punk! Three days, and none could recognize him." Then he set off at rapid pace for Yotsuya.

CHAPTER XXIII

SANZUGAWA BRIDGELESS: THE FLOWERLESS ROAD TRAVERSED BY THE DEAD

It was the hour of the pig (9 p.m.) before Iémon reached the house in Yotsuya. To his surprise he found the *amado* still open on the garden. Some one was lying face downward on the *rōka*. It was O'Hana. To his alarmed inquiry as to what was wrong she answered in the voice of one trying to suppress great pain. " This Hana knows not. Opening a closet to get the spices used in preparing the meal, a rat sprang out. It scratched the face of Hana. Truly the pain is very great." She groaned. Iémon gently raised her. At the look on his face O'Hana said— " There is a mirror in the toilet set (*kyōdai*). Deign to get it for Hana." He did not get it—this dower gift once of O'Iwa —but tried to soothe her—" Let be : the wounds soon will heal. The pain will pass away." She shoved him aside and ran to the toilet stand. She took the hand-mirror to the solitary lamp lighting the room. Aghast she contemplated her features. One side of the face was completely discoloured. It was a dark red, almost black, with the mark of five fingers plainly visible, as if a hand had struck her. No rat had made this wound. O'Hana leaned over, her head resting almost on her knees. Iémon touched her shoulder—" Don't mind it. Truly the pain will pass with dawn. Hana . . ." He drew back from the scowling madness in the face raised to him—" Sa! Sa! Iémon! Iémon! Easily did you get hold of all my property, to waste it on O'Hana. 'Twas like grasping wet millet. Then, barbarous as you were, you sold me to the vile life of a street harlot. Ah! Vengeance!" In fright Iémon retreated. O'Hana, taking herself to be O'Iwa, all her madness had returned. She sprang up. Screens were beaten and torn to pieces. With the heavy mirror she turned on him, seeking

233

vengeance for her imagined wrongs. Iémon narrowly escaped injury as he dashed in to grapple with her. He succeeded in dragging her away from the lamp. Thus did this wild battle rage in the half dark room. The fictitious strength of the ill woman gave out. He held her on the floor, as one subdued. As she relapsed into a sleep, almost of unconsciousness, he ventured to release her. Going to a closet he placed the mirror beside the bamboo stick; both hidden away.

All night he watched over her. Wearied out, with day he sought an aid readily given. The nurse, however, in alarm soon roused him. O'Hana was raving madly in a high fever. The woman could not restrain her. Her cries were terrible, but not more so than the speech from her lips—" O'Iwa, pardon! With the drugs of Suian this Hana would palsy O'Iwa's mind and body; poison the very springs of life, cut off all hope of issue. Ah! Vain the love of a man. All is granted him; body and goods. Iémon sells Hana for a street harlot. Out with him! Help! . . . Ah! Kwaiba aids—in all his rottenness. How horrible he is—huge vacant eye holes, the purple whitish flesh gnawed and eaten. . . . Ugh! He stinks! . . . Nay! 'Tis not Kwaiba. 'Tis Chōbei: Chōbei the leper, who would embrace this Hana. Iémon comes. There is murder in his eye—for Hana to see, not Chōbei. Away! Away! . . . Again, there she comes!'' She grasped the nurse's arm, and pointed to the just lighted *andon* which barely relieved the shadows of the darkening night; was it the woman's imagination? By the light, dimly outlined; sat O'Iwa San. Her hair hung down around face and body half turned aside. The bulging forehead, the puffed eyelids, were not to be mistaken. The woman shook off the sick girl's hand and fled the house. Iémon did not try to prevent her. He was as one paralyzed. He, too, had seen, and was convinced.

To watch through the night was the task of the anxious and wearied man. In the day a *yakunin* had come, with formal notice to attend next day the office of Katada Tatéwaki Dono. His lordship had an inquiry to make. The summons was not to be disregarded, no matter what his own exigencies. O'Hana had dropped into a cataleptic state. As the eighth hour (1 A.M.) approached he thought to clear brain and body by the rest of a few moments. His head had barely touched the pillow when sleep followed. The bell of Gwanshōji struck the hour. It roared and reverberated through Tamiya. Iémon awoke; an oppression like suffocation pervaded his whole body. Opening his eyes they stared into the wide white flat face of O'Iwa. Her eyes were now alive, darting gleams of fire deep from within the puffed and swollen lids. He felt her wild disordered hair sweeping his face as she swayed a little, still retaining her post and clutch on his bosom—"Iémon knows Iwa now! Hana knows Iwa now! Sworn to seize and kill both for seven births—come! Now it is that Iwa completes her vengeance." As she shook and pressed on him he came gradually out of his sleep. With a shout he cast her backwards. Springing up he grasped the sword at his pillow. Madly he dealt blow after blow on the body before him. To the groans he replied by fresh blows.

An uproar without called him to himself. Don—don—don, don, don, don. There was knocking at the gate. Iémon hastily trimmed up the wick of the lamp. He leaned over the body. O'Hana! The young man stooped over her, leaning on the gory sword. Great drops of cold sweat stood out on his forehead. A shout came from without. "In his lordship's name! Open, or force will be used." Why had the summons for the day been anticipated? The unhappy ravings of O'Hana flashed to his mind. Iémon no longer reasoned. A cunning insane light was in his eyes. Softly he made his way to the *amado* fronting on the garden. No one was without. In the rain and storm he might escape. Traversing the darkness he noted, however, the man posted at the gate in the rear. Springing on the roof of the shed he looked over into Teramachi. It was deserted. With the bloody sword he hacked off the sharp points of the bamboo stakes. They now aided his flight over the wall. He cast the weapon aside. In a few minutes he disappeared in rapid flight down the street. When Katada Tatéwaki, accompanied by his men, at last broke down the stout resistance offered by the outer door of Tamiya he found the house empty, except for the dead body of O'Hana, lying in its pool of blood. She was still warm. He took it for mere murder, giving more urgent directions for immediate pursuit. Methodically he searched the house, down to the very rubbish pile. The seal of Tamiya was secured. This meant much. With'sceptical smile he handled the broken bamboo stick found in a closet. He did not show the discovery to his men.

Where did Iémon go? The unhappy man himself could not have told what happened in the intervening days. He came to consciousness in the darkness of a spring night, just before the dawn. The stars were beginning to pale in the East. The landscape had the livid eerie light in which it is uncertain whether day or night is to be the issue. With surprise Iémon looked around him; then shuddered. The stagnant waters of Warigesui's filthy stream lay beneath him. He had found rest on the bank, at the very place where Chōbei had died under his hand.

"The Sanzugawa—without hills or bridges;
On highway traversed by the dead, flowers there are none." [1]

The *yama* (〴) refers to Yamada Chōbei; the *hashi* (﹢﹦) to Takahashi Iémon; the *hana* (﹢ ﹢) to O'Hana, the wife of Iémon. Such was the then interpretation of the old poem.

Iémon could go no further. His course was run. He knew it; but how end life? At heart he was an arrant coward. Determined to cut belly he drew the dagger he had kept with him. A shudder went through him at sight of the steel. Ah! Better the

---

[1] *Sansugawa: Yama* mo nakereba, *hashi mo nashi; shinde no tabiji hana wa nao nashi.* Sanzugawa, the river crossed by the dead.

green slime of the waters below. He thrust the blade back into its scabbard. Moodily standing and gazing down, he gave an idle kick to a stone near by. Dislodged, it swayed, then rolled heavily down the bank, to plunge noisily into the stream, disturb its noisome depths. The effect was surprising. Following its course with his eye Iémon suddenly gave a yell of horror. Eyes starting from his head, arms raised high, he bent toward the stream. Hair standing on end he watched the hideous object rise to the surface. The face of Chōbei, purple and bloated, the lips half gnawed and open in a fiendish grin, looked up at him. Down came the arms, and Iémon put hands over eyes to shut out the fearful vision. A horrid curiosity drove him again to view it. Was he mad? This time the barrel in its slow revolution brought to view the wide flat face, the bulging brow and heavy lids, the tangled, disordered hair of the drowned O'Iwa. Scream after scream of the now frantic wretch rang in the air. These waters! Seek death there! No! No! A thousand times—No! He turned to flee the place, but his legs refused the service. With fell purpose he ripped the blade from its scabbard, tore open his clothes to give the deadly thrust. As he raised the dagger invisible hands seized his arm. When he would release it, the other arm was seized. Everywhere these hands held him fast. He raged, tore, struggled madly to elude their grasp. Then, over-come, he fainted.

Katada Tatéwaki from the top of the bank had been watching the struggle of his men. He came forward and looked down at the bound and helpless creature. "'Tis he: in very fact." On order a bamboo pole was fetched, and run between the bound hands and feet. Thus like some beast was Iémon conveyed to the nearest ward office. The formalities were few and soon over. To avoid chance of repetition of the scene they conveyed him as he was. Thus began the brutal progress across Edo in full daylight. People turned and stared after this escort of the man-beast. At a distance they took the burden as some savage bear, or perhaps one of those reputed "*tanuki*" so noxious in their pranks on humankind. Come closer it was seen to be a man. Any mad struggle to get free was treated to spear pricks applied with no great nicety beyond the avoidance of serious injury. Violent as were his struggles at times, it is doubtful if they could have walked him the long distance. For the days of his flight he had never rested; nor had these men in his pursuit. Yet he was unexpected game. The Yotsuya affair was taking a widening sweep. Tamiya Yoémon and Kondō Rokurōbei were under examination. The death of a girl O'Haru at the brothel of Toémon of Honjō had unexpected effects. In the investigation which followed one of the women, O'Také, had made full confession. The pedlar Mobei had never left the house of Toémon; never escaped from the hospitality of O'Matsu. His goods had aroused her cupidity. The man died by poison, and was buried in the garden of Toémon's house. O'Haru knew of the deed. This knowledge was the girl's destruction. The wife and her substitute O'Kin hated O'Haru. Some remains of a first good looks, her youth, gave her power with the master of the house. The two women worked on his fears to gain consent for her destruction. A charge easily was trumped up, and she was dragged off to the cell of punishment. Under the hands of the wife and O'Kin she suffered so that she died in three days, not without letting her mate O'Také into the secret. Promptly the Honjō police were at work; not more prompt than was the woman O'Kin to disappear from Edo, almost a confession in itself. The rosary, found in the hands of the rector of the Reiganji, was easily traced through different mediators straight to O'Matsu herself. The man Toémon held out, and died under the torture. The woman confessed; and in her confession was comprehended the full story of O'Iwa's connection with Toémon's house. Of her no more need be said. She rotted and died in the jail. The girls were scattered to kindred houses. Two of the women, hunting their pray on Warigesui toward the *yashiki* quarter, had witnessed the murder of Chōbei three nights before. The police had gone to secure the body. Tatéwaki Dono was notified and had accompanied them. To the surprise of all Iémon, then the object of earnest search, was found on the spot.

The affair kept on spreading—to the very source of all these troubles. Katada Tatéwaki in the course of procedure had transmitted the Tamiya case to the jurisdiction of the *machibugyō* of the North district of Edo town, Homma Iga no Kami. With greatest interest the two men in company poured over the innumerable documents now piling up in the case. Old Tamiya Yoémon proved easy game. He readily confessed all he knew. This brought in many witnesses from the wardsmen. It was not exactly what was wanted. The evidence was mostly mere hearsay and conjecture. In those days such testimony had a value not far below that of direct statement. All pointed the way to the real criminal, who after all was the star witness. Against Yoémon at first there was but little. However, in his rage against Iémon and Kondō Rokurōbei—Akiyama was out of his reach—his tongue was too long. The faces of the magistrates grew serious as his connection with the money lender Suzuki was made plain. A *samurai* loaning money on interest! and pressing men to ruin for payment!! The stingy avaricious Yoémon appeared behind the usurer—until in time his own heavy losses had made him a borrower, and placed him in the hands of his once partner. Yoémon, together with the conspirators, was not allowed to participate in the forced restitution made by Suzuki. Nevertheless, at the time no great severity was shown the old man. He was remanded to the custody of his bail, to be kept confined to one room in the house.

The same leniency was shown toward Rokurōbei. When he showed a disposition to be recalcitrant, to equivocate, Homma gave sign to the *dōshin*. Quickly the scourgers came forward with their fearful instrument, the *madaké*. Made of bamboo split into long narrow strips, these tightly wrapped in twisted hempen cord to the thickness of a *sun* (inch), with the convenient leverage of a couple of *shaku* (feet), the mere sight brought Kondō to terms. As he entered he had seen them lead away a *heimin* (commoner) who had undergone the punishment. The man's back, a mass of bruised and bleeding flesh, was vivid to mind. At once he prostrated himself; made full confession. At last they were at the source. Kondō was a witness of the fact. He could and did tell of the inception and progress of the whole plot against O'Iwa San, the source of untold woe to Yotsuya. His story covered the period from the entrance of Iémon into the ward up to the discovery of the body of Kamikura Goémon. The rôle played by Kazaguruma Chōbei was in part dark to him. Of the disposition of O'Iwa to the Honjō master of the *Yōtaka* he pleaded ignorance. Tatéwaki Dono smiled as he counselled indulgence on this point. He knew.

Kondō, however, was sent back to the jail. He was unquestionably a principal. At last it was the turn of Iémon. The weeks had passed. The body had been carefully nursed back to vigour. The mind was in lamentable state. The ill-meant efforts of the jail authorities, the strengthening of the criminal in order better to endure the torture to the confession point, were somewhat baffled by the nightly visions of the wretched man. The two hags, O'Iwa and O'Mino; Chōbei in his final stage of purple bloatedness; these were his nightly companions, to torment and harass him. Sleep! If he could but close his eyes to shut out these horrors! Instead they became more vivid. The jailors put him at the farthest corner of their ample premises. His fellow prisoners, such as were allowed daily exit to the yard, visited him with blows and foul insults for the disturbance he created in the night. But he was cunning withal. Trapped as he was, in his lucid moments he realized that there could be but little against him. O'Iwa? Not even in Tokugawa times was the supernatural cause of prosecution except at the hands of the vulgar. Nor in those days, any more than in these of Taishō *nengo,* was a wife legally protected against abuse of husband or parents-in-law. As for Chōbei—he was dead. His own presence on the scene was no evidence against him as murderer. His only misgivings on that point lay in the confusion of mind as to the few days then covered. But who would blame a *samurai* for testing his blade on a beggar? What were beggars for? He knew nothing of the evidence given by Yoémon and Kondō; of the vile proof in the hands of Katada Dono. He had wholly forgotten the nurse who had listened to the wild ravings of O'Hana in her illness, broken sentences bearing so heavily and dove-tailing so nicely into the completed case. Owing to this woman Tatéwaki Dono had not waited the appearance of Iémon at morning. Iémon also left out of account the characters of the two men before whom he appeared. Iga no Kami sat as judge in the case. Close beside him, a little in the rear, sat Katada Tatéwaki, in whose jurisdiction the case had originated, and who was familiar with every stage. The four *dōshin* sat to one side and the other of these two men.

Homma and Katada were typical of their caste. Cold, callous, cruel, devoted rigidly to the formulæ of the *samurai* code, with strange exceptions granted to the virtues required of the common people—filial conduct and unswerving obedience to a superior— they were not men likely to regard with favour this intruder into their class. The name of *samurai* had been brought into contempt. Hence the serious character of the offence, the necessity of severest scrutiny. To the valued suggestion of Tatéwaki, Iga no Kami nodded assent. Iémon thought of nothing but the murder of Chōbei, the abuse of his wife O'Iwa, the conspiracy against her life and honour. The first question paralyzed his defence. Was he not the son of Takahashi Daihachirō? The whole terrible vista of the consequences of avowal appeared before him, once himself a *dōshin* and familiar with legal procedure. The family had suffered *kaieki* (deprivation of rights). It had been degraded from the caste. Properly speaking Iémon was an intruder into the *samurai* class. He was an impostor. His offence was against

16

the suzerain lord, the Shōgun. All the terrible penalties of treason hung over him. Tatéwaki had been quick to note the opportunity to take this case out of the category of offence by a *samurai*. Iémon was a plebeian and a charlatan. He had insulted Government. At the stumbling denial quick order was given. A *yakunin* seized the rope and dragged down the head of Iémon. Others held him at the sides, to maintain the body rigid. Stout fellows, the pick of the jailors, came forward. With ferocious regularity the blows fell. Welts at once appeared. Soon the blood was trickling from the torn skin. There was no sign to mitigate the severity of the infliction. When at the seventieth blow the body collapsed in a faint the wretched man was a terrible sight. The attendants of the jail, witnesses of the full punishment of double the number of stripes, had rarely seen such severity exercised. The jailors hated this smooth fellow, this disturber of their peace. They kept a jail, not a madhouse. Their superiors showed no sign of the mercy of renewed questioning. Hence they would change the mad nightly ravings to the subdued groans of the punished.

The days passed and his body had healed, though movement caused pain and distress. Brought again before the judges at the very sight of the scourges he screamed out confession. Questioned as to the conspiracy against the caste, his fraudulent attempt to consummate marriage with a *samurai* woman—the actual fact or legality of it was ignored—his ill-treatment and sale of her; all these in terror he denied. Once he had looked upon banishment from Edo as the limit of his punishment. Now decapitation would be a merciful end. He strove to secure the favour of a quick and painless death. Again he was beaten almost to a jelly. He clung to his denial, so important was the issue. At the next appearance he was seized and dragged to a post fixed in the ground not far from the judge's seat. His knees were pressed down on the edges of the triangular bars. These formed a sort of grid, the edges of the bars being just enough blunted to avoid cutting the skin. None of the pain was spared, yet the prisoner remained fit for early future torture. The granite slabs were then piled on his knees. Each one weighed thirteen *kwan* (107 lbs.). As the fifth slab was placed on the body of Iémon, the flesh assumed a reddish tint from the impeded circulation. Froth stained his mouth, mucus ran from his nose. A sixth, a seventh stone, were placed. " How now! How now! " The men pressed heavily on the stones. A *dōshin* bent over him, listening and waiting for sign of the important confession. The criminal was the one important witness of Tokugawa penal law. Without confession he was innocent beyond all other proof. As the eighth stone was placed Iémon began to vomit blood. The doctor raised his hand. The feet were showing signs of blackness, which rapidly spread upward. The man was in a dead faint. No confession had been secured.

Perhaps the examination was thus conducted out of some severity. Days passed. Whether or not the report of the physician was unfavourable, influenced by some means Homma had fear the man might die before a public retribution was secured. When Iémon again was dragged before his judges he had a terrible object lesson before him. A man was undergoing the torture of the lobster. Hands drawn up behind to the shoulders, the feet tightly bound across the chest, he was propped up on a mat. Properly conducted this " effort to persuade " took place in the jail. Homma wished to try the effect of anticipation on Iémon. The prisoner looked quickly at the man under torture, then hung down his head. His lips were twitching with uncertainty. Homma struck hard—" Why deny the plain fact? Is justice so ignorant of the doings and whereabouts of a scamp. Kichitarō, or Kazuma the diviner, as he called himself, murders Chōbei the pimp; a deed carried out before witnesses." A *dōshin* placed the document of the confession of the whores so that Iémon had no difficulty in ascertaining its title. " And why? Because of the agreement with Chōbei to sell the woman he dared to call his wife. The proof? The seal of Tamiya, the document itself." At last Iémon looked up. The *dōshin* placed under his eyes the fatal contract with Chōbei—agreement of exchange of the body of the woman in return for five *ryō* duly received. It had been recovered from the dead pimp's corpse. Carefully wrapped in oiled paper, Chōbei had carried it—sewn in what he called his dress. Iémon unwilling to recognize past services, Chōbei was sure to find it useful. Truly Iémon was young and impatient, and Chōbei was double his age. With bitterness the survivor recognized this primal fact.

Iémon's eyes wandered from the paper to the thief under torture. The dark green of the body was rapidly changing. The doctor present gave a quick frightened sign. Skilful hands at once cast loose the bonds. Over toppled the body. Iémon noted the white, almost livid, colour of death. Restoratives were applied. All were busied with bringing the man back to life. Then he was carried off, expression so unlike that of a human being that the less hardened shuddered. Said Homma—" No confession yet?" He raised his hand to make a sign. Iémon knew the quickness of response. He almost screamed his appeal for further respite. The Law had triumphed. As Iémon put his thumb seal to the confession of guilt to insolence (*futodoki*) the magistrates rose and disappeared. " Futodoki "—they and he knew that it meant the death sentence.[2]

---

[2] A fourth form of torture was suspension—an exaggerated infliction of " the lobster." These official forms are described by J. Carey Hall in the transactions of the Asiatic Society of Japan, vol. XLI., Part V. The native references are the " Tokugawa Seikei Shiryō," " Keizai Dai Hiroku," " Kōjiki Ruihi Horitsu-bu." Cf article on Gōmon in the " Kokushi Dai Jiten." There were other forms. In the examination into the famous conspiracy of Yui Shōsetsu (1651 A. D.) no confession could be secured from Yoshida Hatsuémon. He was brought out, to find his thirteen-year-old son Hachitarō undergoing the torture of dropping water. At the last extremities the boy pleaded for mercy. His father drily told him to act the *samurai*, and not to imperil the lives of others. It was different with Matsubayashi Chuya (really the last heir of the famous Chōsokabé House

Judgment was not delayed. The next day Homma, with Katada and an officer of the Shōgun's household present, gave sentence. Yoémon and Rokurōbei glared hate at Iémon who squatted with head bent to the ground. The sword—that now was his only hope. The first words of Homma showed that no mercy was to be dealt out in this case. Suzuki the plebeian merely suffered stripes and banishment from Edo. He had to make restitution to the amount of his property—such as was left after paying the huge fine to Government. Tamiya Yoémon and Kondō Rokurōbei underwent degradation from the caste. There was no disposition to overlook the offence of usury. Beggary was to be the portion of Yoémon, the destitution of the outcast. For some years the senile old man, the virago of a woman once the wife of Kondō Rokurōbei, were stationed at the Niōmon, to attract and amuse the worshippers passing up to the great temple of the Asakusa Kwannon. Not for long could the woman hold her tongue. Abuse passed with the sun's height to blows, and the by-standers had to interfere and rescue the old man from the severe beating. It was to the profit, rather than disadvantage, of the temple. The pair were an added attraction. The priests left interference to those at hand. Then the old man disappeared; to ornament the highway with his corpse, or be cast on the moor, food for dogs and crows. Such probably was the end of Tamiya Yoémon. The woman had not been seen for some months. Her abilities as scold had attracted those qualified to judge; her transfer to the position of bawd in a low-class house of the neighbouring Yoshiwara soon followed.

Kondō Rokurōbei fared tolerably well, considering his deserts. His confession had been a great aid in unravelling the case. He was not sentenced to cut belly. Degraded he heard with dismay

of Tosa). At sight of his old, white haired, white faced, jail wearied mother threatened with the fire torture, he did for her what he would not do for himself. The old woman willingly would have undergone the torture. Chuya's confession cost the lives of seventy-five men.

the sentence of deportation and exile to the far distant island of Sado. At this savage place, subject to the hell of a Siberian winter and the intense heats of the summer, the once pampered man lived out his last days, few and evil. He who had passed the time idling with tea-cup, or *go,* or flower arrangement, and taking enjoyment in the freshness and coolness of his garden at the Yotsuyazaka, at fifty years now tried to lead the hard and dangerous life of the wild fishing population among whom he was unceremoniously cast. Such life was soon forbidden him. He was but in the road. Then he did such clerical duties as the village at times needed. A wife even was provided for him. The final blow was a palsy, cutting off all effort at making a livelihood. Beatings now took the place of food. The villagers laughed when they heard of the old man's fall from a cliff. They, too, would ·have acted as had the brothers of O'Nabé (stew pan). They took the word for the deed; and at the cliff foot near Negai they erected a wooden shrine to propitiate the spirit of " Jiya Rokurō."

The day of execution had come. When sentenced, bound as he was Iémon struggled forward to plead for mercy, respite from the barbarous punishment to be inflicted on the traitor. His reward was the cangue and bamboo saw—*nokogirihiki;* failing death by this, he was to be crucified. The attendants fell on him. Kicks and blows had little effect on the man frantic with terror. He almost reached the *rōka* at which sat Homma. Then madly struggling he was carried off to the jail. Said a *dōshin*—" His antics in the cangue will find small scope." The last clause of the sentence was due to the notorious unwillingness of any passer-by to give a cut. The punishment had lapsed since the days of the third Shōgun, and was no more successful in Iémon's case. Placed in the cangue at the execution ground of Shinagawa a cut was made in each side of his neck. Smeared with blood the bamboo saw was placed on the cangue in inviting proximity to the head. For five hours people passed, with curious glances, but no movement to release the criminal. An Eta (outcast) butcher sidled up. The guards watched him with curiosity. Picking up the saw he made one pass. At the yell given by Iémon he dropped the implement and fled in terror, amid the laughter of guards and by-standers. Toward the hour of the sheep (1 P.M.) a *yoriki* with his *dōshin* appeared. On signal the cangue was removed. Inert limbs feebly twitching Iémon was bound tight to the double cross, his legs and arms stretched wide apart. This was raised, and again the hours passed in miserable waiting for a death which seemed to recede. If unconsciousness threatened he was given vinegar to drink as restorative. His fevered lips eagerly sought the fluid and prolonged his torture. In the spring light the days were long. As the sun was about to set the officer gave command. A *dōshin* came forward to the cross and made a sign. A guard thrust his spear upward into the belly of Iémon. The limbs made a movement, as in attempt to be drawn up. A guard on the other side in turn made a thrust. Others followed. For some moments they continued their sport, the reward of long waiting. The man was not yet dead. Impatient the *dōshin* gave the shaft of a spear a violent upward thrust. Its point appeared through the left shoulder. The head fell forward on the breast and hung limp. Iémon was dead.

*   *   *   *   *   *   *

These events could not be let pass without notice from either the pious or the timorous. Kyōhō 2nd year 2nd month 22nd day (3rd April, 1717) the Inari shrine built to propitiate the fearful Lady of Tamiya was opened to worship with due ceremonies. It had been erected on the ground of the house once occupied by Matazaémon, facing on Teramachi and on the narrow street paralleling Samonchō to the East. It was almost opposite the entrance to the Shōgwanji. At the family temple, the Myōgyōji, on the Samégabashi side, a grave and stela was set up. With time, however, the opposition made itself felt. It was asserted that the Lady O'Iwa still walked the ward, inflicting

pains and penalties on the inhabitants thereof. Triumphant reference was made to recent public disasters—of plague, pestilence,
famine, and tax levies. The shrine was invitation for her presence. People had grown indifferent as the new paint grew old,
then shabby on the once famous *miya*. Success lay with the opposition, and abolition of shrine and grave was easily enforced. It
was but for a time. The ward was either equally, or more,
unfortunate without the protection of its tutelary Inari shrine.
Just when it was re-established cannot be stated, but in the late
eighteenth century it was most flourishing. It was a favourite
resort of *samurai* women, seeking consolation for unfaithful or
brutal conduct of their husbands, and strength in the reputation
for chastity of the famous Lady of Tamiya. In 1825 the third
Kikugorō made Yotsuya famous by his presentation of the "Yotsuya Kwaidan" as written for the stage by Tsuruya Namboku
(Katsu Byōzō). In the first years of the Meiji restoration period
Shunkintei Ryuō, the famous story-teller, heralded its renown in
the Shin Yoshiwara. O'Iwa San became a feature of the Konha-
rukō fête of that quarter. A grave was again erected to her at
the Myōgyōji. As she had no *kaimyō*, or posthumous name, the
rector of the temple gave her that of "Tokushō-In Myōnen
Hishō Daishi," which can be interpreted—"She, pleasing of disposition and earnest in prayer; a woman of greatest brilliance."
Let the reader not judge this composition harshly; or its truth.

The editor to the reproduction [3] of Ryuō's story speaks of his
difficulties. Placed in his hand for judgment he saw at once the
power of the tale. But—how avoid incurring the divine anger
of the Yotsuya Inari; how avoid being charged with the divine
punishment? This question was solved by the publisher assuming
the burden of both inflictions; under the spur of what *he* regarded as publication in inferior and untrue form. He answered
these questions with a laugh—"Afraid? Not so: I, too, am

---

[3] Hifumikwan (Tōkyō), Meiji 29th year 2d month 15th day (28th
March, 1896).

human. Though the unusual is an object, yet I would not rejoice at incurring the divine anger by publishing what should not be published. Though the divine anger be incurred by publishing the Yotsuya Kwaidan, and the divine punishment be inflicted, yet who would not gladden the eyes and ears of the land? Hence in haste the true record is to be printed; owing to emission of unfounded stories. The true record being put forth, the people profit by it. How then is the divine wrath incurred by publication? Certainly not: the protection of the divine one is secured." The editor trusted in his argument; as does the present scribe.

More than once the remark has been heard as to these shrines of Nippon—" Their temples? Those dirty, shabby places, without architecture or interest, the haunts of snotty, ragged children?" The sun-helmeted gentleman and lady, or collection of their kind, rush them by in haughty contempt, and with some ridicule and ridiculous comment. Good Sir and Madame, you are passing history on the road. At this Kwōgwanji, in its rather shabby guest hall, Kusonoki Masashige and his devoted followers spoke their last defiance and then cut belly. Kobé? It is noted as a place to take ship, and not be too long in doing so. This other, barely a mile from the Tōkyō-Yokohama railway, is contemporary record of Nitta Yoshioka, who carved his bloody protest on the Ashikaga before he killed himself in the trap set by their treachery at this spot. Here behind the Kōraiji near Oiso is a very shabby and tiny shrine nestled at the foot of the cliff. This had better be avoided. It is dedicated to the small-pox god. But more than history is neglected in the indifference and contempt shown these minor *miya*. A vein of thought inwoven into the minds of this strange people is instanced by this modest shrine of the Tamiya Inari. Wandering along the amusement quarter of some great city, a theatre is seen with a *torii* gorgeous in its red paint standing before the entrance. Within this entrance is a small shrine and a box for the practical offerings of cash or commodities. The theatre is decorated inside and outside with flags as for a festival (*matsuri*). Such is actually in progress. The representation is that of the Yotsuya Kwaidan. From manager and actor (even in the presentation of the figured screen of the moving picture) the malevolence of the O'Iwa Inari—the Fox-witched O'Iwa— is to be averted. Hence all the signs of worship as at her very shrine; hence the unwillingness of author or publisher to handle the story, at least in its full form. This is but a remnant of the fear of "black magic" still found and practised in Nippon. On the beach at Kamakura at times can be found straw chaplets with gaudy cloth attached to the centre; a copper coin, and rice offering are accompaniments. Or such will be found at the crossroads of town or village, or on the Yokohama Bluff. Or in times of epidemic in numbers they are laid on the wayside shrine of the god of measles or other disease. The latter disposition conveys its own warning; the others are *majinai* or charms by which it is hoped to transfer the disease to some other child, thus insuring the cure of the first sufferer. The coin has been rubbed on the body of the little patient. Dogs usually dispose of the food offering; and passing children are only too likely to pick up the nefarious coin. The road cleaner comes along at his rare intervals and sweeps the chaplet into the hole for refuse. It is to be regretted that the ignorance and malevolence indicated by these charms cannot as easily be gathered in and disposed of. With these remarks the Yotsuya Kwaidan and its tale of ill-fortune is brought to an end.

YOKOHAMA,
5th June-4th July,
    1916.

FINIS

APPENDICES

A

[In printed copies of the *gidayu* the characters are to be distinguished by their theme, only the term *kotoba* is used to mark a speaker. The shading into descriptive writing is at times vague. In the present translation the characters are indicated. The original figures in most *gidayu* collections. Cf., " Gidayu Hyakuban," p. 271.]

The Gidayu:

Tsuruya Namboku was a writer of drama. Many are the persons called Namboku. The three preceding generations were actors who played in buffoon parts. In the fourth generation for the first time was taken up the literary work of play-writing. The Namboku in the fourth generation, Yōmyō Genzō, later known as Inosuké, was born at Motohamachō. The father carried on the business of *katatsuki* dyer, (handling the cloth to be more or less gaily patterned). Anei 4th year (1775), entering at the Kanai Sanshō no Mon he (*Yōmyō*) took the name of Katsu Byōzō. Later he received the name of Nan Tsuruya Boku. When he became a playwright he was about fifty years old. His plays are most ingenious, and are very numerous. Among them are the " Osome Hisomatsu," " Iro-yomi-uri," " Sumidagawa Hana Goshō," " Yotsuya Kwaidan." In the playhouse they are known (collectively) as the " Namboku Mono."

IÉMON SUMIKA NO DAN

(Scene in the house of Iémon)

Now to present it:—Already on that day—kō, kō—the bell of sunset had issued its call. In the hedges were heard sounds of the swarms of insects. Still more lonely was the deserted

251

mansion. O'Iwa, disturbed, anxious, when was her countenance to be open, her breast cleared of its darkness? She brought forth the *andon;* took out the sulphured slivers of wood from the box holding steel, flint, and tinder. In the depths of her husband's mind no flowers bloomed. She thought it was her woman's temperament that made her brood. In her anxiety she gave expression to her gloom:

O'Iwa—"Truly as 'tis said, it is a fleeting world; the flowing of water the future of men. Before this I performed the service of the inner apartments of the Hosokawa House. The marriage! Connected in thought with Iémon Dono the honoured dismissal was requested, that I should become a bride. Without fortune is that Inosuké, heir of the master, such object of delight to bring him to maturity. In the end all affection is absent. Nerve-racked from birth, with the pains of child-birth, the blood clot, such sickness has seized upon me. Then suddenly—one without a home, shorn of all ornament. Overcome completely by the struggle, effort and end have culminated. Parent and child, husband and wife, these (relations) master this self. Detested is the fleeting world, gloomy one's existence."

As she pondered, unbidden the tears mingled with her depression. Without restraint, gradually rising-rising-rising, mounted the flow of blood:

O'Iwa—"Ah! Ah! Again the ever-present disease shows itself. Deign—a remedy! Oh! Oh! That! That! That same remedy of aforetime, stirred and mingled with pure water. Two sips, three sips; if one drinks poison—one becomes divine; life comes to an end, but pity is aroused."

The curtain before the dressing room was gently raised. Without speaking Gombei seated himself close to O'Iwa.

"Eh! Who is that? Iya! No one is announced. Hana, I say! Hana, I say! Oh! 'Tis he—of all men! Gombei San, has he come again? Vengeance is satisfied, no longer exists."

As she would depart he held her sleeve to stop her.

Gombei—" Ah! Ah! I say—please wait. A little while ago, at Iémon's coughing and clearing his throat, I was frightened away. Trembling, at that time I went round to the rear. Thinking him really absent, with stealth I have entered. The motive of a man lies at the bottom of the heart. Just think to grant me a little affection. Alas! Ma! Submitting it is deigned to hear what I have to say. Heigh! A woman like this, her whole mind on Iémon, she would be the chaste wife. But the affections of Iémon are elsewhere, far distant. Ya! Hoi! Hoi! Hoi! To fly! Ho! Ho! Ho! Ho! Ho! Oh! Moreover the disposition of Gombei is not wicked. He seeks to be the husband. Other purpose there is none. Condescend to be easy in mind."

But his words carry no weight. The face of O'Iwa in the light has a glare.

Gombei—" As usual: Ma! One deeply distrustful. Iya! These matters, though in thought, are not to be put in words. The state of affairs is too urgent to be put into words. Sa! But I hear you say—' Iémon probably goes to Hachiman. Groundless all these censures.' Do you really believe this? The intrigue is with the only daughter of Okumura Kinai, by name Koúmé. She is indeed a beauty; whether one regard the shape of her face, her manners, or the carriage of her loins as if the willow of spring. The intimacy with Iémon could go no further. The proof spoken of is here. This letter—the sealed envelope: it fell from the sleeve of Iémon. Stealthily I picked it up, by accident. Now then! Whereabouts is it? A lengthy thing—Sa! Let's see what's in it. The coquettishness of the sentences! But let's see what she does say. Eh! What's that? ' The night is source of pleasure. Great the pleasure at sight of you. With compliments.' Assuredly there can be no mistake, when she talks this way—' The day comes. Soon we will be husband and wife; morning and night to be at your service. With compliments.' [1]

---

[1] *Mairase Sōrō:* " I take the liberty of . . ." Brinkley's Dict. A purely formal expression used in the letters of women writers.

—' Thus are the gods invoked. With compliments.' Eh! What's this? ' When distant from your side but for a moment, painful Time's course. Place this signature next your very person (*hadaka*) '—' To-night—come quickly; your advent is awaited. With compliments.' What a miserable creature is this! Is she not? But there's still more. ' O'Iwa Sama and matters with her, this is a punishment due to offence in a previous existence. Condescend to be relieved in mind. Be sure thus to view it. The spiteful brush (pen) stops. With compliments.'—' It is hard (my lot); very hard. With compliments.'—' The honoured master comes; the ever-present desire.' How now, O'Iwa Sama? Sa! Is there no outbreak as to this? The occasion is no pleasing one. Is there no harsh remark forthcoming as to one who holds illicit intercourse with the husband of another? Eh! You are a woman of marvellous patience! Oh! Oh! Oh! Oh! At all events say what you think. ' As yet in this matter, as yet in this affair, you are certain of nothing.' Is that it? That Koúmé and her mother plot together. Eh; but she has a beautiful face! And you—you are bloated, eyes wide distended, one side of the face caved in, the hair of the head all fallen out. That—and that—how describe the ugliness of your face! The affection of Iémon has worn out. Ah! What is the name of that poisonous drug, begged of Suian until secured? That, too, has been learned. Oh! Fearful, fearful, fearful! This is to act as one without care. Life is not something which lasts forever. Send from this house dismissal to Iémon, the act of separation. This the finality! Surely the intrigue is proved. Mere thought, easily exhausted, is to no purpose. Make up your mind; express your feelings. At all events your reputation is preserved. Act and decide as one indifferent. More and more have in mind the *susuki* of Masuo. Deign to yield. Do this—just this—O'Iwa Dono! "

O'Iwa—" No! and always, No! Firm the stand taken. In no way is this to be endured—to be endured. To hate a person is unreasonable; 'tis unjust. But—the embracing arms, the closely clinging, this is to act the lover."

With fingertips she thrust him off. Angry the tears; her voice trembled.

O'Iwa—"Ya! 'A woman, and the object of contempt; one treated by her lord with rudeness beyond measure. The husband has become wearied. Here's the proof. Are you a woman lacking sense?' One so unmeasurably rude—out with you! One's whole frame vibrates with passion. At one's very feet, the fact is made plain. Quick—away with you! Delay—and this shall be the guerdon."

With violence she drew the dagger of Kosuké. Gombei, wicked as he was, weakened forthwith.

Gombei—"Eh! Treated thus one's purpose is brought to naught. Listen now to reason, self-willed as you are. A little while, and it will not be the time for a snarling face. Very well: notice is given that soon your spirit will be broken. The petition is lodged at the Daikwan's office. There will be difficulty in gathering principal and interest. Just wait." He said these words on leaving, ready to make a bolt of it. With zōri (sandal) on one foot and a wooden clog (geta) on the other rapidly he ran away. Left alone O'Iwa rose in haste. To the conflagration burning in her bosom, was added the fuel of a woman's temperament. If it were true! How learn? Pondering over the details filled her with anxiety.

O'Iwa—"Ah! Ah! Ill feeling seeks to destroy—already it turns to wickedness. Gombei's face betrayed him. His talk was specious. At sight of the letter he read the doubting heart learns the truth. Burdensome the knowledge for one's heart. The mind tastes the bitterness of adversity. The hair of the head, behind the temples, is affected by the feelings. To draw out the dressing stand to hand: the little combs of willow, where are they? Sorrow effects change; as does entanglements of the heart. The fine-toothed comb which holds the thousand strands of hair—how now! It has been forgotten."

Again she took up the hair. To get it out of the way she took the front hair in both hands, making space to see.

O'Iwa—" Alas! I fail to understand. To-day the vertigo is more pronounced than usual; especially with the hair like this. Did sickness cause the loss?"

As she spoke, she drew the cover from the mirror. Reflected in it was a face to inspire fear. Ha! Frightened, she rose and drew back. Though she looked around her—there was no one. Alas! How strange! Thus she stood. Then leaning forward carefully she scanned the mirror. "Ya! Ya! Since when has my face been like this? It is completely altered." As if she could repair the ravages to self and features squint-eyed she stood and gazed. To sight she seemed a woman of evil. "Hai! Ha!" She fell prostrate. "How now! How pitiful!" Like one crazed she arose. Her body writhed in pain, at the pit of the stomach. These stomach pains, of frequent occurrence, now seized her. Thus long she lay writhing where she was.

While she twisted in agony; knowing nothing of what has happened, and hearing the wheedling voice of a crying child, Kosuké had returned and was at the entrance.

Kosuké—" Honoured lady, long have you been kept waiting. The honoured priest had matter to relate. In Yotsuya I went from this place to that, in effort to coax supply. But just now. . . . Is she suckling the child?" While speaking he drew close—" In the meantime the honoured illness has developed beyond measure. After retiring for the night you walk in your sleep. Eh! Deign to be a little prudent."

Softly the child came to her side. On seeing in what agony she was:

Kosuké—" Ya! Alas! Alas! Have you again one of those hysterical attacks, now so frequent? Okusama! I say!"

To restore her from the fit to consciousness he raised her in his arms. Regarding with attention her frightful appearance:

Kosuké—" Yo! Yo! Yo! Yo! This face of the Okusama: Ma! What can be the matter?"

He staggered in bewilderment.

Kosuké—"How changed! The Danna is absent. Heigh-ho! Ma! How has this occurred? What can be done? The cold water in the kettle here . . ."

Opening her mouth he made her swallow a mouthful. He placed his mouth to her ear.

Kosuké—"Okusama! Your ladyship!"

Gently he stroked her back. Thus nursed, the breath of the heart-broken O'Iwa faintly returned.

O'Iwa—"Hei! Has Kosuké returned? Why do you stroke me thus? I had but gone to sleep, just now."

"Oh! Oh!" said he—"Ma! Ma! How joyful. Ah! Iya! I say, Okusama; how long have you been in that state? Your face inspires fear."

At his question again she was the woman. The tears in her breast rose high and overflowed. For a time she did not answer. When a little calm:

O'Iwa—"Deign then to listen. As usual Iémon Dono went forth to worship at Hachimangū. Subsequently my vertigo was too pronounced. Two or three drinks were taken of the medicine prescribed by Suian Dono. Secretly at the rear entered Naosuké no Gombei, to make illicit courtship. Various were his pleas. Thus—Iémon Dono was deeply in love with the daughter of Okumura. The worship (*kami-mairi*) was all a lie. He was contracted to Koúmé. Hence his affection for me was at an end. This change was due to the drug. Hear what is to be done. Love unrequited is to be satisfied by revenge. Thus did Gombei put the matter. But it is not likely that my husband is so cruel. Heart again will turn to heart. The attack of vertigo was strong. The hair was pulled out. Moreover, suddenly the face became altered. . . . My appearance: Ma! Gombei then did not lie. By the plotting of the Okumura, parent and child, I have drunk poison. They have an understanding with Suian. Eh! At the thought—at the thought—anger rises. My husband, a man of note, with him she commits adultery. Hence the hatred of these

17

people. Since the poison has been quaffed; as serpent, as demon, none shall be my equal. The Okumura, parent and child, are you the kind thus to act!"

Suddenly she sprang up, and would have dashed out at the front. At her act the frightened Kosuké put his arms around and stopped her.

Kosuké—"Heigh! Heigh! I say, Okusama! The expression of your face has changed. Heigh-ho! Whither away? Alas! It is plain that she would go to the *yashiki* of Okumura. Evil her purpose. She would confute the malice spoken by Koúmé, by parent and child. She would fetch away with her Iémon Dono. Iya! Ho, there! Your honoured judgment strays. She believes in what Gombei has said; that he is with the Okumura. Does she not remember times past, the reproof of the Danna? Sa! As before! As before! As before! Put on outward seeming. Deign to be calm. No! No! No! Though there be shame; display a smile. Do but this. The prudence of the lady carries the day. The colour, the perfume, of the flower has no effect. Sa! She won't stop! She will go! Thither she will take her way! The conflagration of her wrath is in her glare. She goes, and Kosuké remains behind!" At a sound she looked around. The little boy was weeping bitterly at his mother's state. The tie of blood, her affection, prevailed.

O'Iwa—"Oh! Bonka! Bonka! Bonka! The pretty fellow grieves."

She drew near to embrace him. Earnestly he looked in his mother's face.

Child—"Iya! Iya! My lady mother is not like this. I'm afraid! I'm afraid!"

Weeping, the little boy dropped from her knee.

"Bei-yo! Please call my real lady mother."

O'Iwa—"Aré! Aré! Aré! Deign to hear that! In heart children are without discernment. My appearance changed, he fears the presence of his mother. To her side he will not approach.

How, how comes this face! Meeting with Iémon Dono one would think—one would think—my very self meets with retribution for some deed done in a past existence. Husband and beloved child—alas! they avoid my sight."

With lamentable cries she wept. Kosuké, too, was moved, and joined in her tears. O'Iwa again inspected the appearance of her face.

O'Iwa—"To continue living thus in the world would be one unending shame. Dying the grudge will be repaid. Holding thus the skirt prevents my leaving. This must not be. To that place I go."

As the two struggled the girdle (obi) came loose. The contest was brought to an end. At this juncture returned Hamiya Iémon. He had little disposition to enter his home. Thus unexpectedly, without premeditation, the two came face to face. Mutually they gazed at each other. "Ho! The Danna: good day." Kosuké remained where he was, uneasily twisting. O'Iwa clasped tight the breast of her husband's coat. "Heigh! Iémon Dono."

O'Iwa—"Complete has been the silence toward me. Every night, every night, polluted. With Koúmé have pillows been exchanged." Speech and voice vibrated with jealousy. She glared at him. Without showing alarm:

Iémon—"Ma! I don't understand. This way of acting is unusual. Why look like that? In that manner painful the change in appearance."—"Why? Why? Eh! You pretend ignorance. You pretend ignorance of the joyful result. By the artifice of Koúmé, of parent and child, in unison with Suian, a poisonous drug has been given me to drink. By this means I am made unrecognizable. Would that never I had been born, to live so deformed . . . all due to the feeling aroused in these people. Sa! Sa! Sa! Restore my former appearance! Bewitched, seized by anxious care, it remains but to withdraw."

Iémon—"Ya! What mad talk! In my absence, loosening the cord of the obi, secretly you indulge your lewdness. Detected by the master's eye, disloyal as you are, death is the weighty punishment. Make ready!" At hearing the unjust proposal the upright Kosuké with tears held tight his knees.

Kosuké—"Heigh! Danna Sama. Iya! I say, Iémon Dono! This Kosuké an adulterous fellow? Heigh-ho! It is unreasonable! Unreasonable! Unreasonable! You speak for your own purpose. I, the mere servant, have been to call the honoured priest to the Yotsuya. Returning home I found the Okusama unconscious. When she learned the true state of affairs the Okusama would have rushed forth. To stop her I seized the end of the *obi*. And that is to be unchaste! Iya! A paramour—heigh-ho! That is too much! Too much! Too much! It is to go to excess. Truly, truly, for these years and months you have gone forth in the world. Such has been your conduct. You have allowed a sight of you—at the Bon Matsuri, at the New Year, in accidental meetings on the street when on some mission. Why! The very dogs bark—the honoured constables of the night watch—eh! they administer reproof."

O'Iwa—"Lamentable the distress. How many times! Sleepless the nights—the time when one should slumber. But this does not move him. Hence the unkindness of his speech."

Kosuké—"Eh! He don't listen. Danna Dono, beating the *tatami* one weeps with regret."

O'Iwa forthwith sprang up in haste—sprang up—sprang up.

" Superior is the concubine to the lady wife. Below the basely mean is one placed. In the relation of husband and wife, the thought is to treat the husband with respect. Such is the duty of woman. To you the poverty and distress are not displayed. Obtaining her means to live by washing and occasional tasks, yet the wife is discarded. The sum total of the sunshine transforms the flowers; invisible their change. Regardless of self-distrust of the past is put aside. But you act with cruel motive; a grudge as lasting as a night without moonlight. From the clouds the drizzle falls on bamboo and on village. And between the intervals of rain there is naught but weeping."

Iémon refused to listen:

Iémon—" Ya! Mere excuses these; mere excuses these. In the master's absence the cord of the *obi* is loosed. Madly you go your rounds. The lewdness is evident. Sa! Make honest confession."

At the outrageous words of the husband the voice of O'Iwa trembled still more:

O'Iwa—" Eh! 'Tis your own sin you would conceal. Regardless of self you would impute evil reputation to me. Having driven me out, you would make Koúmé your wife. But by that you shall gain nothing. Miserable one! Unblushingly do you join in the hate of the Okumura, parent and child? "

With a rapid motion she snatched his dagger. She half turned:

Iémon—" Ya! Whither? Whither? Here one must pick one's words. This is not the time to inquire into the facts. Iya! Iya! Iya! Where do you go? "

At their quarrel Kosuké was perplexed. Said the child in troubled voice:

Child—" Honoured mother—where go ye? Honoured father—forbearance, patience."

He clung to their garments in kindness and affection. The eyes of the two in Shuradō (Hell of fighting) were blinded. On this side and that they pulled at the scabbard of the sword. In the wrestling, the springing in and recoil, the sword slipped from the scabbard. Without intention to five or six inches it pierced the shoulder. Atto! The wife fell—" Namu Sambō! "[2] Plucking out the sword O'Iwa cast it aside. By the action of retributive fate the point of the weapon pierced the chest of Kosuké. The wound was fatal. Seven revolutions and a fall: alas! he was dying. Close under his feet the blow of Iémon had reached the child. With but a single cry forthwith he died. At the

---

[2] The three holy things—Buddha, his Law, the priesthood.

accident the husband was at a loss what to do. He stood stupified. With difficulty O'Iwa rose from the ground.

O'Iwa—" Heigh-ho! Heigh-ho! Heigh-ho! You would kill me! Oh! Since you would kill, put into deed the ardent wish. Wretch! An idea—Koúmé, the parent and child: these are to be seized and put to death. Be it so!"

With eyes of hate, her hair fallen down, jealously glaring, in appearance she was just like a female devil. Blood curdling, she inspired fear. The husband gave vent to his inner thought:

Iémon—" Though one kill without intent, yet the brandishing of the sword is one's own deed, one's very act. It is the punishment of Heaven for unchastity and jealousy. Bear it in mind."

At the cruel words Kosuké, drawing painful breath:

Kosuké—" Eh! To us, to us, to us, such speech applies not. Unkind, unrighteous, is this death punishment. There is naught to compare to it. Very wicked and unprincipled, surely you are possessed of a devil! Seldom is the life of a serving man grudged him; unconsidered as he is. Forgetful, the evil reputation of lechery is attached, and death the portion. Eh! How regrettable! The sight is unseemly. 'Twas you who inflicted the wound! To the Okusuma also, evil the name. Thus, without intention, the end of your life is not witnessed by your child."

Iémon—" By the hand of another your wound, by one your parent! On my part—on my part—had I aught to do with this? Heigh! Am I not grieved? Eh! Cold? Unfeeling? A wound to myself could not pain more."

Vainly writhing he raised and embraced the body of the child. As sadly he lamented, O'Iwa crawled up close. Tightly her arms clasped the dead body of her child.

O'Iwa—" Alas! Alas! Inosuké! Inosuké! The selfishness of your father; the temperament of the mother; foolish their thoughts. Thus have you ended life. . . . How great is the grudge. Heigh! Exercise forbearance! Exercise forbearance! Deign to show forbearance. Parent and child are related for but

one life, 'tis said. Now separated, again in what world will there
be meeting? Men are born into the wide world. There is such
a thing as sympathy, 'tis said. Before your eyes lie *kerai* (retainer), wife, and child. Now, on the very brink of time, not
once do you recite the Buddha's name. Abandon your inordi-
nate desires. Is your heart that of a demon? Eh! A snake?
Cruel and cold to your wife, you reckon up your various hates.
With Kosuké I am the one to lament. Tears overflow. Steady
the fall of rain of Yōsuji, of *sumidare* (the rainy season). When
dying the chief of birds vomits forth blood with his song: so I."
Iémon—" Ya! The song she sings inspires no regret. A prayer
said and the child enters Nirvana. Namu Amida Butsu! As
for these two—I would kill them by inches; as they twisted, and
staggered, and fell grasping at the air, and in every way showed
their agony. In the next world may they meet with a mountain
set with sharp-edged swords, so cruel as to inspire pity."
Just then came running to the front entrance Suian. He gasped
for breath:
" Heigh! Heigh! Iémon Dono!"
Suian—" O'Iwa Dono's appearance has changed. It was the
drug, our own secret nostrum, administered at request of the
honoured mother of Okumura. Though sorrow was felt, unexpected the good luck in killing the honoured wife. Henceforth
come out openly. Who would not drain the *saké* cups with
Koúmé Dono! The three lands (China, India, Japan) are the
inheritance of one who was but an adopted son. All in good
order! All in good order! All in good order! Ha! Ha! Ha!
Ha! Ha! Sa! To set about it at once."
The husband concealed tears of regret for past conduct.
Iémon—" Plain it is that wife, child, and *kerai*, though deserving
compassion, have found death. 'Twas determined by fate in a
previous existence. But to obviate fear of future disaster, though
not the original purpose, the dead bodies of these two are to be
nailed to a door panel, with the inscription—' unchaste and jeal-

ous.' Let them float away on the current of the Nenashigawa.
The entrance of the house is close to the inner room. Make
ready: it will be best to leave by the rear. Quick! Quick!
But . . ."

Suian—" It happens that the neighbor Dansuké comes." He bent
and peeped through the entrance. " Dansuké! Dansuké!" Dansuké Mizuo in presence, mouth to ear he was informed. "Namu!
Namu! Namu! Namu!" He nodded consent. The two men
talked in whispers. The dead bodies of the two (O'Iwa and
Kosuké) were carried into the inner room. For some time Naosuké Gombei had been watching what went on, peeping out and
listening. He appeared from the shadow.

Gombei—"Yai! Unjustly have the blameless wife and *kerai*
been punished by Hamiya Iémon. Complaint is to be made at
the Daikwan's court."

When he would rush forth he was pulled back by the girdle (*obi*).
"Ya! Ya! Whither would you go? There is matter of importance to hear."—" The intent is plain. You would kill me." One
had the long sword of the soldier. Two or three passes and he
was nearly cut down by the skill of Hamiya. When he tried to
flee, from behind he received a cut through the shoulder. It
finished him. Then he (Iémon) would hide the dead body of
his child from the eyes and reproach of men. Close at hand was
a heavy stone trough. For funeral rites—" Namu Amida Butsu!"
Into the well crib he threw it. Aré! Marvellous! Suddenly the
house creaked and trembled. From somewhere came swarms of
rats. Heigh! Incomprehensible! Iémon wavered. Singling him
out they flew and seized him. Sha! Confused he slashed in
attempt to drive them off. Lightning blazed around the sword;
many phosphorescent lights—in wreaths, double, triple. To the
end of the worlds his retribution.

Thus the causes, origins, are made known of what remains as the
Yotsuya Kwaidan.

END OF THE GIDAYU

[It can be noted that Japanese thought and expression are not very different from that of the West. An idea perhaps can be obtained from this *gidayu* as to why the native waxes enthusiastic over the pose and vivid gestures of the *geisha,* who is the one to interpret these dramatic recitations. To her falls the *"kotoba."* The descriptive lines are recited by a chorus to the harsh and effective twang of the *samisen.* The *samisen* may not afford music, but it can give expression to the emotional in feeling. The *gidayu* recitation is a favourite art with the Go Inkyō Sama. Symposia are held, before which the old gentleman recites, often enough without chorus; for he, and the *geisha,* at times have to fill the rôle both of *"kotoba"* and chorus, modulating the voice according to the theme. Symposia is not an unbefitting term. Meetings are held for public competition in *gidayu* recitation; but in the privacy of one's circle and hobby the banquet is an important feature—at least to the guests. In his history of "Japanese Literature" (Dai Nihon Bungaku Shi, pp. 591–596) Suzuki Chōkō gives a long extract from the play, as sample of Tsuruya's powers as a dramatist. Adopted into the House of the actor Tsuruya Namboku, and marrying his daughter, Katsu Byōzō in turn assumed the name Tsuruya Namboku.]

B

[In the original the story by Momogawa Jakuen is found in the Kwaidan Hyaku Monogatari, vol. ii, p. 83 (Kokkwadō-Tōkyō). This collection has already been referred to, as sketching a number of the best known Japanese *kwaidan.* The present example furnishes a specimen of *kōdan* style, and has application to the present subject. It also instances how the Japanese stage boldly faces situations, the exigencies of which call for the greatest adaptation and facility on the part of actor and stage manager. The "Yotsuya Kwaidan" in the stage representation presents a number of critical scenes in which both qualities are severely strained. Rapid metamorphosis is a *siné qua non*. And it is effected—somehow.]

The *kōdan:*

ONOÉ KIKUGORŌ NO YŪREI

From former times and generations the Otowa [1] House held a monopoly in the representation of ghosts. Its representative in the fifth generation was the most skilful of all at spectres. This man of the third generation lived at Mukōjima no Terajima. He was commonly called Terajima no Kikugorō; his stage name was Baikō. This man's daughter was the mother of the fifth generation. Thus it can be seen that he was the maternal grandfather of this fifth representative. This third Kikugorō was the first to act the Yotsuya Kwaidan, in Bunsei 8th year 7th month (14th August–13th September, 1825) at the Nakamura-za (theatre). The author was the noted Tsuruya Namboku, who constructed the very famous " Tōkaidō Yotsuya Kwaidan." O'Iwa San, the attendant (*wakatō*) Kohei, and Enya no Rōnin Satō Yōmo Shichi, these parts fell to Kikugorō. Matsumoto Koshirō, he who strutted it at the Kōraiya, did the Naosuké Gombei. Iémon was the part of the seventh Danjurō; later Ebizo, who was the real father of the ninth of the name. The staging of O'Iwa Sama includes— 1st scene, the combing of the hair; 2nd scene, the Sunamura Ombōbori; 3rd scene, Iémon ill in the dark room at Hebiyama; 4th scene, the *yashiki* of Naosuké Gombei at Fukagawa Sankaku. O'Iwa appears at the scene of the combing of the hair as mentioned, in the incident where the guests are received, and in the 3rd scene at Hebiyama. Iémon is ill. Splitting apart the lantern set out during the Festival of the Dead (Bon Matsuri) the ghost of O'Iwa appears with the child in her embrace. Iémon receives them as would a stone Jizō. O'Iwa, at sight of the fright of Iémon, laughs—ki, ki, ki. At once they fade away; and at once the ghost of Kohei the *wakatō* takes her place, he who was charged

---

[1] Another reading of the characters for Kikugorō—to the initiated.

with unchaste conduct with O'Iwa. It was the part of the performer to please the uninitiated by some strenuous effort. The first performance at this theatre was for three months—from the seventh to the ninth month. On consideration the drama is of interest. O'Iwa is killed at Yotsuya. With the dead body of the *wakatō* Kohei she is fastened to a door, and from the rear the scoundrel sets them adrift. Fishing at Ombōbori, Iémon sees them float by. From Yotsuya to Sunamura is a very great distance. It would occupy a woman's legs for the space of a day; or faint-hearted fellows, water drinkers, such of the kind as would try it. Winding along what rivers, by what intersecting canals had they floated here? In no way does one conceive. All the more the reasons influencing the author's design are not known. Very interesting is the story, to the cheerful character, and those not to be chilled by apparitions. At all events they get to Ombōbori? The third Kikugorō, the first to take the part of O'Iwa, was a superlative actor, skilled in capturing the people. In the third scene, the dark room at Hebiyama, the ghost comes forth from the *Bon* lantern. Every day the *kozō* (man or boy as apprentice) of the utility shop in Asakusa Umachō slowly took down the lantern covered with white paper. In a straight line, before the eyes of all, he passed along Kuramaédōri, crossing Asakusa. From Yokoyamachō he crossed to Daimaru no Mae. Passing through Norigyōchō he reached the Nakamura-za in Sakaichō. As he passed along these streets crowded with people, the eyes of men were attracted:

No. 1—"Every day, every day, the *kozō* goes by carrying that Bon lantern. Where does he go?"

No. 2—"He? Kikugorō now is playing O'Iwa Sama at the Nakamura-za. The ghost issues from that Bon lantern. The lantern used is brought every day by the *kozō*."

No. 1—"Ha! A practical application. We must be sure and go see." Through this advertisement the guests came readily. As fact, every day but the one *Bon* lantern was used. Split apart, it was repaired. From the first day, up to the performances of a thousand autumns, one lantern answered all purposes. Truly Kikugorō was more than a clever actor. He was wonderful in securing the good will of people. No actor was equal to him. Tradesmen, Government officials, learned men, refined people— he was skilful at gaining their support. Hence he did not lack money. His *status* did not affect him. When as usual the Bon lantern one day was to be carried out, Kikugorō made his pupil Onozō the bearer. Said Kikugorō:

Kikugorō—" Onozō, don't I frighten you somewhat in this shape? "

Onozō—" I'm not in the least frightened. Every day acting as your assistant I'm not afraid."

Kikugorō—What? Not afraid? Say that you're afraid."

Onozō—" Patron, that is unreasonable. One not afraid—is not afraid. Hence it cannot be helped."

Kikugorō—" Anyhow, say you are afraid."

Onozō—" I'm not at all afraid."

Kikugorō—" An obstinate rascal, this."

While speaking—*pokari*, he gave *Onozō* a whack on the head. As it was he went through the performance. Coming to the green room, at once he called Onozō.

Kikugorō—" Fool and low fellow."

Onozō—" Why is it then you would strike a fool and low fellow with a stick? "

Kikugorō—" You are just like a fool. A little while ago when told to be afraid of me, you would not say you were afraid."

Onozō—" Patron, that is to be unreasonable. I attend you. Every day I see you."

Kikugorō—" I know you are not afraid. But you are the very one who acts as my attendant. In public you are to look at me as one frightened beyond measure. If this be not widely published, will not the theatre be deserted? An actor who is good only at acting, he is not to be called a clever man. He must draw people. Fool and low fellow!"

Onozō—" Naruhodo! Since you say it—I'm afraid."

Kikugorō—" Your answer now is to the purpose."

Hence on considering the matter, was not Kikugorō in every way a talented man? For the space of eighty days this theatre turned away guests. Later, in Tempō 7th year 7th month (12th August to 11th September, 1836) again this drama was produced. The actor was the same as at the previous production. On this occasion Kikugorō took thought. As it was the second time, it must be changed in presentation to an audience. *Dōmo!* There was the coming on of the ghost. It is clad in a grey robe. If O'Iwa wears a gray robe, and the *wakatō* Kohei wears a gray robe, both being the same to view this would fail to interest. He continually worried. Nevertheless it would not do to wear armour; and a ghost in *kami-shimo* [2] raises no chill. Some contrivance must be hit upon. Day and night the matter worried him. Habitué of the gallery of this Moritaza was a man named Tsutaya no Yoshi, commonly known as Tsutayoshi. An extraordinarily dissolute fellow he borrowed to the four sides and eight directions. At this time in the Yoshiwara Sumichō was a tenement placed in the rear of the prostitute houses. He removed thither, and soothed his troubles by living alone. His face washed in the morning, at once he ran forth. He ate his meals at a cheap eating house. A varied meal consumed he made his way to the Morita-za. Lunch was eaten in the theatre. On the return he took a drink and then went home. In truth he was a lively fellow. The Yotsuya Kwaidan had just been determined on for the close of the sixth month (July). At sundown he returned to his home in the Yoshiwara. On the way he drank—the strongest of liquors. At once he hung up the mosquito net and

---

[2] " Top-bottom ": the beautiful lozenge shaped X dress of the *samurai* when on court service, or for other ceremony: full dress.

went inside. Not knowing front from rear he went to sleep. Pressed by a necessity the sound of the wooden clappers (*hyoshigi*) made him open his eyes. It was the harlot quarter, the 9th hour and more (after 3 A.M.), and the liveliness of the night was over. The quiet of the place inspired fear. From evening he had not stirred from the mosquito net, but had slept. The light had gone out, and it was pitch dark. Soundly had he slept. In the jar was fresh water for drinking. Greedily he drank.

Yoshi—" I have slept—in a way to cause fear. It is now past the 9th hour. I still can sleep without stint."

Again he entered the net. He drew the tobacco box close to his pillow head. He would smoke. Looking toward the *andon*, beneath it, faintly outlined, he saw somebody.

Yoshi—" Who is there? This place used to be a brothel. Now it is a tenement. I rent it. It don't do to have it taken for a brothel. Oi! You—whence do you come?

At the words—he! It disappeared.

Yoshi—" I say now! A marvellous thing—that over there. A kind of dream—extraordinary: I don't remember having a grudge with anyone. Yai! If the spirit which just came entertains a grudge I have never even dreamed of such. I am a dissolute fellow, but remember no grudge with anyone."

Thus loud and wrathfully he shouted out. As one without fear he went to sleep. Waking up, the next day he left the house to go to the hot bath in Umachō. On the way he breakfasted. Then he went to the Morita-za. Although the performance had not begun, as it was a first representation the theatre was crowded with people. Said a friend:

Friend—" Yoshi San, the colour of your face is bad. Are you affected by the heat?"

Yoshi—" Liking strong spirits, I feel badly. Moreover, last night a strange thing was witnessed. I feel out of sorts."

Friend—" What was it?"

Yoshi—" In the middle of last night I opened my eyes. Dimly outlined beside the lantern (*andon*) sat a rascal; some fellow who had been amusing himself at a neighbouring brothel. I thought that being drunk with wine he had come there by mistake. ' Who are you? ' Thus I shouted. It disappeared. *Dōmo!* It was a strange occurrence. Was it a ghost, thought I? I could remember no grudge with another person. Anyhow, in all likelihood it is no ghost, thought I. However I look at it, I don't understand."

Friend—" Hei! Yoshi San, it was your own imagination."

Yoshi—" Though I considered it a vision of my own, as strange I mention it."

Friend—" If you feel bad it will be well to stay away for tonight."

Yoshi—" I don't think I feel badly in any other way. To-night—for the whole night—I'll make the test."

That day he returned to the Yoshiwara house. That night no one was seen. But when he did see it, was the thing a matter of his own imagination? The next day he came to the theatre. The friend was waiting for him.

Friend—" Yoshi San, did it appear at night? "

Yoshi—" Iya! At night it did not appear. In the middle of the night opening my eyes I looked with especial care to the eight sides. Nothing that could be considered suspicious was to be seen."

Friend—" Then it was as I said. It being at one time a brothel, would not something appear in this house? Having this wholly in mind, the thing presented itself to your eyes."

Yoshi—" Doubtless it is but that; a freak of the imagination."

That night returning to the Yoshiwara, nothing happened. A space of five nights passed. His habit was to return early; and as his thin dress was wet with sweat he would change it. Going upstairs he took out the thin garment from the clothes-basket (*tsuzura*). With this in hand he was about to descend. Now as at one time the place had been a brothel the steps were broad and wide. Seated on the lower step, lying face downward, was somebody.

Yoshi—" Ah! Has it come? "

Being a courageous fellow, while speaking he raised his leg.

Yoshi—" You're in the way."

Pon: he gave a kick. There was not the slightest resistance. Forthwith—ha! it was gone.

Yoshi—" *Domo!* Remarkable: it is a strange occurrence."

While speaking he changed his robe and lit the fire. Making the water boil, with Echizen peat he heated some wine he had bought on the road and brought home with him. With *tsukudani*,[8] or something of that kind to eat, he drank and thought.

Yoshi—" To-day it is no product of my imagination. Who can that rascal be? "

Talking to himself, he drank the *saké*. Attending to preliminaries he would go to bed. He went to the necessary and opened the door. Some one stood there, with his back to him.

Yoshi—" Here again? "

At the words it disappeared. No matter how brave he was, that night he felt badly and did not sleep. Awaiting dawn he was quick to go forth. On coming to the theatre—

Friend—" Good day: how goes it with Yoshi San? Are you not very much out of tone?

Yoshi—" At night it came. Moreover it appeared twice."

Friend—" Did it appear? "

Yoshi—" At first it was seated on the stair. The second time it was inside the necessary."

Friend—" Hei! That is marvellous. Probably it is the work of fox or badger (*tanuki*)."

This talk abruptly terminated. Tsutayoshi was a bold fine fellow. Unmoved, he retired to his own home in the Yoshi-

---

[8] " Small fish boiled in soy in order to preserve it (named after Tsukudajima-Tōkyō—famous for its preparation)."—Brinkley's Dict.

wara. After that nothing was seen for several days. Just as he was forcing a way into the theatre—

Man—" Yoshi San! At the Bairin (Plum Tree) over the way is the master of Otowaya. He is urgent to see you; so he says. It will be well to go at once."

Yoshi—" Was he told I was here? "

Man—" Ah! "

Yoshi—" How annoying! The Otawaya San has lent me money. Dōmo! A meeting, 'tis bad news."

Man—" As nothing was said about it—go. Surely the return of the loan is not involved."

Yoshi—" It's not to be avoided. I'll go and see."

Opposite to the theatre was the tea house called the " Bairin." He went in.

Yoshi—" Good-day."

Maid—" Oya! Yoshi San. As the master of Otowaya is waiting upstairs for you, just condescend to go up."

Yoshi—" Ah! Is that so? Condescend to pardon."

Don, don, he climbed the stairs. At the end of a six-mat room was a man fanning himself. He was alone. It was Kikugorō, the third of the name. He had been noted as a handsome man. However, at this time he was an old man. The white summer garb of that very fine quality of cloth-grass known as *jōfu* was girded in by a *chakenjō obi*.[4] Of his profession there was not a hint.

Kikugorō—" Sa! Yoshi San, come here, please."

Yoshi—" The patron: *dōmo!* truly it has been rude not to come and see you. I have not crossed the threshhold."

Kikugorō—" Iya! Why speak so? You now live in the Yoshi-wara."

Yoshi—" That is so; for a long time I lived in Fukiyachō. The neighbourhood was a bad one. I had borrowed money. It was

---

[4] Brown, with stripes—a favourite pattern with men and women.

18

like running away in the night. A one-time brothel now the rent is ridiculously cheap. *Mikoshi* (carriages) are kept in it now."

Kikugorō—" The Yoshiwara is a gay place. For people who would amuse themselves there is none superior. It is an excellent locality."

Yoshi—" One can find whatever is desired."

Kikugorō—" So Yoshi San, now you live alone."

Yoshi—" Hai! I'm alone."

Kikugorō—" I've just heard the talk of people. A ghost appears at your place."

Yoshi—" Who said such a thing? "

Kikugorō—" Iya! It was heard, by accident. Is it true? "

Yoshi—" Hai! First it was seen beside the *andon;* then on the stairway, and in the necessary."

Kikugorō—" A strange matter! Is it man or woman? "

Yoshi—" Dōmo! That I don't know. It was seen as in a mist. Whether man or woman, I don't know."

Kikugorō—" Are there male and female ghosts? "

Yoshi—" Male or female—I know nothing about it."

Kikugorō—" What its nature? When it appears this time, condescend to take a good look at it." He continued (then)—" The present drama of the Yotsuya Kwaidan—as to my part, as you well know, O'Iwa and Kohei before the very eyes must change places in an instant. For both to wear the grey *kimono* lacks interest. Which of them is to change? It is on my mind. Dōmo! Thought fails to solve the question. Hence the request to you. What kind of dress does that ghost wear? That is what I want to learn."

Yoshi—" Hei! "

Kikugorō—" But Yoshi San: It is no mere request. I loaned you ten *ryō.*"

Yoshi—" Patron, do you condescend still to remember it? "

Kikugorō—" Deign not to jest. Who would forget such a rascal?

I'll wipe out that ten *ryō*—and give you five *ryō* in addition. How now? Condescend to observe."

Yoshi—" Thanks are felt. When it appears I'll take a good look at it.

Kikugorō—" With the month's change the first representation takes place. It must be ascertained in the intervening time. Probably in four or five days it will be seen."

Yoshi—" That is so. Dōmo! The opponent being a ghost, will it appear to-night? Or has is ended by going away? That I don't know. Having found out its dwelling place, I'll send a postal-card."

Kikugorō—" Don't jest. As just said, I'll give you five *ryō*. Be careful; and please take a good look."

Yoshi—" Respectfully heard and understood. This time I'll get a good look at it."

Thus agreed Tsutayoshi returned that night to the Yoshiwara.

Yoshi—" A pleasing thing! Ten *ryō* wiped off, and five *ryō* received in addition. Thanks: a fine bit of work. It will be well if the rascal of a ghost comes to-night. Anyhow, just before the *Bon* it suffers distress beyond measure. For several days nothing has been seen of it. Its purpose may have changed: Yai! If the ghost is to appear, please show up at once. Don't it yet appear? Oi! Ghost!"

The ghost was not to be drawn out by this display of energy. Several days passed without the slightest sign of it. Every day Kikugorō came to the Bairin and sent for Tsutayoshi.

Kikugorō—" Yoshi San, has it not yet appeared?"

Yoshi—" Dōmo! The patron is vexed. Every day, every day, it is awaited; and not a sign of it. Feeling out of sorts, has it not died? That's my idea."

Kikugorō—" Oi! Oi! Yoshi San. Being dead, is it not a ghost? Once dead, does the rascal die again?"

Yoshi—" Dōmo! Patron, nothing is known of one's spirit. For it not to appear is annoying. Spirits (*ki*) suffer pain; and suffering pain they don't show themselves. It seems that you want it to appear before the first representation. If I see it, I get five *ryō*. I would like to have it show itself before the *Bon*. My purpose is to get through this year's *Bon* [6] by means of the ghost.

Kikugorō—" Anyhow—have a care."

Yoshi—" Agreed."

That night he went home and drank wine.

Man—" Yoshi San, is he at home? "

Thereupon without ceremony entered an intimate friend, from Sakaichō near Fukiyachō. He had loaned money to Tsutayoshi, and now sought the repayment.

Man—" Yoshi San, you say you will bring it, you will bring it; and you make no sign of bringing it. That was my money, and the failure to return it is vexing. Will matters change before the *Bon?* "

Yoshi—" Wait but a little. If to-night something materializes I get five *ryō*. The money in hand, at once I will pay you back."

Man—" What is going to materialize? The five *ryō* you spoke of? "

Yoshi—" In fact at my house a ghost appears. The Otowaya San heard of it. As of immediate use to the theatre I am carefully to observe what the ghost wears. He says he will give me five *ryō*. The money obtained, at once the two *ryō* will be repaid. Wait until that happens."

Man—" Oi! Oi! Yoshi San. Does a ghost really appear? "

Yoshi—" It really does."

Man—" What kind of a ghost? "

Yoshi—" As to that—right before one; a most blood-curdling thing. Anyhow, I shiver all over at sight of it. Just like this—"

Man—" Where does it show itself? "

Yoshi—" Just where you are seated."

Man—" Yoshi San, jokes don't go."

---

[6] Feast of the Dead. This festival is held in July—in the country in August, the old calendar seventh month.

Without waiting for an answer he fled. Seeing this said Tsuta-yoshi:

Yoshi—" A ghost is a very profitable object. Do but speak of it, and he who would collect borrowed money takes to flight. If it appears, money is obtained. Hence a ghost is a remarkable thing. After this when the dry goods man comes for repayment, I'll chase him out again with the ghost. Anyhow this house brings good luck. The rent is cheap, and there is a ghost which enables one to dodge paying loans. Thanks: henceforth in renting a house I'll confine myself to haunted houses. So much for that. Will it show itself to-night? "

Tsutayoshi hung up the mosquito net. He drank a glass. Thus reinforced, tranquil and pleased he laid down on the pillow. After sleeping awhile he opened his eyes. All around was quiet. The bustle of the night had ceased. There was not a sound. Outside the mosquito net the wick of the *andon* had burned low and gave a faint light. Suddenly the bell of the eighth watch (1 A.M.) was heard on Bentenyama. Thereupon—de! . . . the sound was heard and the light of the *andon* went out. Then as a mist an object like to a human being (*hito*) was visible. Ha! Tsuta-yoshi was frightened. Was this the ghost? He rolled up the mos-quito net, the pupils of the eyes intent. Thus he had it in plain view. The hair of the head was in wild disorder. To sight it was certain it was a man. He wore a grey cotton garment.

Yoshi—" That's it! "

At the sudden exclamation—Ha! It disappeared. The *andon* having previously gone out truly it was the very blackness of night. Coming out from under the mosquito net he (Yoshi) lit the wick. Smoking his tobacco he staid awake until dawn. In time the East became white. At once he left the house. He entered the bath at Agechō, breakfasted as usual at the cheap eating house in Komégata, and then went to the Morita-za in Kibikichō.

Friend—" Good-day."

Yoshi—" Iye! It's hot to-day."

Friend—" How now, Yoshi San? The O'Baké? "

Yoshi—" As usual—it came in the night."

Friend—" Is that so? When Otowaya San hears that, he will rejoice."

While in talk a message came from Kikugorō. At once Tsuta-yoshi went to the Bairin. Otowaya was waiting for him.

Kikugorō—" Yoshi San, how now—the ghost? "

Yoshi—" Patron, condescend to rejoice. It appeared in the night."

Kikugorō—" Did it appear? The rascal is brave. Is it man or woman? "

Yoshi—" A man in all likelihood."

Kikugorō—" The dress? "

Yoshi—" Was seen to be grey cotton—positively so."

Kikugorō—" That's interesting. A *kimono* of grey colour just suits the ghost of the *wakatō* Kohei. Sa! Yoshi San, in accordance with the bargain I give you five *ryō.*"

Yoshi—" Dōmo! Thanks are felt."

Kikugorō—" There they are. Yoshi San, you are a brave fellow. Life in a haunted house is unpleasant. It will be well to remove elsewhere."

Yoshi—" Iya! A haunted house is splendid. A friend just now came for the return of borrowed money. When told of a ghost appearing, he fled. Again, merely for noting what the ghost wears, you tell me I will get five *ryō.* All this is due to the honoured shadow of the ghost. Thus regarding (my) Yurei Dai Myōjin Sama,[6] to abandon such a splendid ghost and remove to some other place would change my luck. My purpose is to go on living with this ghost.

Kikugorō—" In that case, Yoshi San, it would be well to have the house cleaned. Dōmo! Don't you think it is the work of fox or *tanuki?* "

Yoshi—" Naruhodo! At all events I'll have the house cleaned."

So receiving the money from Kikugorō, rejoicing Yoshi returned

---

[6] Apparitional divine lord.

to the Yoshiwara. On the way he took a glass or so. Somewhat drunk, he entered the Tanaka no Mikawaya, a *tabi* (sock) shop. The house was the owner of the place where Tsutayoshi lived.

Yoshi—" Good-day."

Mikawaya—" Oya! Yoshi San. Are you on your return? Ma! Condescend to enter. Dōmo! The theatre now pleases the people. The audiences are large."

Yoshi—" Thanks are felt."

Mikowaya—" What your business, Yoshi San? "

Yoshi—" Danna, I would like to have the house cleaned."

Mikawaya—" Cleaned? "

Yoshi—" Dōmo! At present a supernatural object appears. It is vexing. As I will furnish the wages of the workman, I thought it would be well to have it cleaned."

Mikawaya—" Hei! What appears? "

Yoshi—" At times a ghost shows itself."

Mikawaya—" A ghost? "

Yoshi—" Once it showed itself beside the *andon*. The second time it was seen in the necessary. At evening it was seated at the entrance to the stairs. There is nothing to fear, unless it be the work of fox or badger. It would be bad for outsiders to get wind of it; so I would like to have the place cleaned."

Mikawaya—" Is it man or woman? "

Yoshi—" There is no doubt of its being a man, of small stature. His dress plainly is of grey cotton."

Mikawaya—" A dress of grey cotton—the man of small stature. Un! Jō! It is that low fellow."

Yoshi—" Oi! Oi! Danna, did you know him? Was he a wicked fellow? Setting up in the ghost way—pray excuse me."

Landlord—" Ma! Yoshi San, please hear what I have to say. The house that I rent to you originally was a brothel called the Yamashiroya. The landlord was an unrighteous fellow. One night an *oiran* lacked any guest.⁷ He took her with him to the

---

⁷ The expression is technical—" *hitoban de mo o cha wo hikeba.*" All night a mere tea-server.

semeba—(punishment room) and treated her most cruelly. No one called the place 'the Yamashiroya.' It was known as the Onimisé (devil-shop) of Fushimichō. It was just this time last year that a *wakashū* (attendant) named Tokuzo fell in love with a woman named Kotsu no Wakataké. Pressed for money, to get it he had an eye to the pillows of the guests. From the low brothel mentioned perhaps he would get a *bu*—a couple of *shū*. A restitution privately effected would have been well. He was roped up and carried off to the town hall. In every way a low scoundrel he was sent to Temmachō. Soon after he died in the jail. Subsequently there were nothing but unpleasant happenings at the Yamashiroya. It was completely ruined. Later I bought it. Undecided about setting it up, I divided it into two houses and rented them out."

Yoshi—" Hei ! "

Mikawaya—" That Tokuzo, as the *wakashū* was called, when sent to the town hall was dressed in the thin grey cotton robe given as present to him by an *oiran*. I knew Tokuzo. He was flighty and good natured; an interesting fellow. Of low stature, he was a good worker. Probably he failed to carry out his purpose."

Yoshi—" Is that the case? It is a wonderful affair. Anyhow condescend to make everything clean."

Mikawaya—" Agreed."

After this workmen came from the Mikawaya, and the cleaning up was performed. Tsutayoshi at a subsequent meeting with Kikugorō told him the story of Tokuzo. It would be well to have a funeral service held. So the memorial service for Tokuzo was conducted at the family temple of Tsutayoshi. The figure was never again seen. Kikugorō in the rôle of ghost of the *wakatō* Kohei came out dressed in a grey robe marked with *kokumochi* (the badge of the white disk figured on coloured ground). Before one's very eyes he changed to O'Iwa. As ghost and arrayed in the family crest it was restricted to the Kohei of the " Yotsuya Kwaidan." The theatre was packed. Such was the crowd that the upper gallery of the theatre collapsed. Even though an actor, everywhere he (Kikugorō) was spoken of as a great man. To favoured guests of Kikugorō the matter was so related. Thus the tale is a true one.

TAKUAN

Three great priests of influence figure in the rule of the first three Tokugawa Shōgun. Tenkai Oshō of the Nankwōbō, bishop of the temple foundation at Ueno, was all powerful under Iyeyasu. His successors, Nikkei Sōzu of the San-en-Zan Zōjōji at Shiba, and Takuan Zaishō of the Daikokudō, the Tōkaiji of Shinagawa, were the priestly influences under the 2nd and 3rd Shōgun. It is the last-named cleric who is responsible for the hard and palatable yellow preparation of the *daikon* (radish) known under his name of *takuan*. The *daikon* is soused in brine and rice bran, kept weighted down under heavy stones, and allowed " to ripen " for some weeks. A way station in its preparation and edibility, and to be experienced in every Japanese household, is the unspeakable and unbreathable soft *nukamisozuké*. Its presence always arouses suspicion of a pressing defect in the house drainage.

Takuan deserves esteem and appreciation for other than culinary reasons. On a visit to the castle one day the old friar noted the depression of his valued and intimate friend Yagyu Tajima no Kami. The aging *ōmetsuke* (suzerain's eye) and fencing teacher to the third Shōgun opened out his woes. His second son was dead. His third son was worthless. At least the father thought so at this time. His eldest son, Jubei, as great at arms as himself and his legitimate successor, was a madman— gone mad over his own excellence. Takuan heard the particulars. At once he volunteered to act as physician. " Be of good heart. This Takuan will prescribe." The grateful Munenori, in the course of the next few days sent to the prelate's quarters to know when the journey to the far-off Yamato fief would be made. He would make provision for the prior's comfort and conveyance.

Said a sleek scribe and substitute—"The lord abbot has long since departed. It is useless to attempt to overtake him. He travels fast." Such was the message to the pleased but discomfited Munenori. Meanwhile at Yagyu Masakizaka in Yamato there turned up a shabby travel-stained old fellow. The gatekeepers were inclined flatly to refuse admission. However, the *karō*, or chief officer of the fief, had to be notified. He was unwilling to let slip any chance of relief to the condition of Jubei Dono. With some misgivings the old fellow was ordered around to the garden. The *samurai* code made little account of cutting down a retainer, a beggar, or an outcast. In the first case compensation was allowed; the last two were honoured by the experiment. Priests and women were not covered by the code; matter of omission, rather than of importance. The wanderer had taken his seat by the little pond in the garden. Here to all appearance he remained in a meditation which was roughly interrupted by the irruption of the lord of the mansion into a room close by. Jubei kicked the *shōji* out of the frames, and strode to the edge of the verandah. His hair was in wild disorder. He wore armour on his shoulders, and was stark naked below the waist. Face twitching and eyes flashing he hailed his visitor, to demand on what mission he had dared to intrude on the time and patience of the great man. Let the excuse be a good one. Otherwise— But at abuse the cleric was a good hand himself. He, too, had heard of Jubei Dono; he who posed as the great man of Nippon. This was poaching on his own ground, for he set himself up to be the match of any number in the land. At this Jubei broke into angry jeers and invectives. The priest made answer with equal roughness. "How face two opponents—to right and left?" Jubei snorted with contempt. He was active enough to neglect the one and cut down the other before aid could be brought. The Yagyu-ryū, or style of fencing, made provision for such occasion. Aye! And for four—and against eight . . . "And against sixteen, and thirty-two, and sixty-four, and a hundred and twenty-eight opponents . . . against all the many fighting men of Nippon? How would Jubei face all those?" To this Jubei could but answer that he would die fighting. The priest in his turn snorted with contempt. "Die fighting: by such words Jubei admits defeat." But he did not allow Jubei to turn questioner in his turn. Swiftly he shifted the argument. He, the cleric, considered Jubei of small account. He would prove to him what a fool he was by the interpretation of a mere thirty-one syllables of poetry. This should be the test of intelligence. The Knight's Way (Budō) had its inner and cryptic meaning expressed in verse. So had the Way of the Buddha (Butsudō). Of this latter Jubei knew nothing; and he doubted if he knew anything of the former. At least let him display some sample of his wit. Jubei leaped at the test to prove his greatness. Now he scorned to deal with a priest in arms. How was this:

> "By night storm of Narutaki broken,
> The scattered jewels, e'en the moon, it harbours."[8]

"Is there but that to prove wit?"—"How then with this one?"

> "Tree leaves on Yamakawa's flood:
> The self, abandoned, does but drift—lo!"[9]

The priest threw up his hands. "Such stuff will never do! And this fellow considers himself educated!"

> "Rain seen, impeded not to flow away;
> The snow breaks not the stem of willow green."[10]
> "Various and many though the ways of teaching be,
> There is but one true stroke of sword."[11]

---

[8] [Narutaki no yoru no arashi ni kudakarete;
Chiru tama goto ni tsuki zo yadoreru.]

[9] [Yamakawa no nagare ni ko no ha shizumu tomo;
Mi wo sutete koso ukabu se mo are.]

[10] [Furu to miba tsumoranu saki ni haraekashi;
Yuki ni wa orenu aoyagi no ito.][3]

[11] [Sama Sama to oshie no michi mo ōkeredo
Uchikomu tokoro shin no ittō.][4]

Jubei gleamed most homicidally at his questioner. The priest only said—"A child has such by heart." And Jubei knew 'twas so, and was rebuked. Now he was in less haste:

> "The heart, how judge it?
> An ink sketch of the breeze amid the pines." [12]

A shrug of the shoulders was the reward of this effort.

"Though barrier mount, the leafy mount, the inner mount, be dense with leafage;
What e'er one wills, naught hinders." [13]

The priest shook his head as with grave indulgence to childhood's thoughts. Jubei burst into a rage. He turned to his sword-bearer, and laid hand on the weapon. The lad knelt with bowed head, uncertain whether the sword was to fall on himself or the visitor. Without paying the slightest attention to the hostile attitude the priest cut matters short. "Jubei Dono would question the priest's right to judge. Come now! The cleric's foolish head against the wits of Nippon's great man. O warrior, interpret!" A sign; and ink stone and poem paper (*tanzaku*) were put before him. Jubei in turn took the scroll in hand. He read:

> "*Tatazumuna, yukuna, modoruna, isuwaruna;*
> *Neruna, okiruna, shiru mo shiranu mo.*"
> "It neither stands still, nor goes forward, nor
>   goes backward, nor remains as it is;
>   It sleeps not, rises not: known or unknown."

Jubei started with a bellow; and ended in a whisper. The retainers looked in each other's faces. Who was the maddest—their lord or the shabby *bōzu?* A long silence followed. Jubei no longer stood in grandiloquent pose. He squatted down before

[12] [Kokoro to wa ikanaru mono wo iu yaran;
     Sumie ni kakitsu matsu kaze no oto.] [5]
[13] [Tsukubayama, Hayama, Nakayama, Shigeredomo;
     Omoiru ni wa mono mo sawarazu.] [6]

the ideographs. At last he said—"The poem contains much matter. Deign to allow time for the solution." His voice was gentle and courteous to this future victim of his intelligence. The priest nodded a genial assent. Before he withdrew Jubei gave emphatic orders as to ward and entertainment. The pleasures of anticipation, of solution of the poem and slicing of the cleric, must have compensation. His tread was slow and stately as he left the room; his looks were contained and thoughtful. The man of black robe was carried off to a better reception than so far experienced. With scorn he sent away the scanty meal of vegetable food; and ordered matters to his taste with a manner that none cared to obey, or dared to disobey.

Meanwhile Jubei started in on the poem. With the progress of his efforts ideas of his greatness disappeared. No matter what might be his skill with the sword—and the priest already had shown its limitations—his inexperience in literature was patent. Ah! If he could but win the head of this scurvy cleric. His mind now was totally removed from thoughts of himself. For two days and two nights he never closed his eyes, which were fastened on the infernal ideographs—palpably so full of a meaning he could not grasp. Then he was worn out. He went to sleep, and slept for a full twenty-four hours. On awaking he was a different being. The cobwebs of the mind were clean swept. Its vague shiftings had been brought to concentration—to thought. Now it was the household which was mad with joy. It was Jubei, lord of the manor, who sought interview with his saviour. Prostrate he gave thanks, apology for the poor entertainment; and expressed his hope and wish to keep always by him the holy man. Who was he—this man who had given him back mind and power of thought? Just then a messenger from his father, Tajima no Kami, was announced. Those assembled leaned forward at sight of the man in amazed prostration, first before his lord, then before the shabby old priest. "Takuan Oshō Sama at Yagyu! And yet this Kyūtarō has made all speed to Yamato to make report of his lordship's coming." All fell on their faces, including Jubei. Takuan smiled, a little grimly. " The garb makes not the cleric. Jubei Dono will forgive the presence of the humble priest who now must leave him, pressed by affairs, none of which have been more important than the mission here." And leave he did—but ample gifts to the temple followed after. Jubei never could take his father's place close to the Shōgun's side. His one-time madness forbade assumption of such office. Indeed on rare occasions the mad fit again would threaten; but the infallible remedy was at hand. To Jubei's question Takuan had answered—" The meaning? The poem has none. If there had been verily Takuan would have lost his head. But find one, if you can." The joy of Tajima no Kami was completed by the return of his third son Matajurō, restored to normal health. Later this Matajurō became the famous Hida no Kami and successor to his father as the Shōgun's fencing master. Of these three men—more anon.[14]

---

[14] Cf.—" Araki Mataemon—Ueno Adauchi," by Masui Nanzan. There is little reason to believe that Jubei's madness was assumed, a rather extravagant explanation of the more than probable fact that his well-known travels were inspired by the Shōgun's government. Actual knowledge and inspection of the conditions and feelings in far-off Satsuma, made by an expert, was much desired. Okubo Hikozaemon also travelled as the Shōgun's private eye. Jubei undoubtedly found his reputation for one-time madness very useful, and played upon it.